POSTCARD HISTORY SERIES

Around DuBois

POSTCARD HISTORY SERIES

Around DuBois

DuBois Area Historical Society

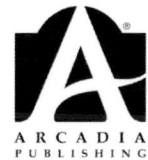

Copyright © 2005 by DuBois Area Historical Society
ISBN 978-0-7385-3716-0

Published by Arcadia Publishing
Charleston, South Carolina

Printed in the United States of America

Library of Congress Catalog Card Number: 2005920048

For all general information contact Arcadia Publishing at:
Telephone 843-853-2070
Fax 843-853-0044
E-mail sales@arcadiapublishing.com
For customer service and orders:
Toll-Free 1-888-313-2665

Visit us on the Internet at www.arcadiapublishing.com

Contents

Acknowledgments		6
Introduction		7
1.	DuBois in the Beginning	9
2.	Street Scenes	19
3.	John DuBois	27
4.	Business and Industry	37
5.	Community	51
6.	Railroads	67
7.	Brady Township and Falls Creek	73
8.	Sabula and Penfield	91
9.	Reynoldsville and Sykesville	101
10.	Miscellaneous	113

ACKNOWLEDGMENTS

Our sincere thanks go to the following people for the use of their postcard collections and other materials: John Morgan, Linda Dixon, Robert DuBois, Marilyn Challingsworth, Edwin Brubaker, Shirley Clark, Mary Jo Pifer, Doris Fye Andrulonis, Cleora Bolam, Emma Miller, James and Jane Bonsall, Jean Hayes, Mona Cramer, Harold and Alice May Muth, Rick Sierzega, and Lenny Federici. Without them, this book would never have been completed.

Special thanks go out to Todd Thompson, Dave and Nellie Beer, Beecher Kingensmith, Evo Facchine, Tom and Ginny Schott, Audrey Lott, and Judy Leech for the time they spent doing write-ups, scanning, layout, and research.

Thanks to Erin Loftus and the staff at Arcadia Publishing for their help, patience, and encouragement.

Finally, we acknowledge the DuBois Area Historical Society for allowing us access to all of their resources.

INTRODUCTION

The DuBois area, located in scenic western Pennsylvania, has a rich history that dates to 1785, when Brady Township was settled. That same year, Luthersburg was settled by James Woodside, whose land was in the area known today as Helvetia. George Shaffer and his family arrived in 1812 and settled on the land now called DuBois. John Rumbarger came to the area in 1873 and settled on what is now the south side of town. John DuBois followed in 1874, settling on the north side.

Sidney Fuller bought land in the area of Washington Township that would later be known as Falls Creek. Joseph Taylor, known as the Father of Falls Creek, was another important person in local history. The Sabula area was originally developed as a splash dam for the DuBois Lumber Mill. It was later turned into a summer retreat for the more affluent residents of the DuBois area. Penfield was incorporated in August 1899. Some of the early pioneers were Hiram Woodward, Ebenezer Hewitt, Rufus Lucore, and John Hoyt.

The DuBois area was known for its lumber, coal, and railroads.

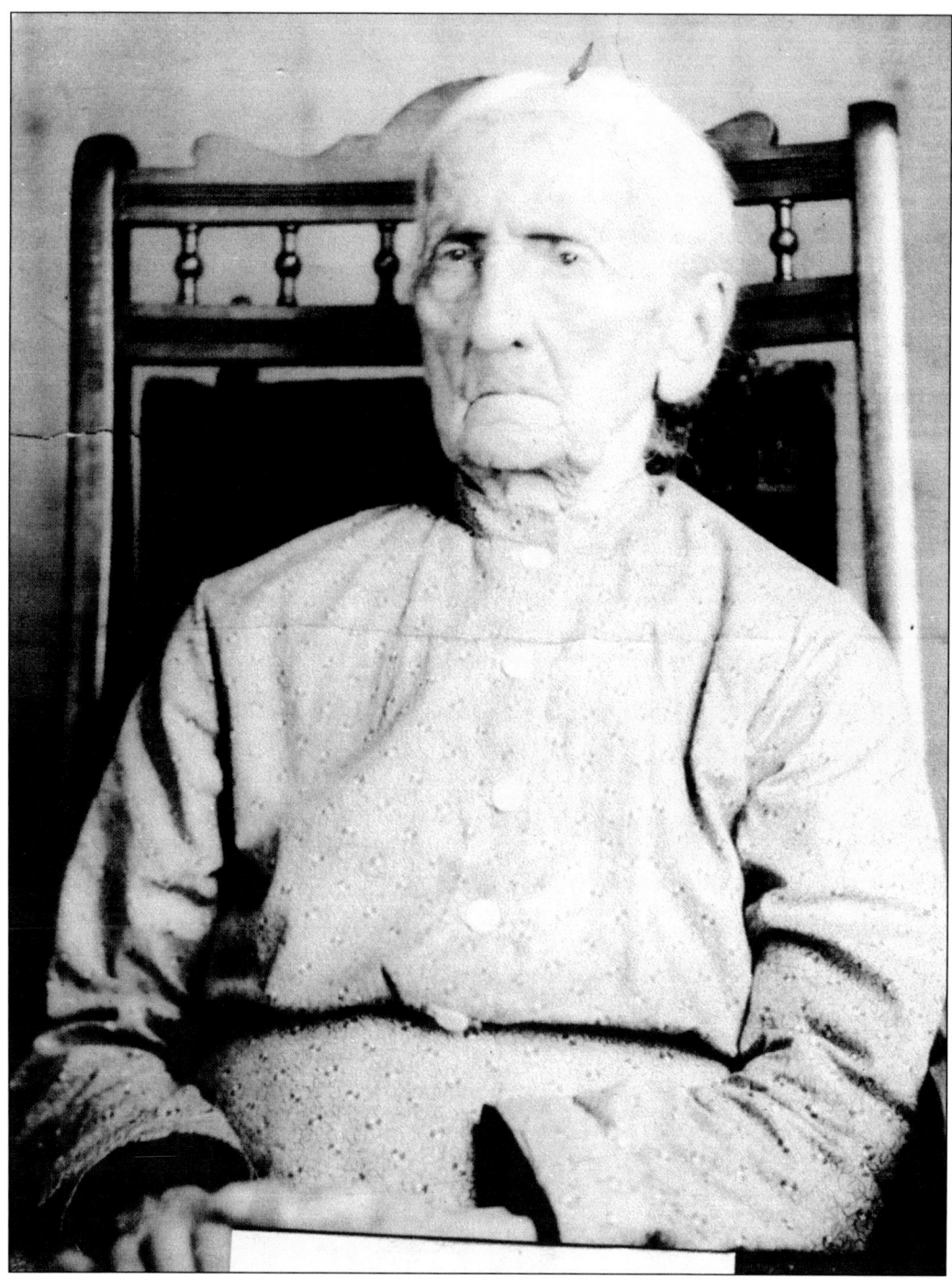

Katy Shaffer Reasinger, a descendant of George Shaffer, lived her life within a five-mile radius of her birthplace. She was one of the last members of the Shaffer family, who were early settlers in DuBois, and she was well known and respected. She died in 1931 at the age of 102.

One

DuBois in the Beginning

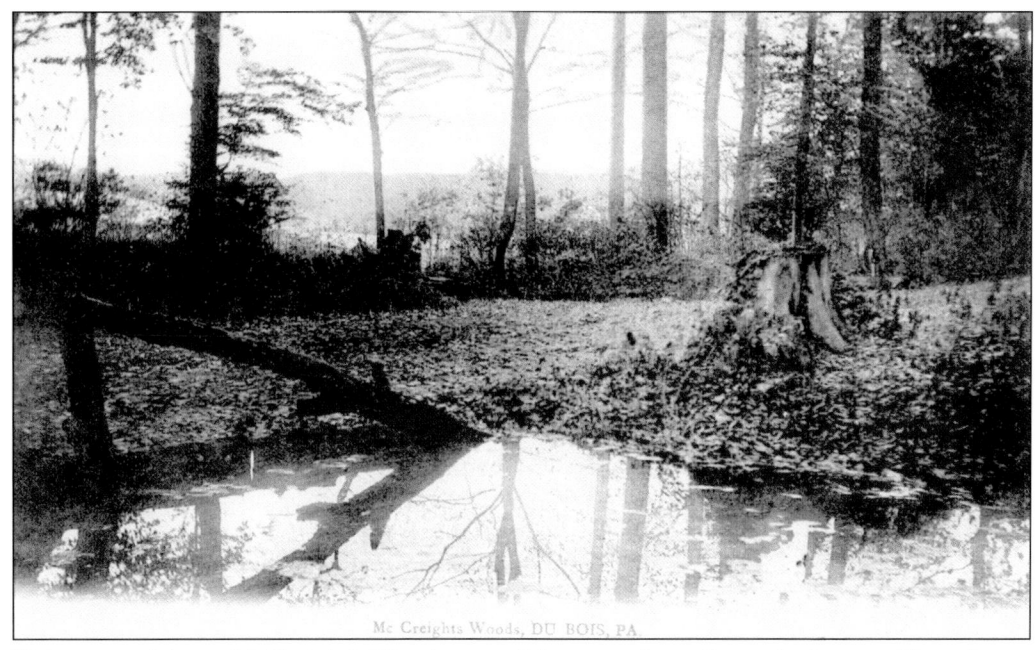

This postcard shows McCreight's Woods, one of the many dense forests in the area. These forests were home to numerous varieties of hardwood and evergreen trees.

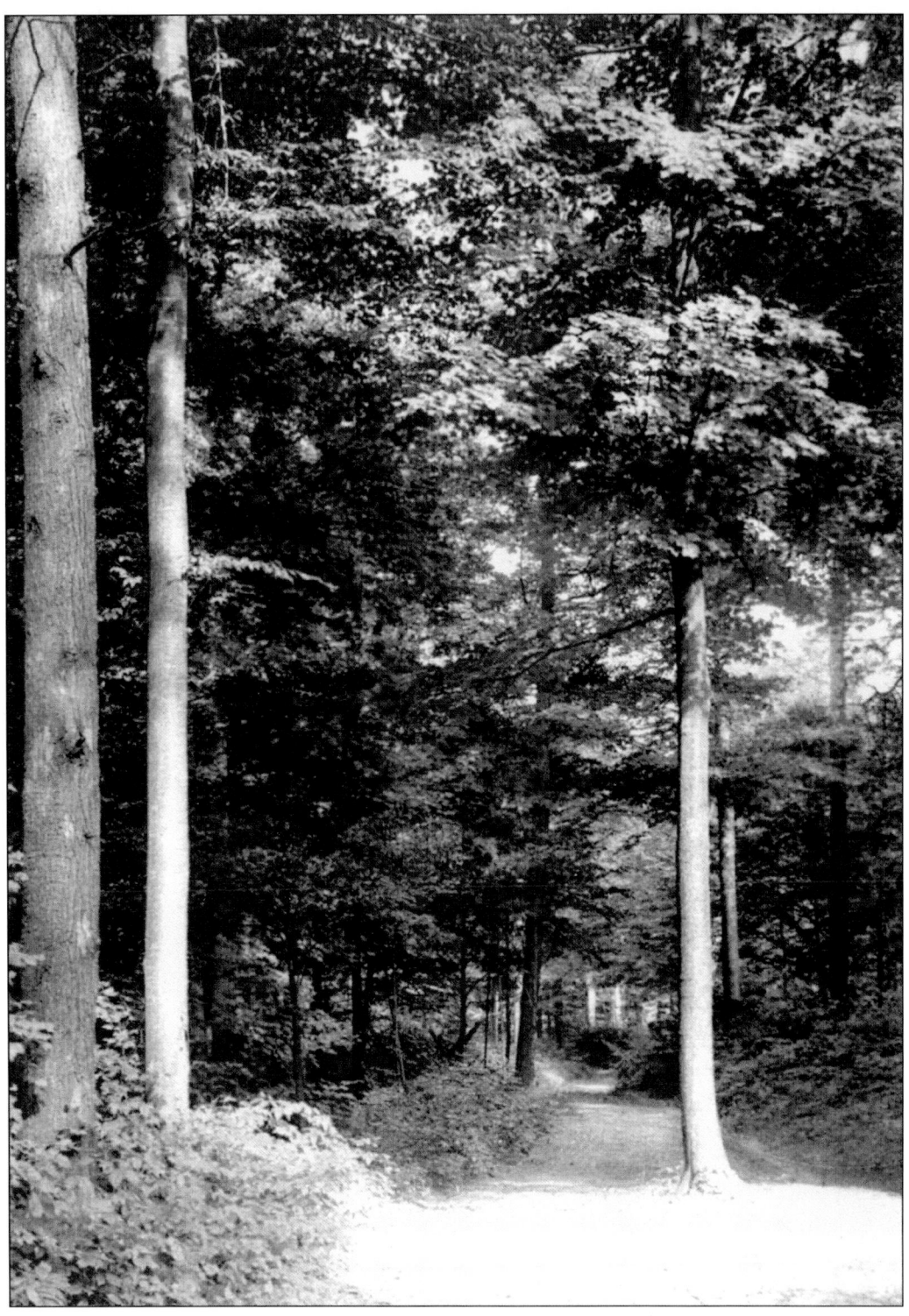
This roadway in McCreight's Woods was constructed by loggers. The road was cleared so that settlers could take advantage of the plentiful timber.

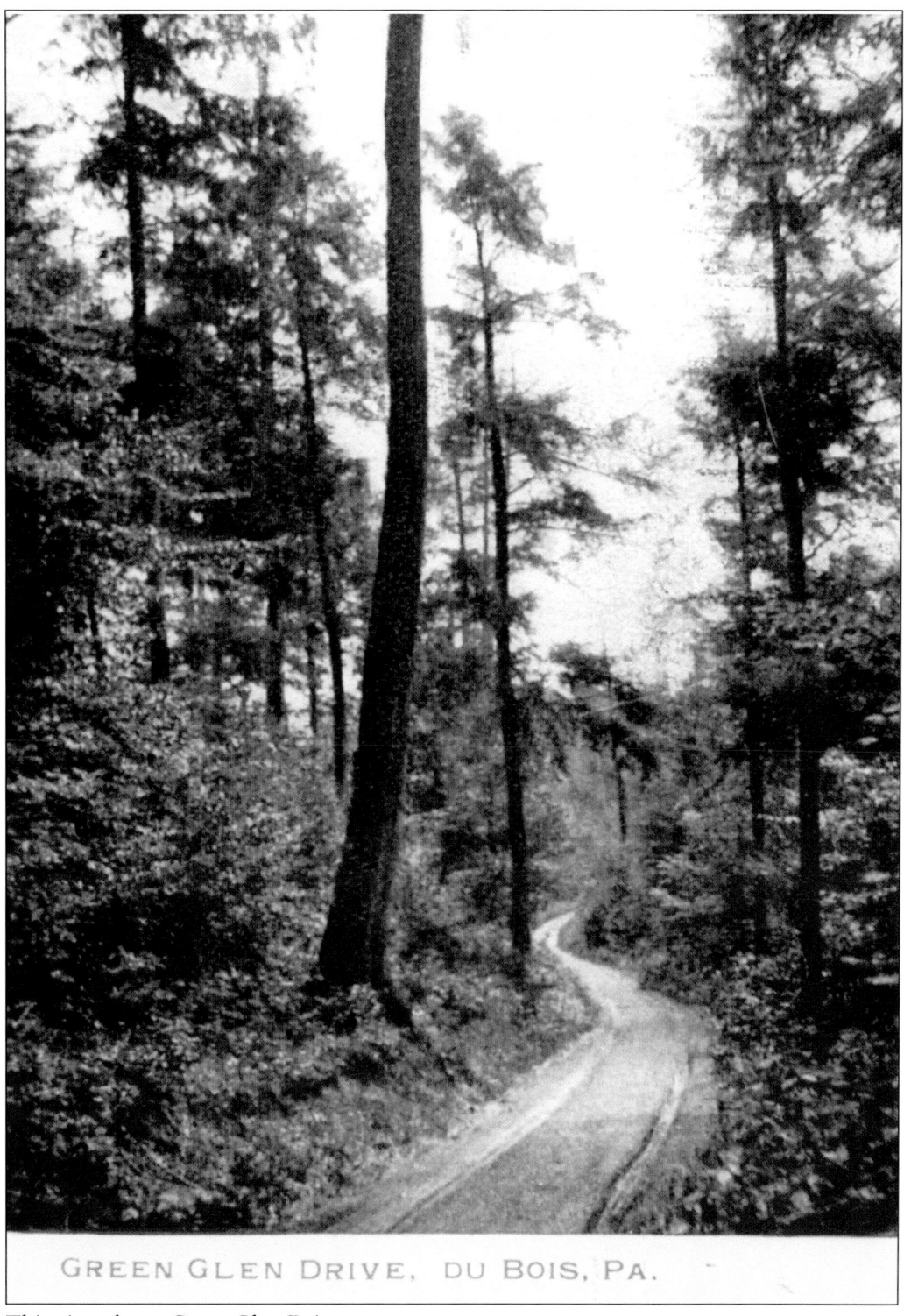

This view shows Green Glen Drive.

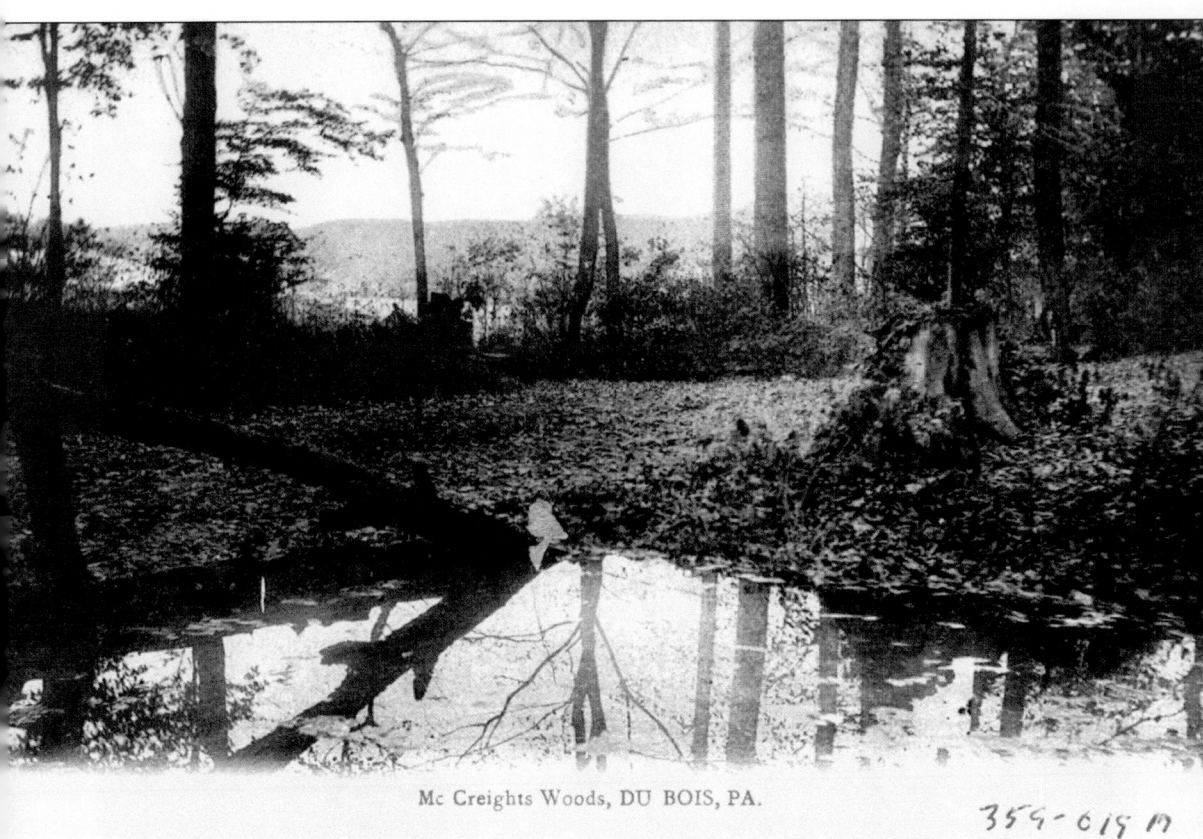

Mc Creights Woods, DU BOIS, PA.

These four postcards of wooded sites provide a glimpse of what early pioneers saw when they first arrived in this area. There were dense forests of all varieties of hardwood and evergreen trees, but pines were predominant. In the early years of the 19th century, the trees were both an obstacle to be removed and a source of fuel for those who cleared the land for farming. It has been estimated that more than 30 percent of the timber was burned or cut and wasted. When John DuBois and other lumbermen came to the area, they systematically logged the timber from these dense forests and sent it to market. Logging operations in the DuBois area continued nonstop from 1872 to 1900.

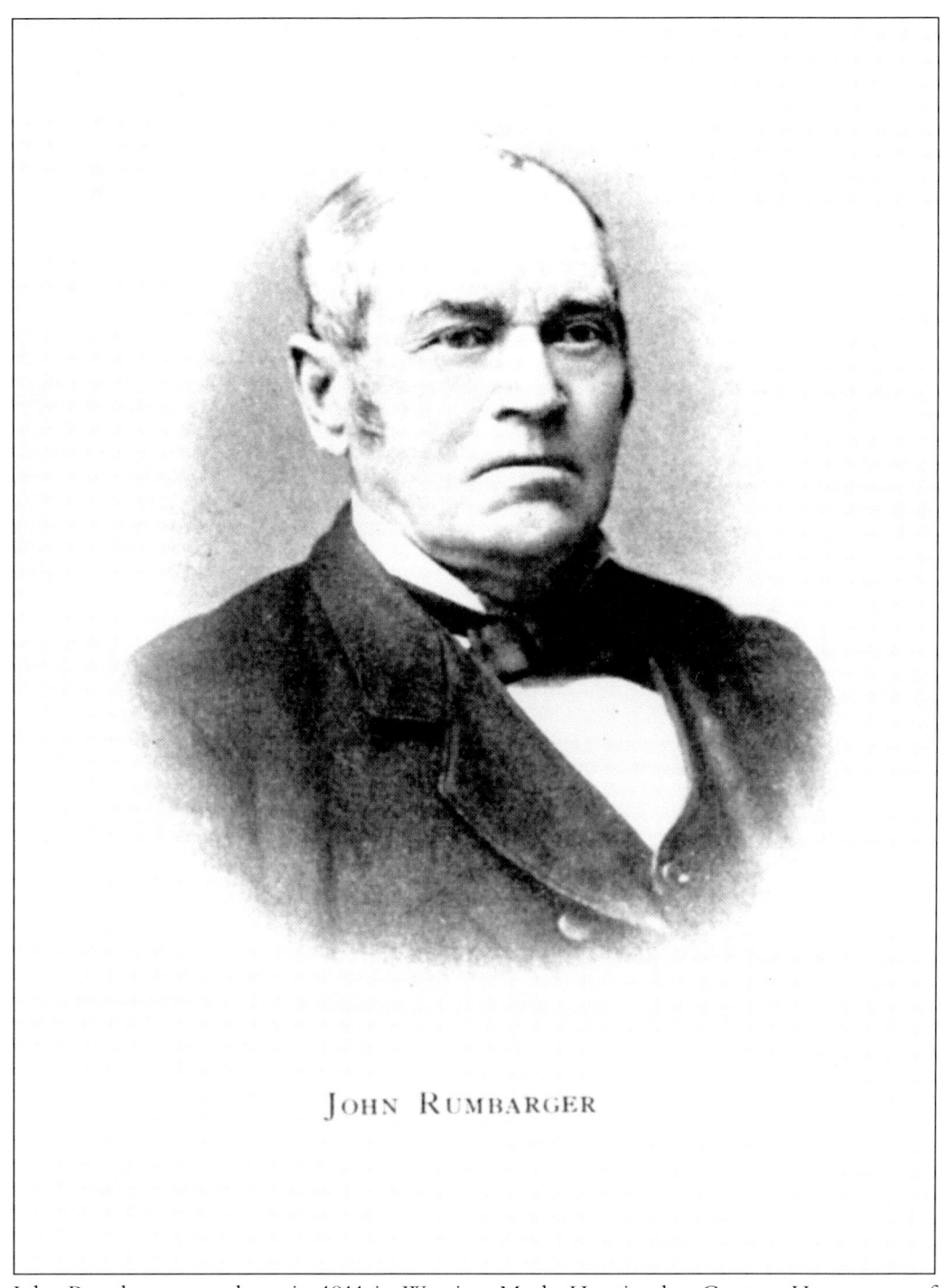

JOHN RUMBARGER

John Rumbarger was born in 1811 in Warriors Mark, Huntingdon County. He was one of 10 children. Rumbarger settled first in Armstrong County near Kittanning. Then, in 1865, he purchased the Heberling farm in Clearfield County. In 1872, he hired George C. Kirk to lay out lots for a town he named Rumbarger, and he advertised the lots for sale in the Clearfield and Brookville papers. Coal miners and their families settled in this town.

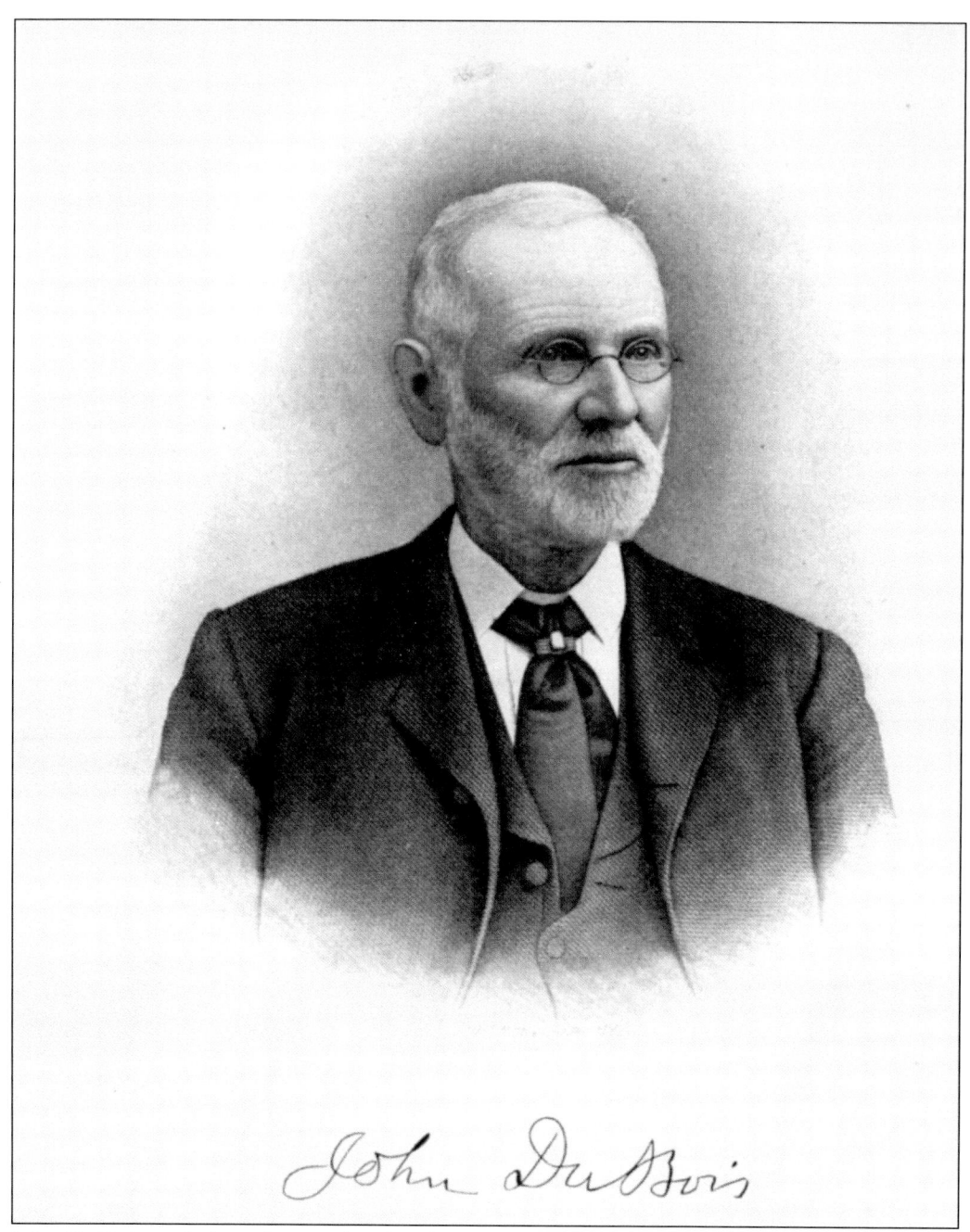

John DuBois settled on the north side of town, which was known as the Swamp Siding. In 1874, he built the Big Sawmill for his lumbering business. He later built what was called the Little Mill, along with the box factory, the sash and door factory, and, later, a tannery. These industries were necessary to use the by-products from the Big Sawmill.

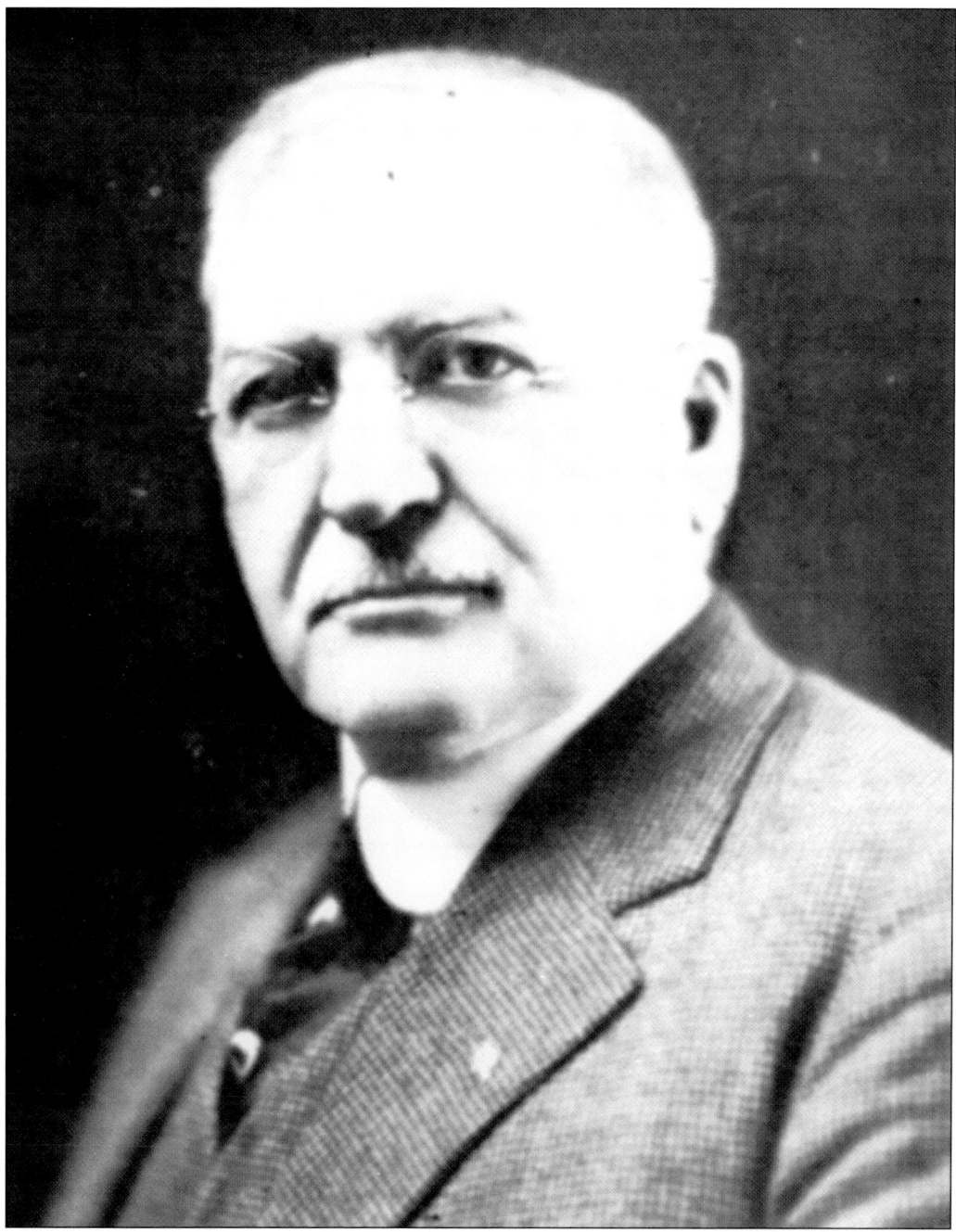

Major Israel McCreight was born on April 27, 1868, in Jefferson County. He was a well-known member of the DuBois community, taking on the roles of banker, prolific writer, candidate for Congress, and businessman. "Major" was a nickname given to him by his family when he was very young, not a military title. He preferred to be called by his initials, M. I.

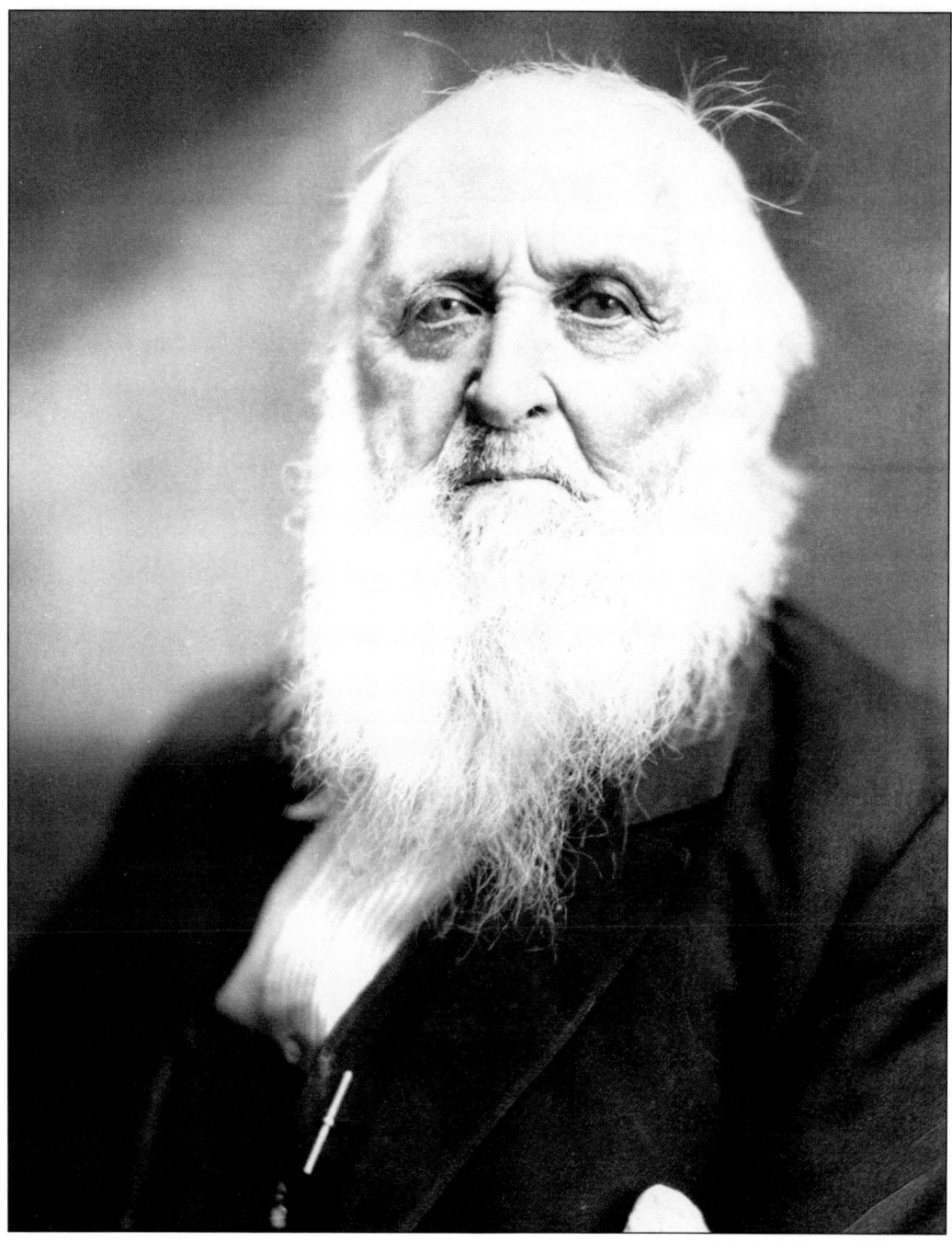
George Kirk was born in March 1837 and died in 1936. He was the author of *Pioneer History of Brady Township*. John Rumbarger hired him to lay out the lots for the town of Rumbarger.

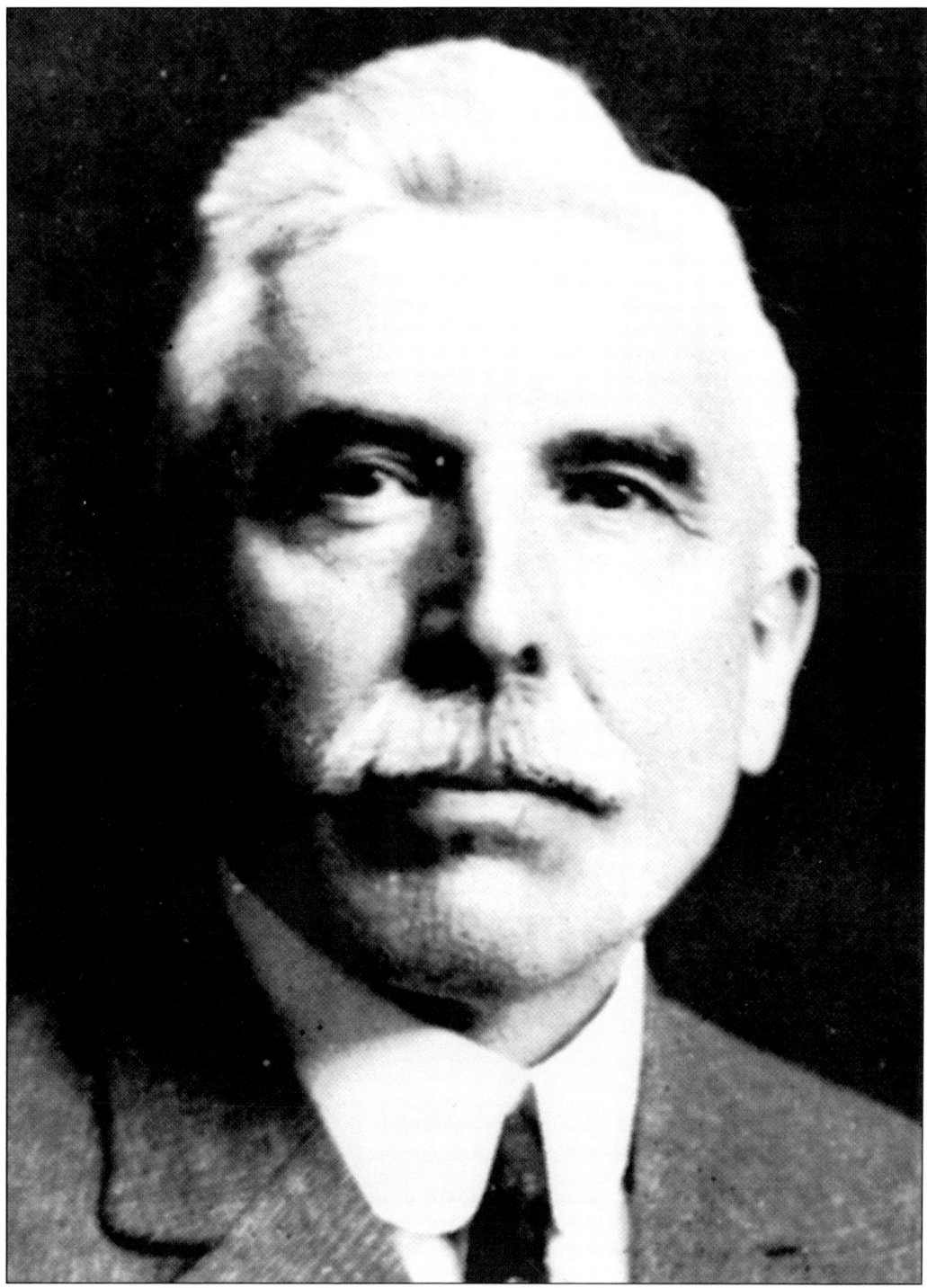
Frank Hahne Sr. arrived at the port of New York on May 3, 1875, from Bremen, Germany. He came to America to learn more about the brewery trade. Frank married Caroline A. Trom of Chicago, and they spent several years in Chicago before coming to Pennsylvania. In 1890, Hahne started building the DuBois Brewery, and in 1895, the first beer was ready for market.

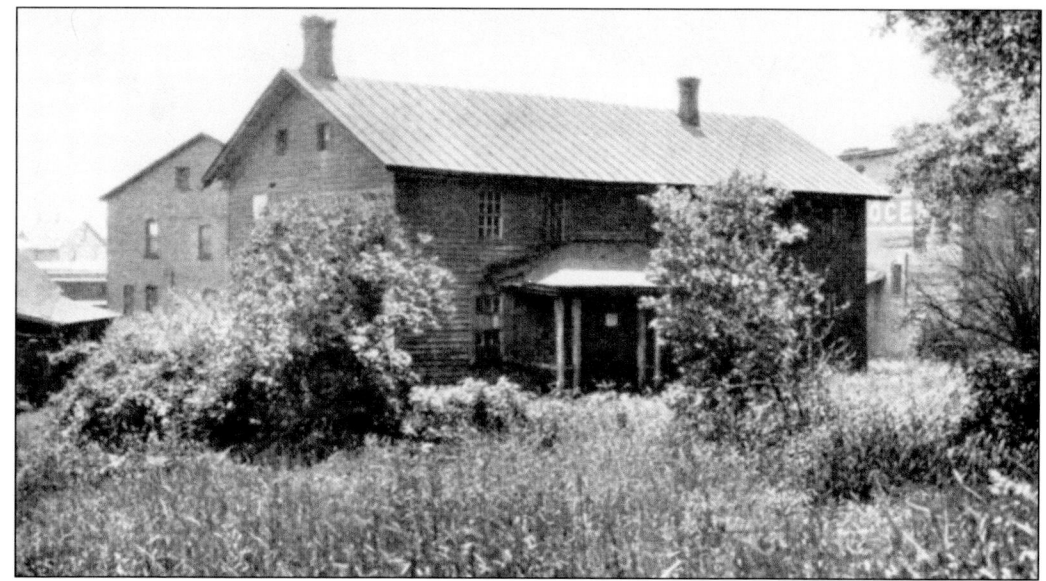

The old Rumbarger House, for many years the oldest house in DuBois, was located where Riverside Market now stands. It originally belonged to Jacob Heberling. In 1865, it was sold to John Rumbarger, who lived there until he built another residence on South State Street.

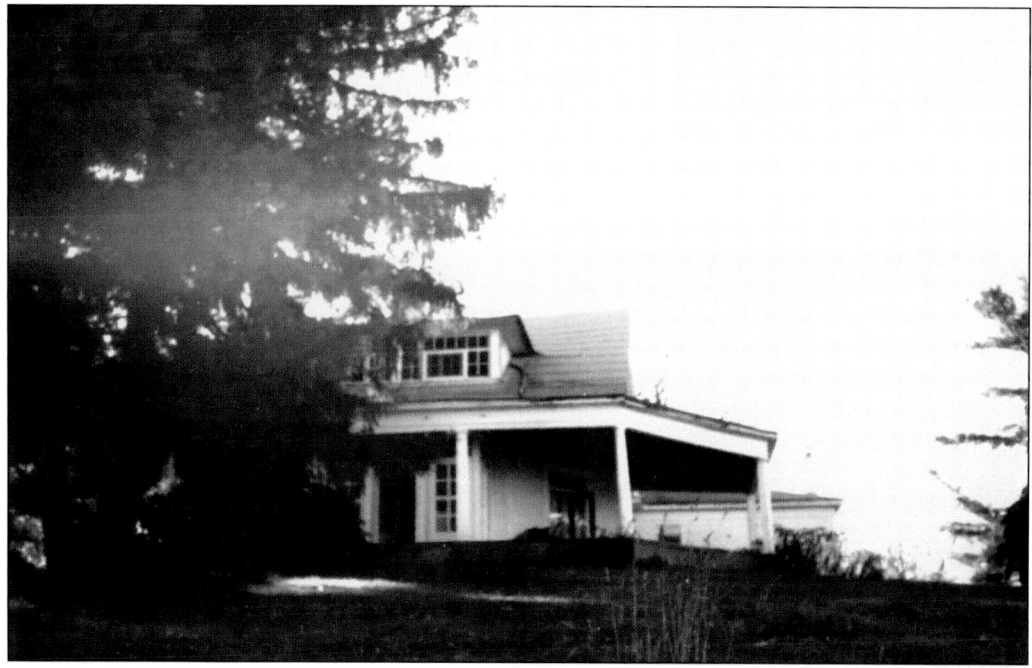

The M. I. McCreight home was called the Wigwam and was built in 1906 on a hill overlooking Lincoln Drive. McCreight was a great friend of the Sioux Indians, and he obtained a large collection of American Indian artifacts that he displayed at the Wigwam.

Two
Street Scenes

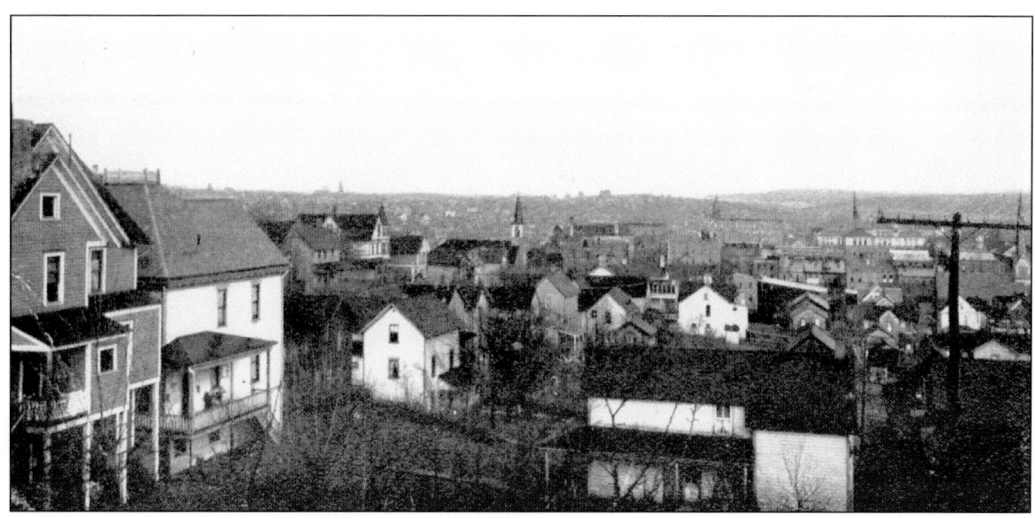
This postcard offers a bird's-eye view of DuBois.

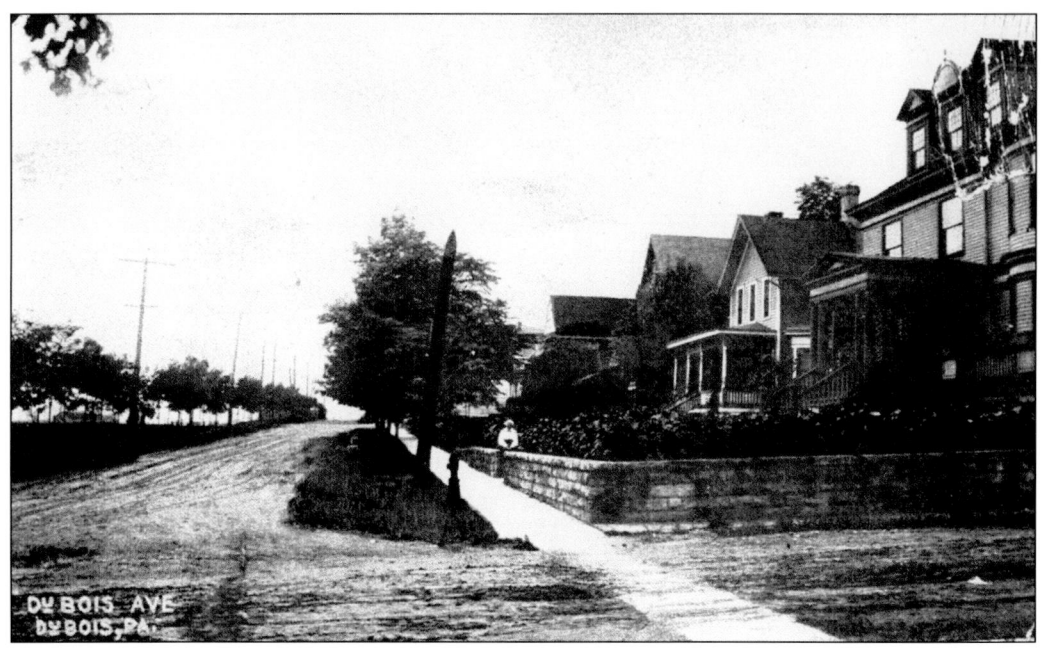

DuBois Avenue, located not far from the present Penn State campus, was once a dirt road. Many of these homes are still standing today.

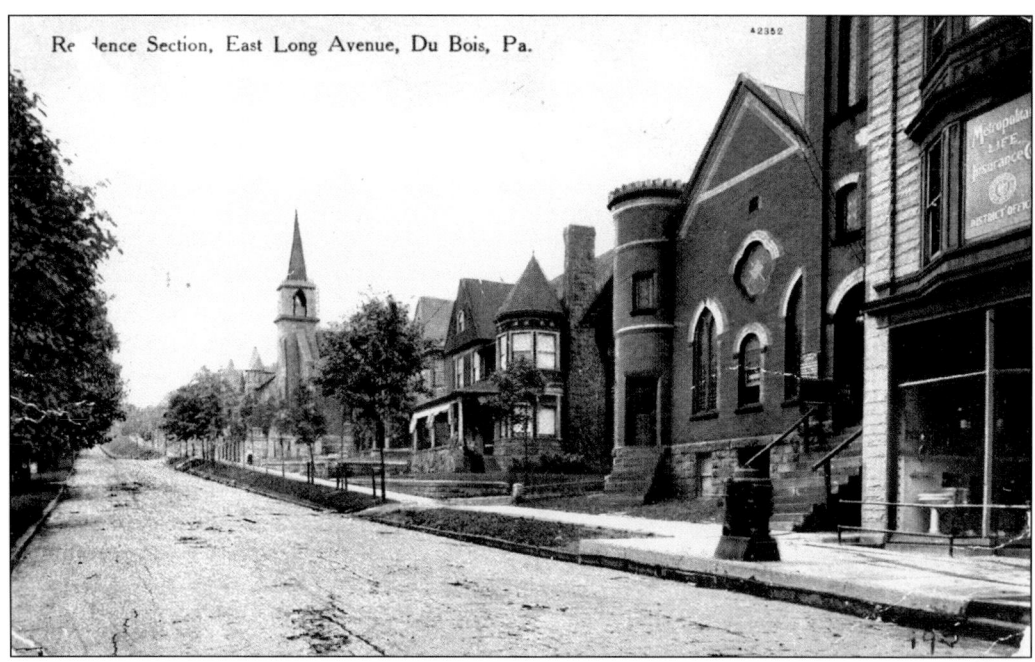

East Long Avenue is a residential section of town. The Baptist church shown here was once the Fuller Opera House.

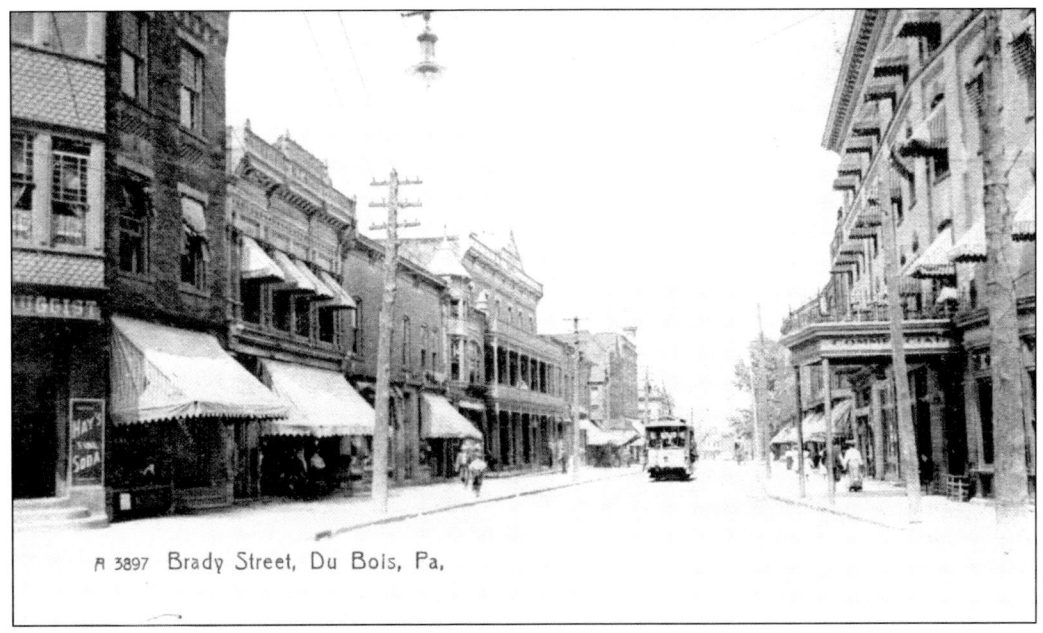
The Commercial Hotel on Brady Street is shown here. The local trolley is in the background.

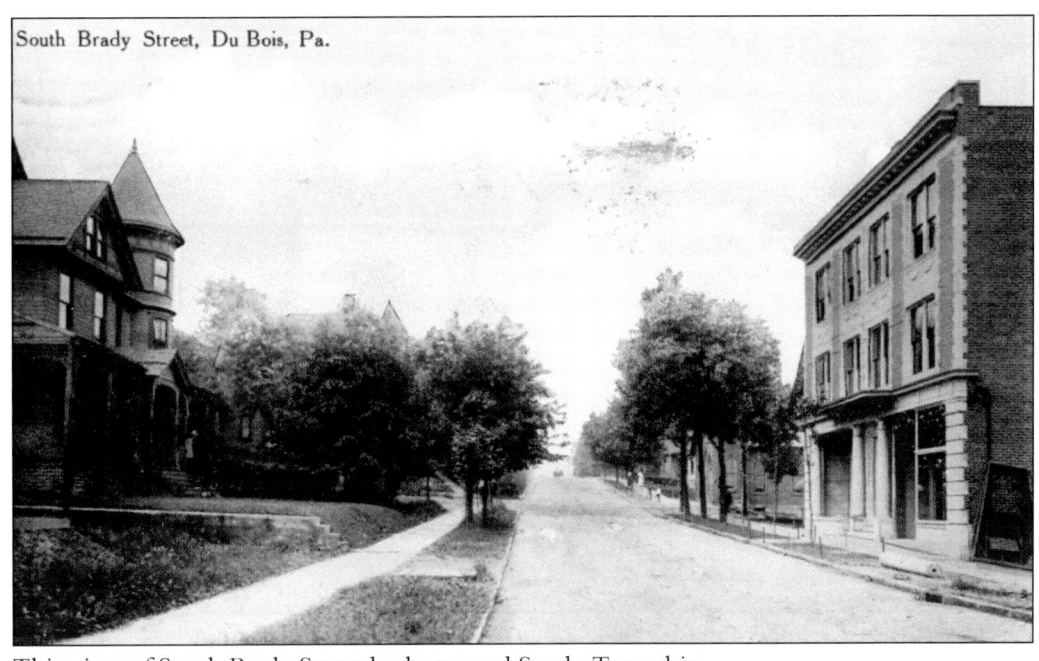
This view of South Brady Street looks toward Sandy Township.

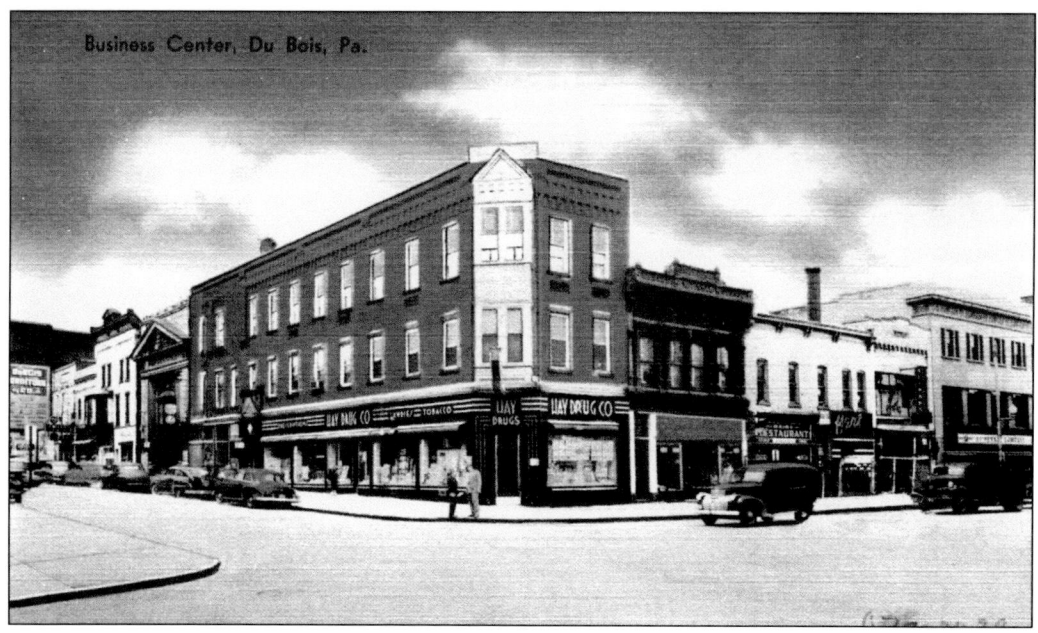

The Hay drugstore is shown in this image of the business center of DuBois. The store was located on the corner of West Long Avenue and North Brady Street.

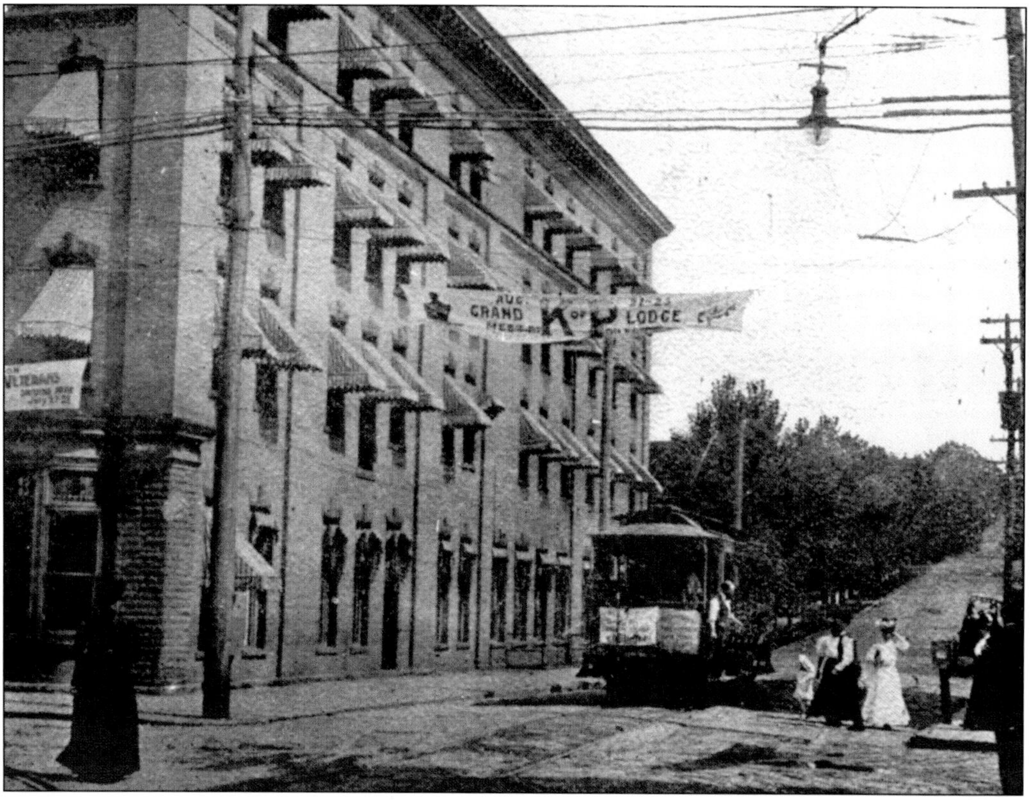

This view of East Long Avenue looks up the hill toward Stockdale Street. The Commercial Hotel is on the left.

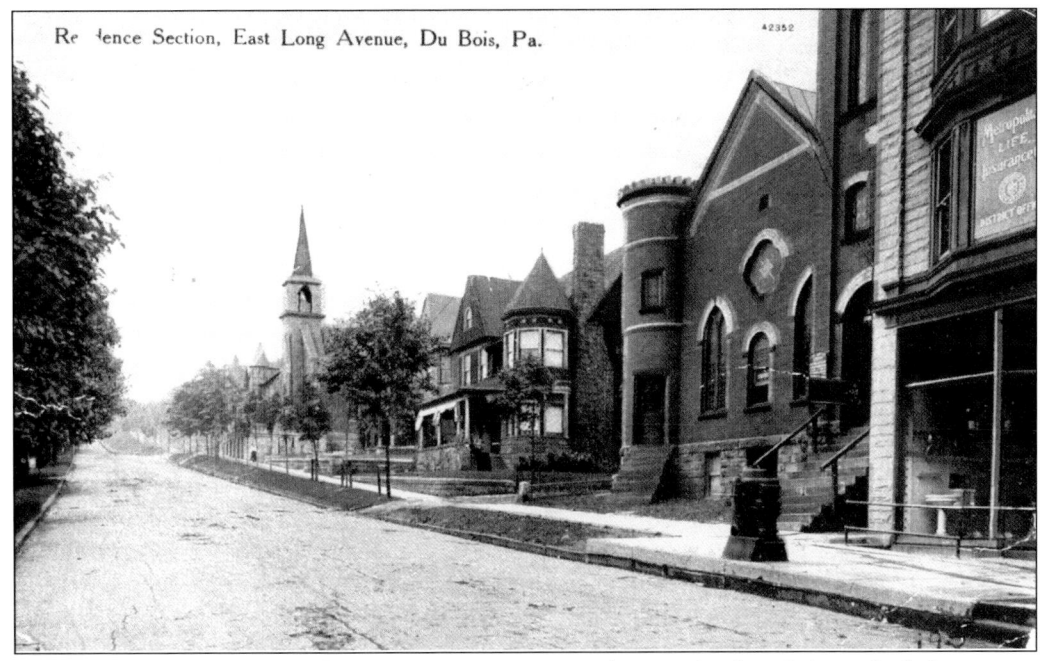
The downtown area is seen from East Long Avenue. The Baptist church is on the left.

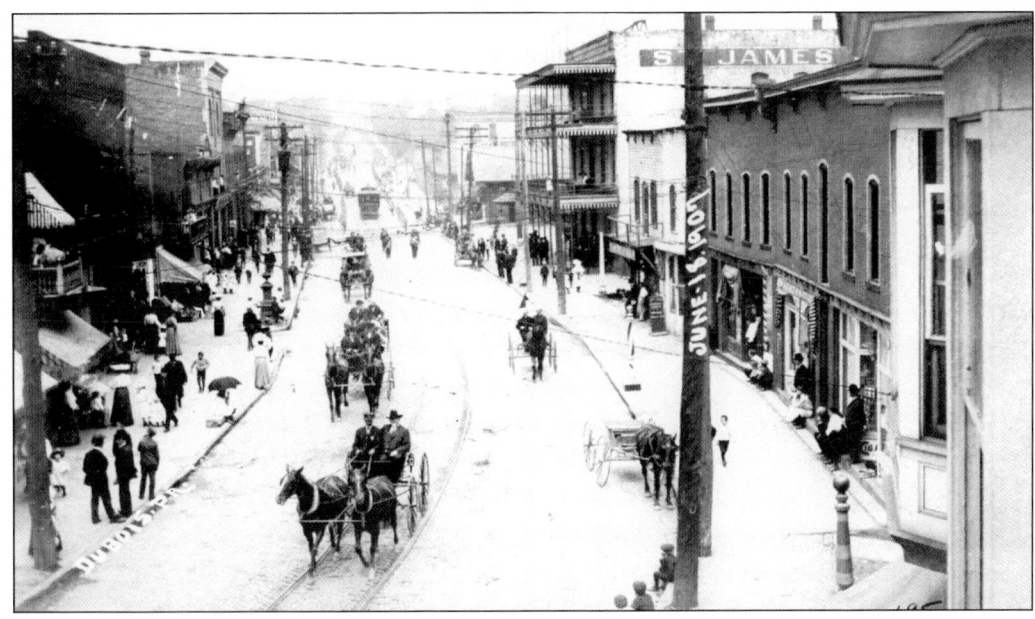
This parade took place on West Long Avenue in 1907.

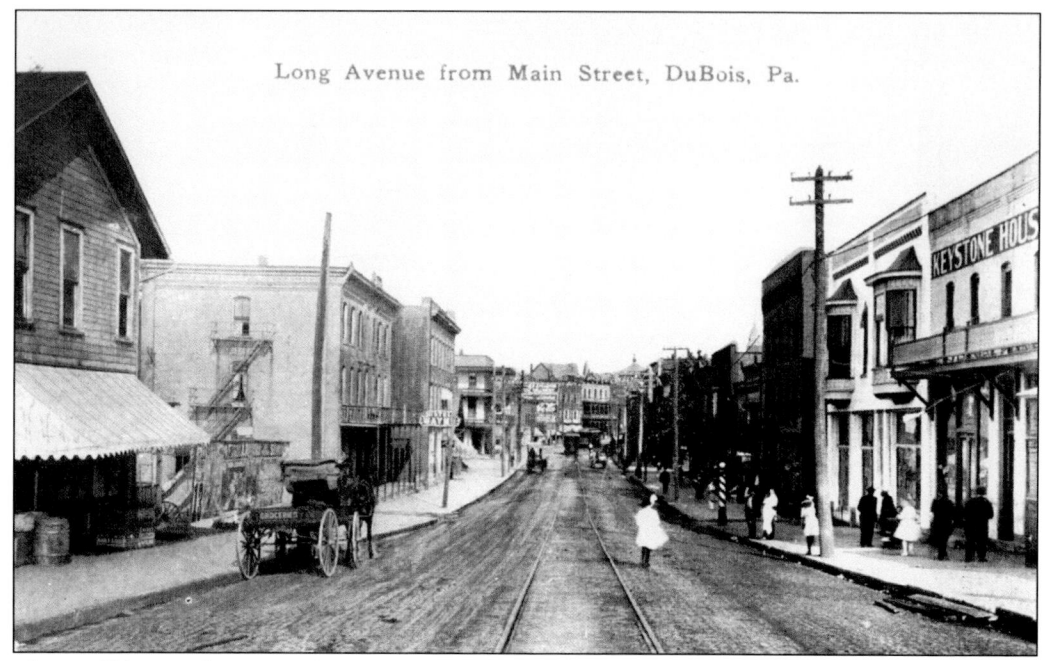

The Buffalo, Rochester, and Pittsburgh railroad terminal is seen here from Long Avenue.

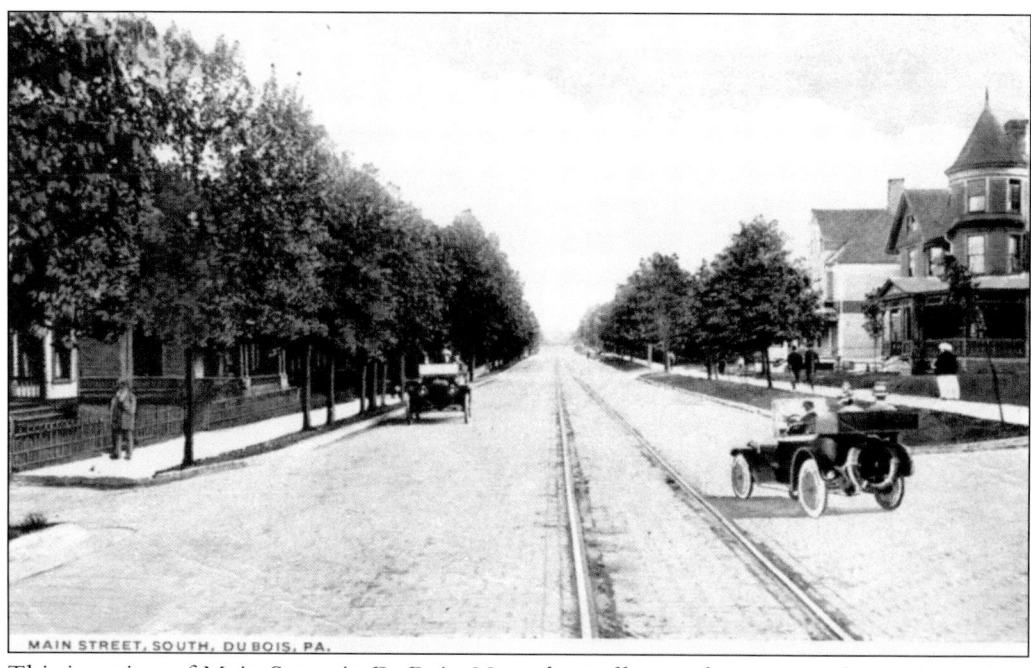

This is a view of Main Street in DuBois. Note the trolley tracks running down the middle of the street.

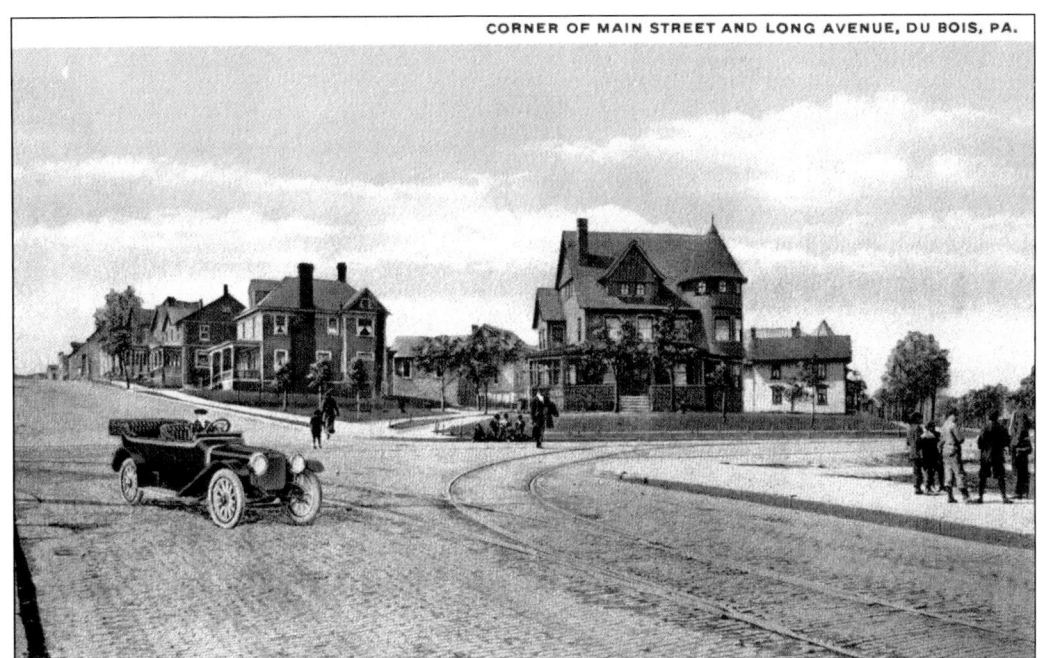

Coming up Long Avenue, the trolley tracks on the right go to Falls Creek, and the tracks on the left lead to Sykesville. Dahrouge's store is on the left, and the Merris mansion is ahead on the right.

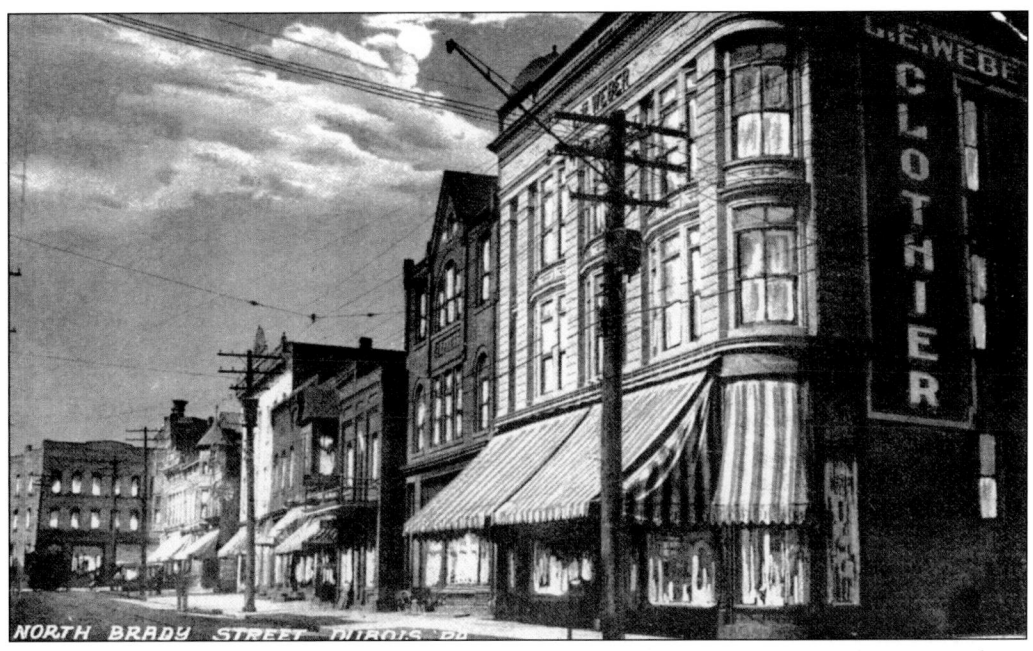

L. E. Weber Clothier is seen here on the corner of North Brady Street and West Scribner Avenue. The store was originally located in a different building, but it moved into this building on August 25, 1898, after the great fire of 1888 destroyed the business district of DuBois.

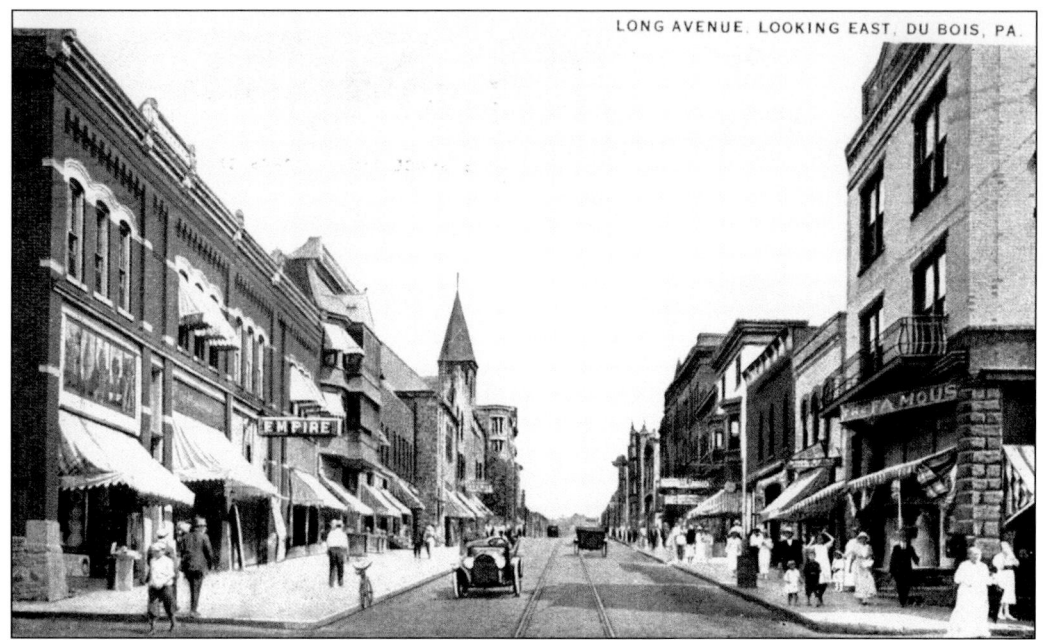

This is a view of Long Avenue looking east from Jared Street toward High Street. The Empire Hotel is on the left, and Avenue Theater is on the right.

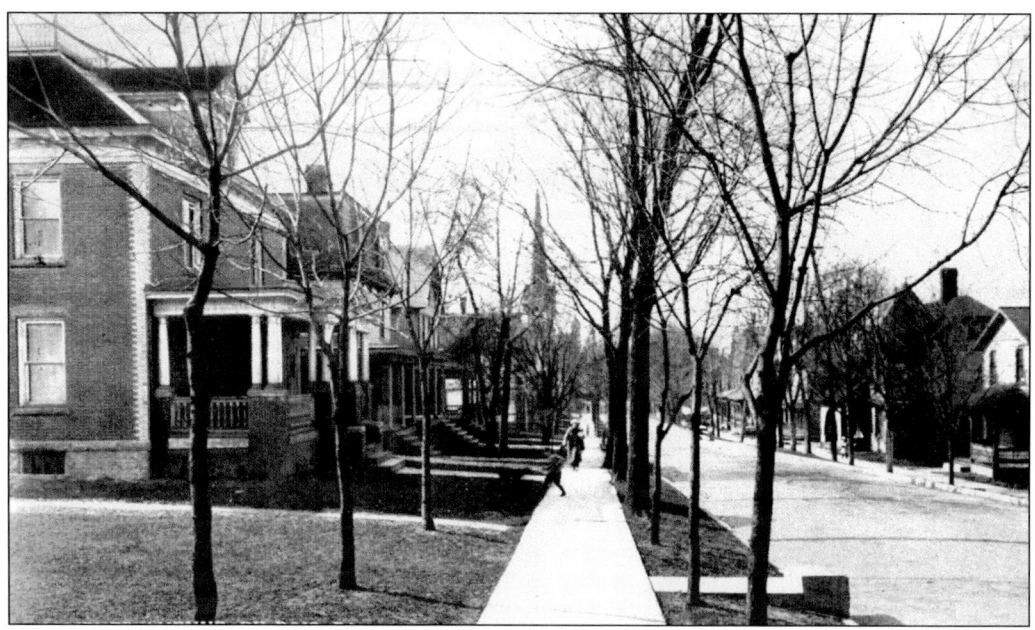

East Scribner Avenue is a residential area with many beautiful homes.

Three
John DuBois

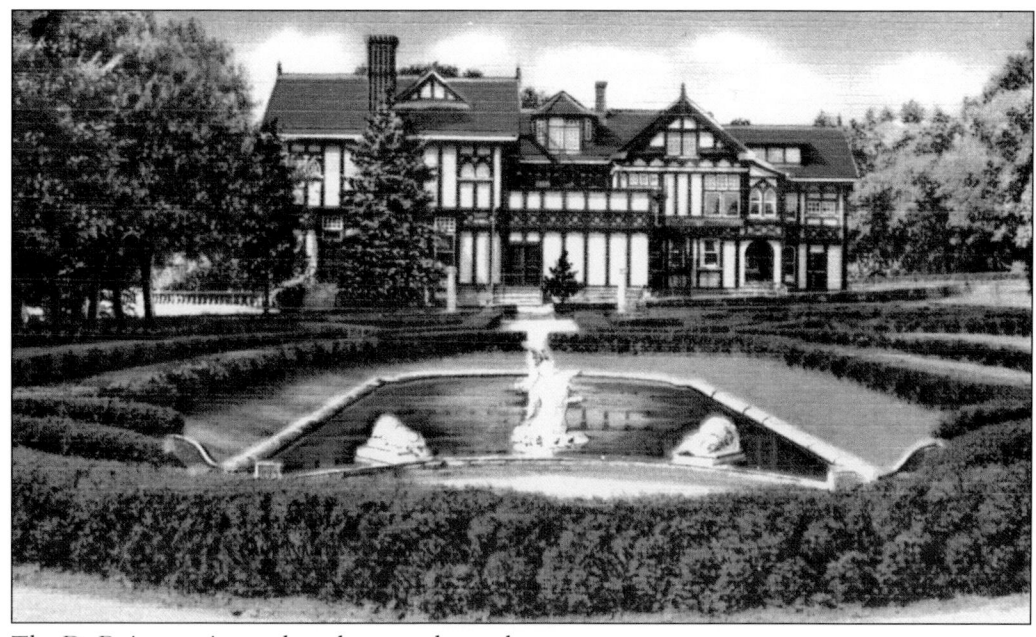
The DuBois mansion and gardens are shown here.

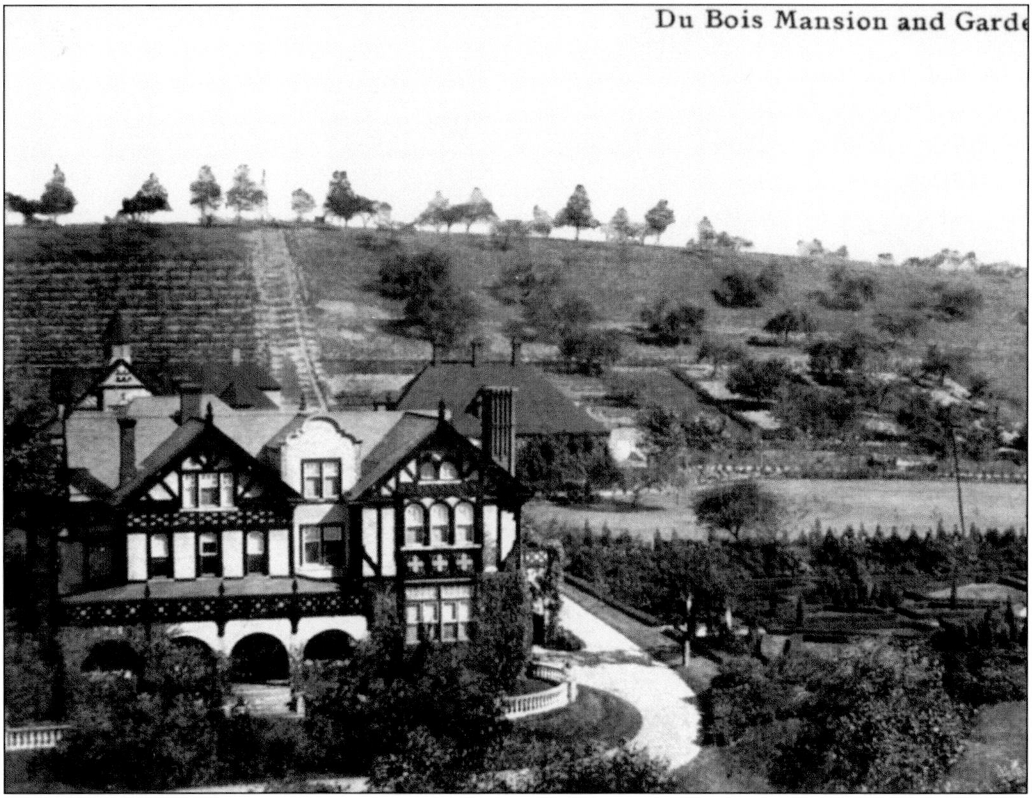

Du Bois Mansion and Gardens

The many gardens and orchards of the DuBois estate are shown here. To the right of the mansion are the beautiful gardens and goldfish ponds. Behind the mansion are the carriage house and the barn. On the hillside, in the rear, are apple orchards and grape vineyards and the monument that marks the burial site of John DuBois, founder of the town of DuBois.

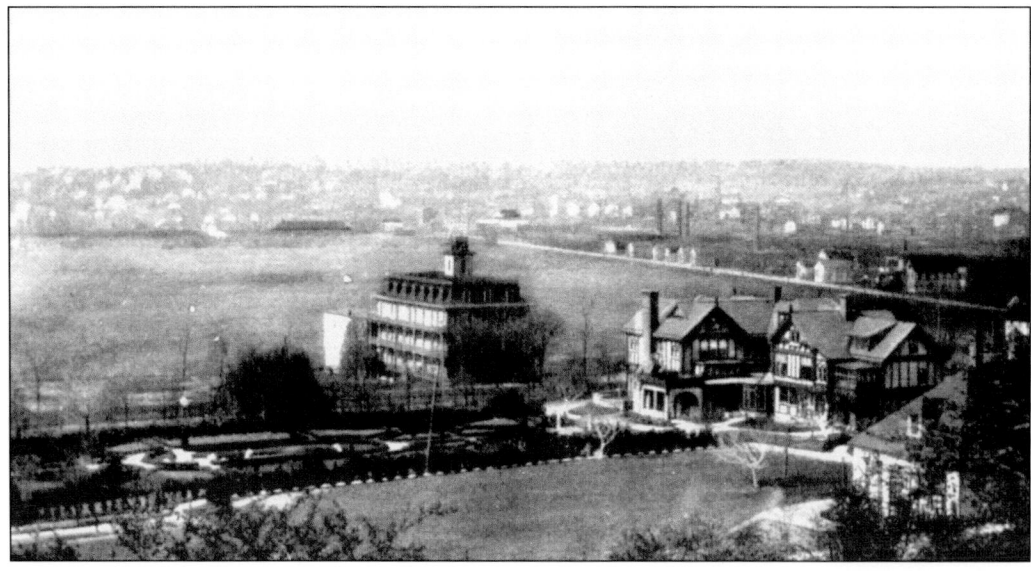

This view of the John E. DuBois estate shows the mansion and gardens. In the background is the DuBois House Hotel.

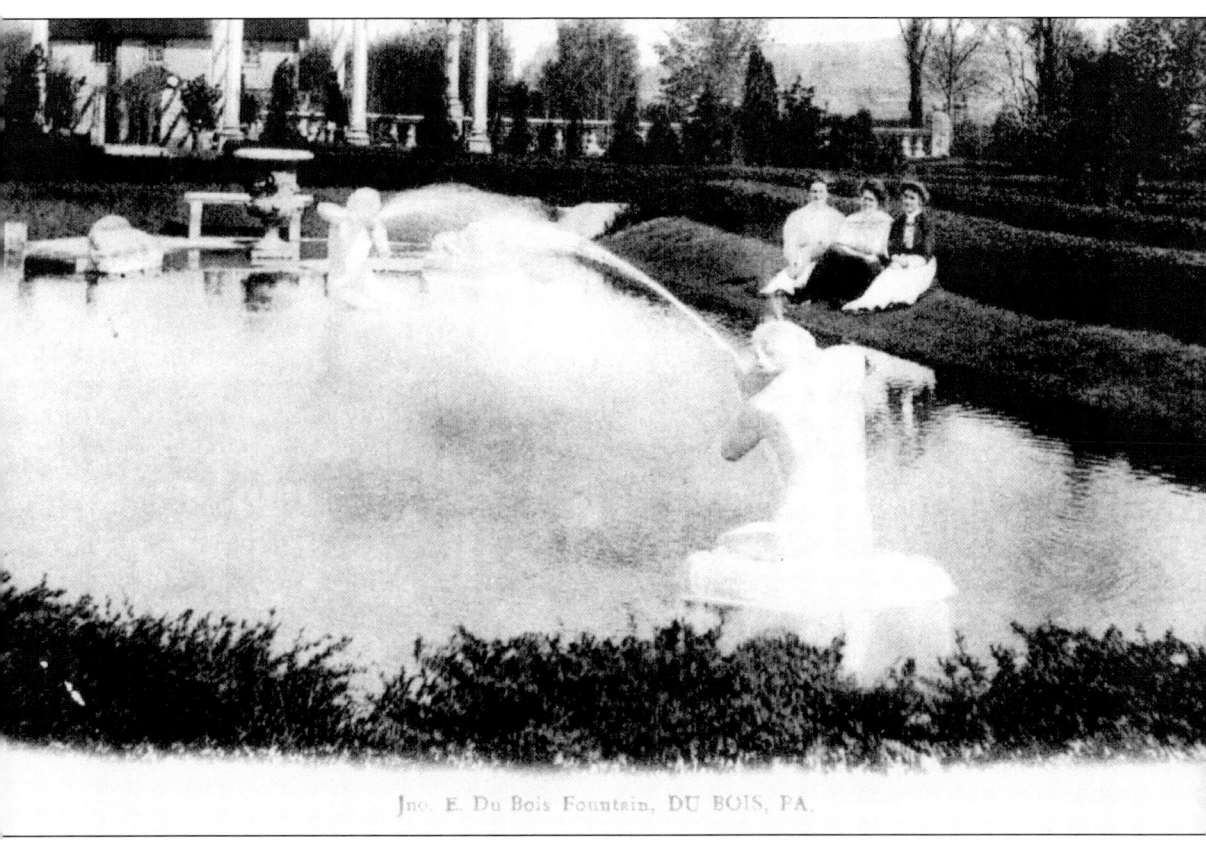

Willie Gamble DuBois, the wife of John E. DuBois, poses with daughters Sarah and Caroline in front of the fountains on the DuBois estate.

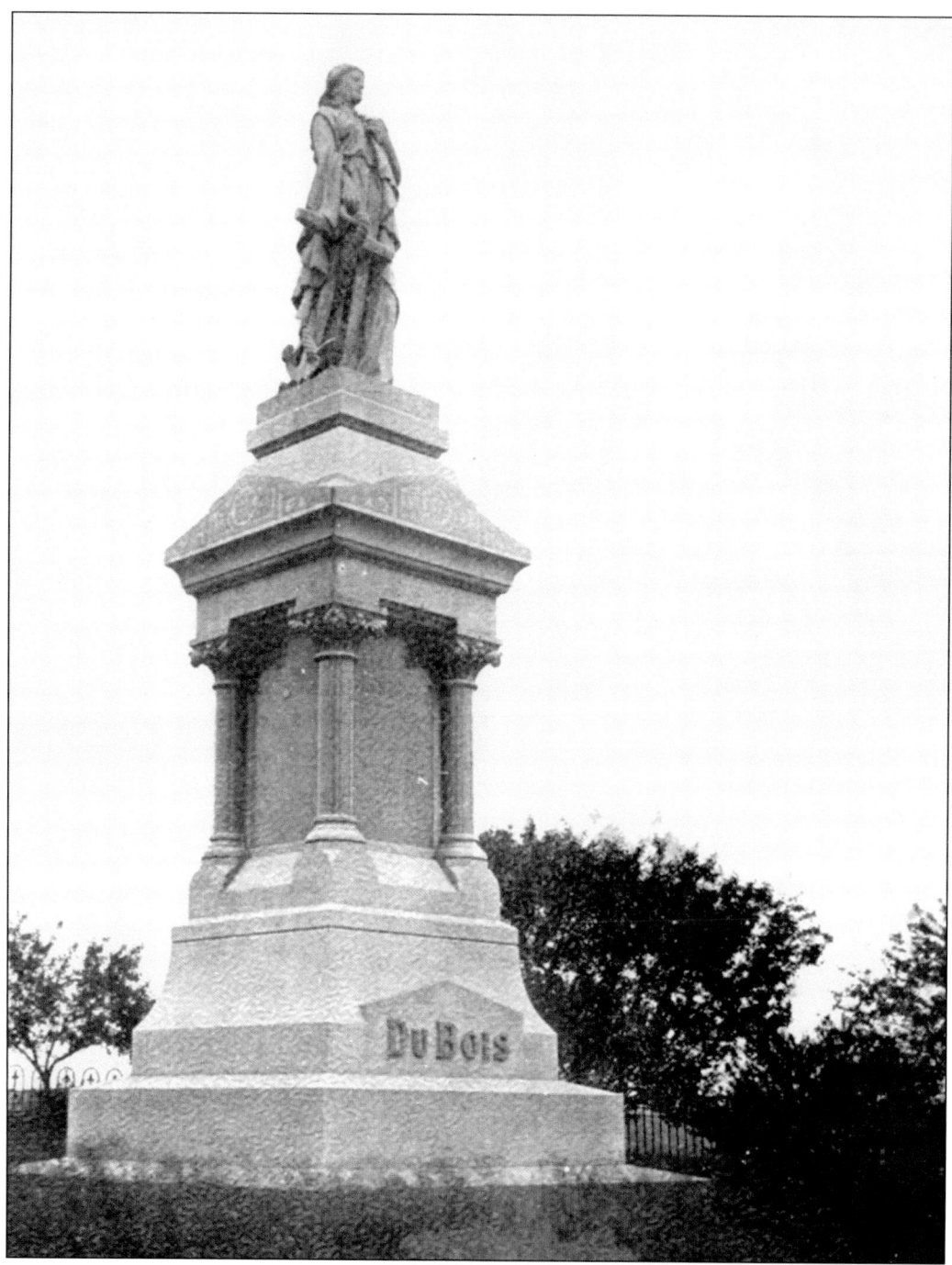
This monument was built in memory of John DuBois at the site of his grave, which is located on a hill overlooking the town of DuBois.

John E. DuBois took over the lumbering business and other enterprises after the death of his uncle, John DuBois. Known as a generous and caring man, John E. DuBois made many contributions to the community. He donated land for the Maple Avenue Hospital and funded the creation of the pipeline to the reservoir to supply water to the community.

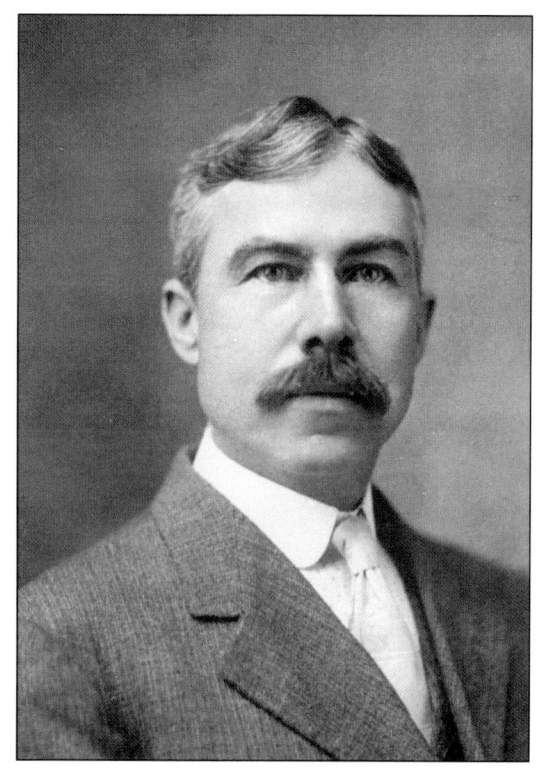

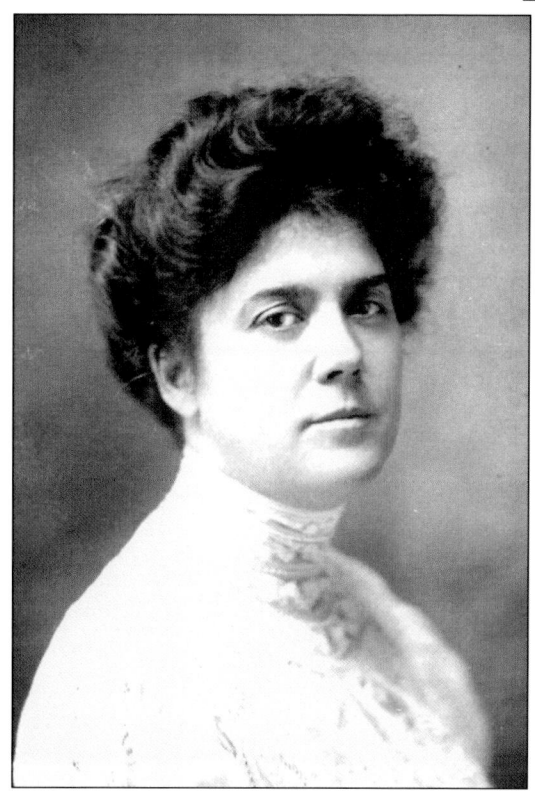

Willie Gamble DuBois was instrumental in the remodeling of the DuBois mansion into a Tudor country estate. She was also a prime mover in the DuBois Chapter of the Daughters of the American Revolution, at one point serving as regent.

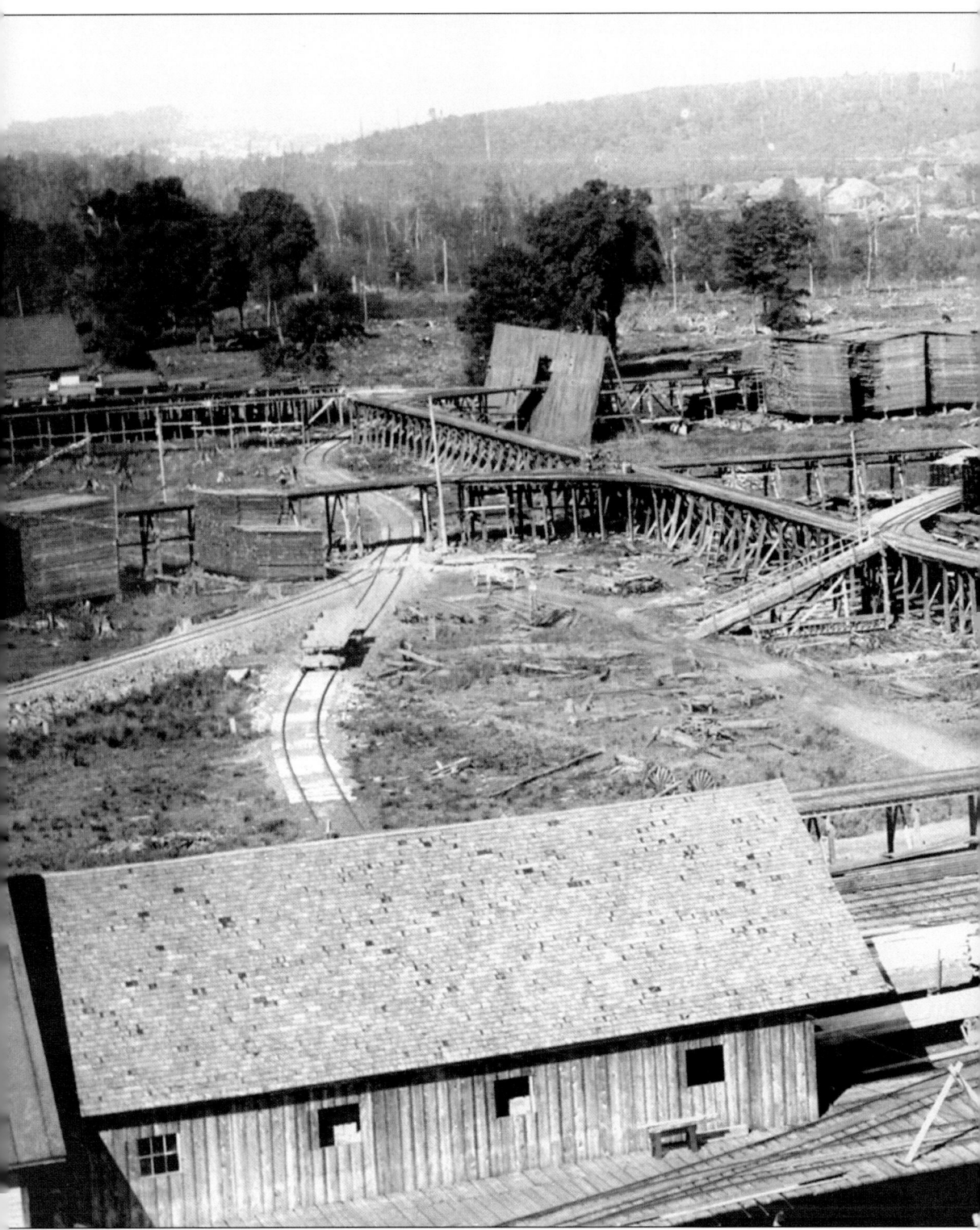
The large John DuBois Lumber Mill was located on the east side of what is now Liberty Boulevard.

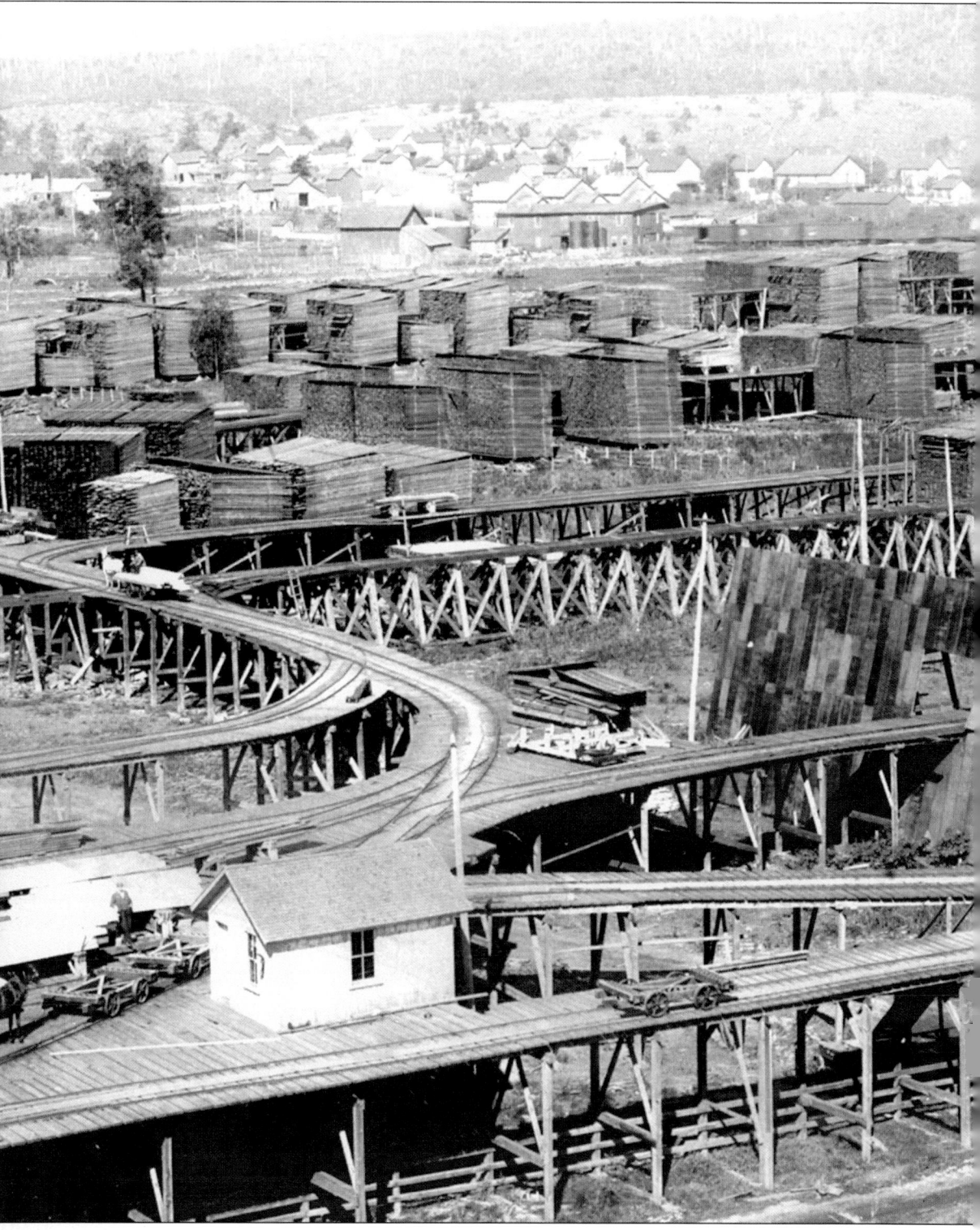
Built in 1874, the mill operated for 20 years. On June 13, 1904, the mill whistle gave its last toot.

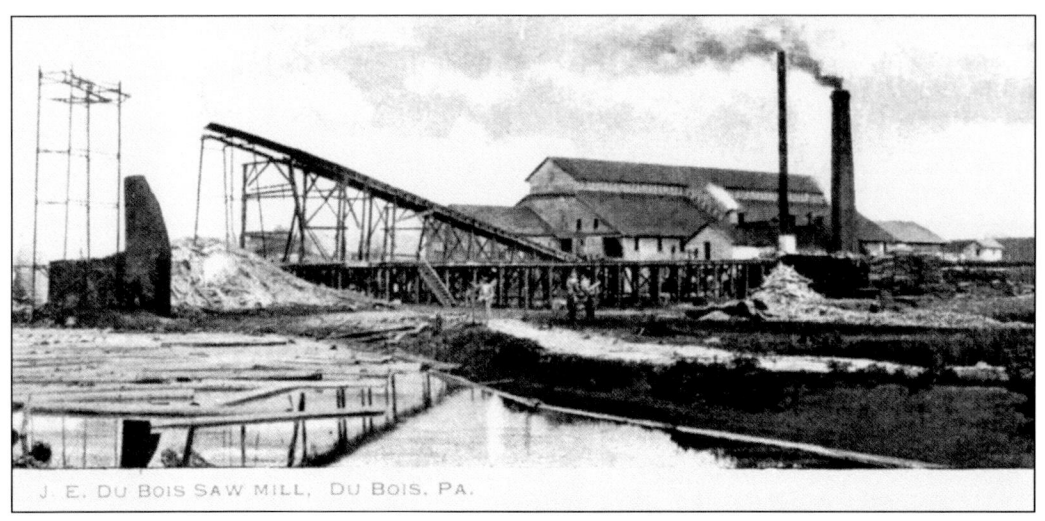
This mill was called the John DuBois Big Mill, and production began here in 1874.

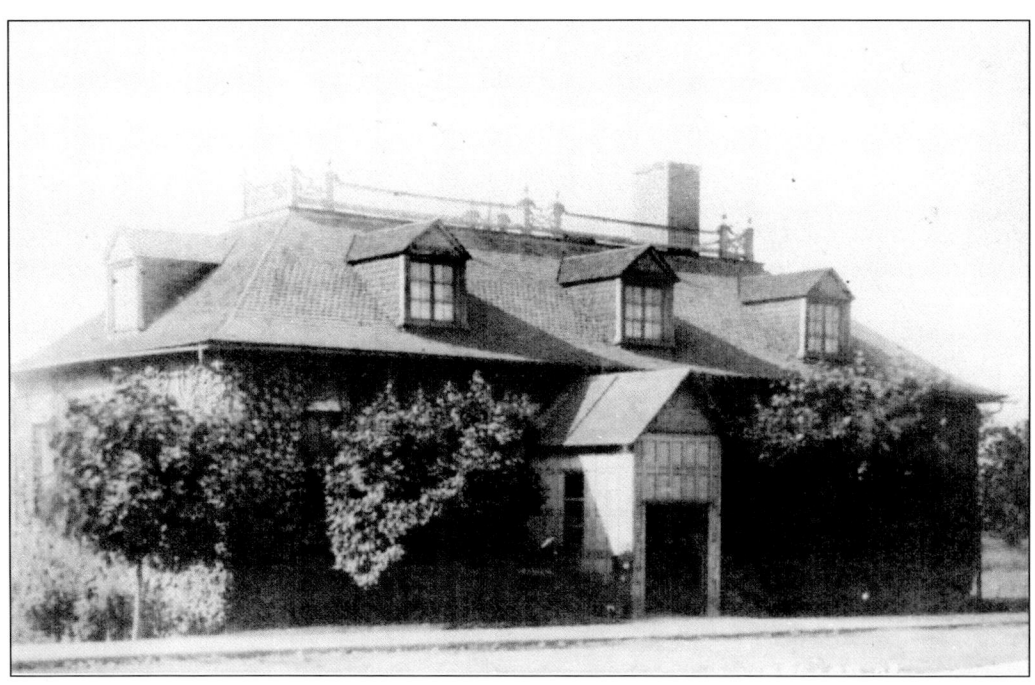
John E. DuBois's office is pictured here. It later became the WCED radio station.

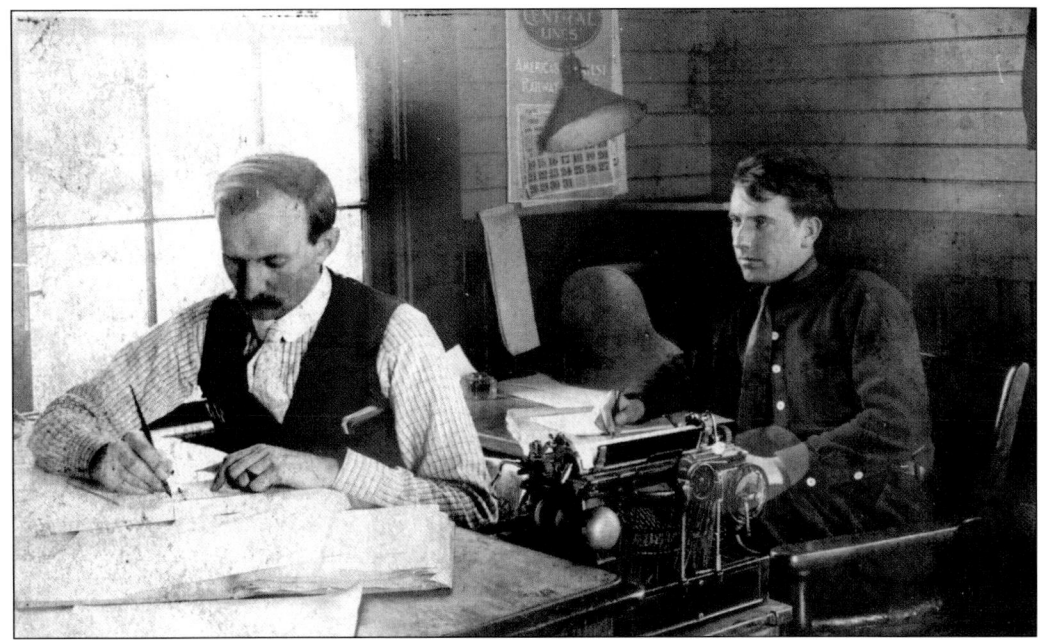

Chief clerk Leonard Resinger is seen at the typewriter and general yard manager Edward Barlett is at the other desk in this view of the DuBois yard office.

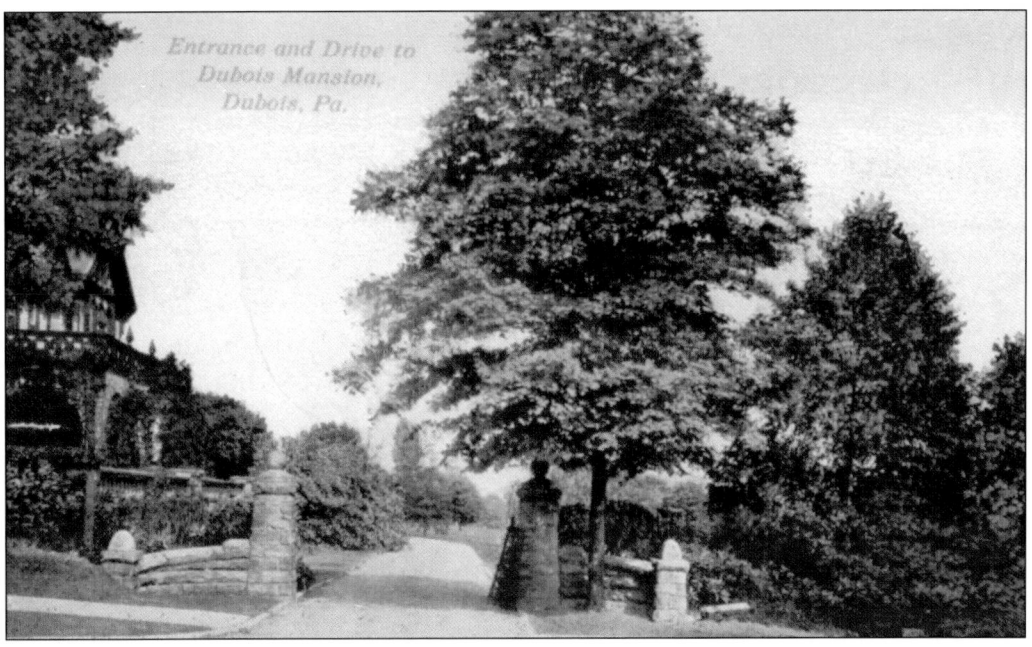

This is the entrance to the DuBois mansion.

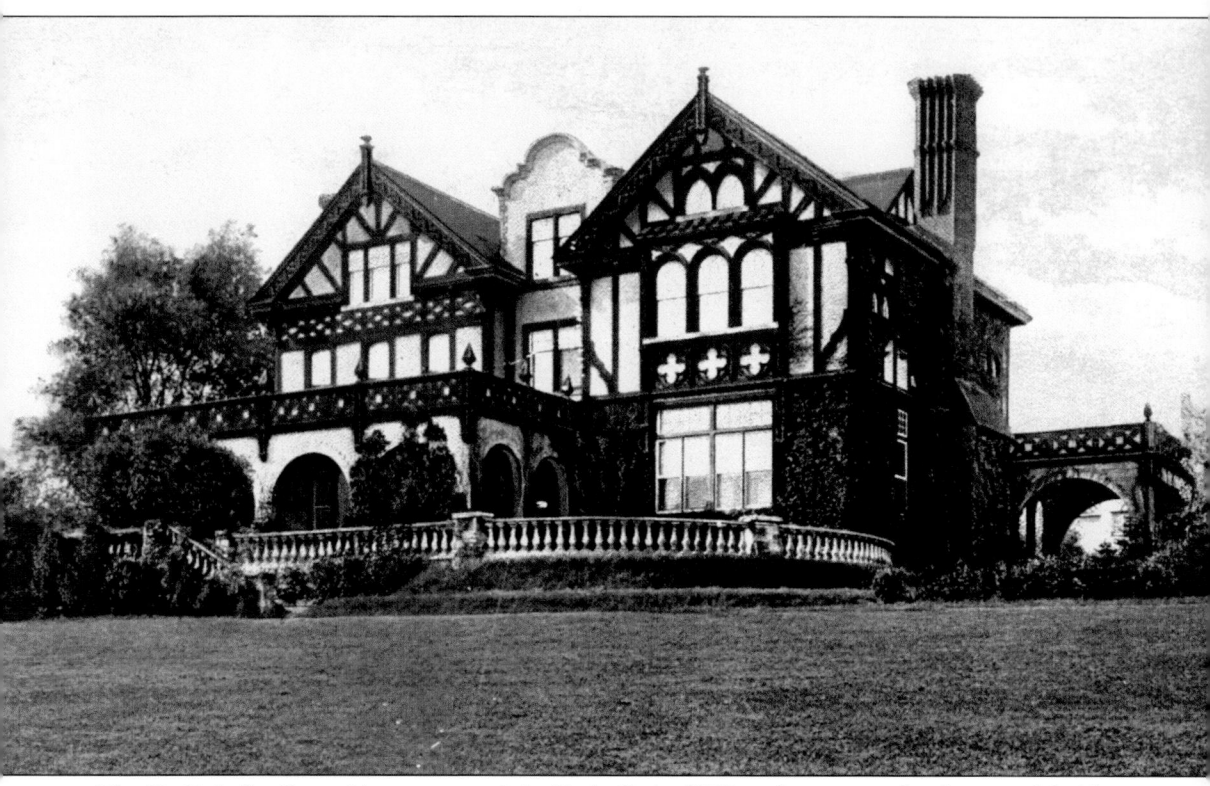

The DuBois family residence was originally built in 1876 and was completely remodeled by John E. DuBois and his wife, Willie, in 1902. When the renovation was complete, the house had more than doubled in size, and a ballroom had been added downstairs. The mansion was demolished in 1979.

Four
Business and Industry

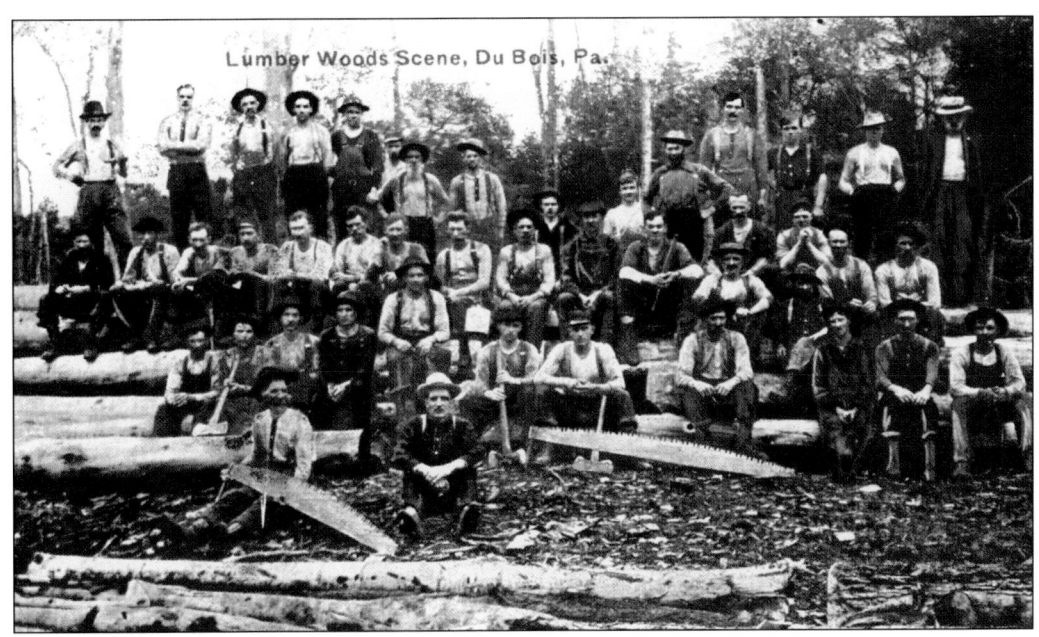

Some of the employees of John Dubois's lumbering business are shown in Hicks Run in the early 20th century.

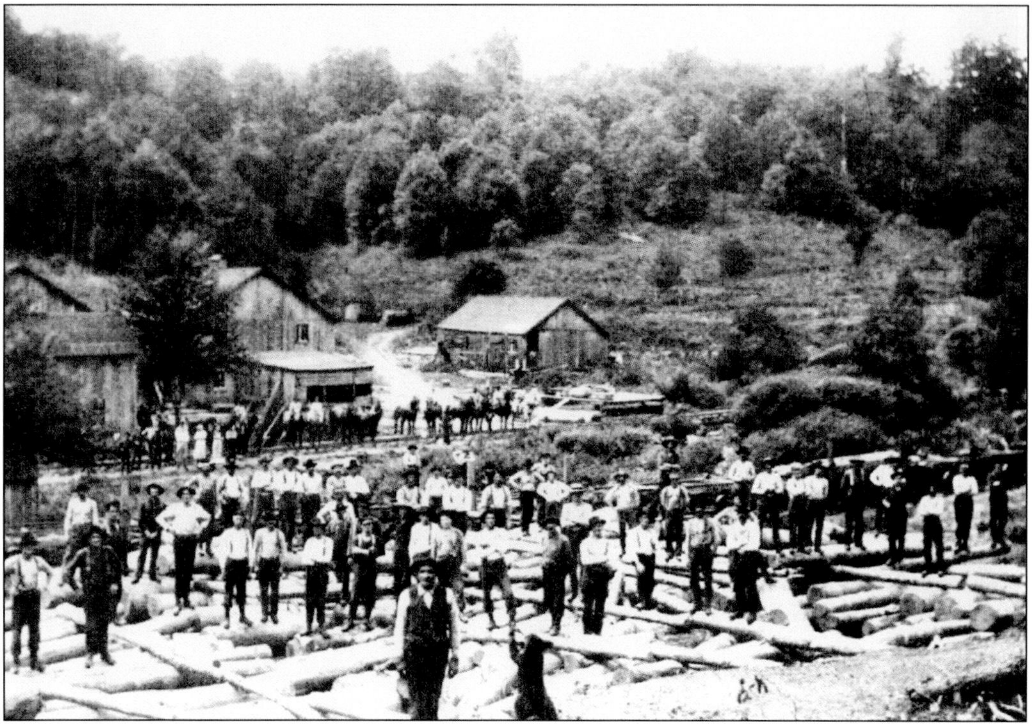

This is the J. E. DuBois Lumber Camp. The bear in the foreground was the camp mascot.

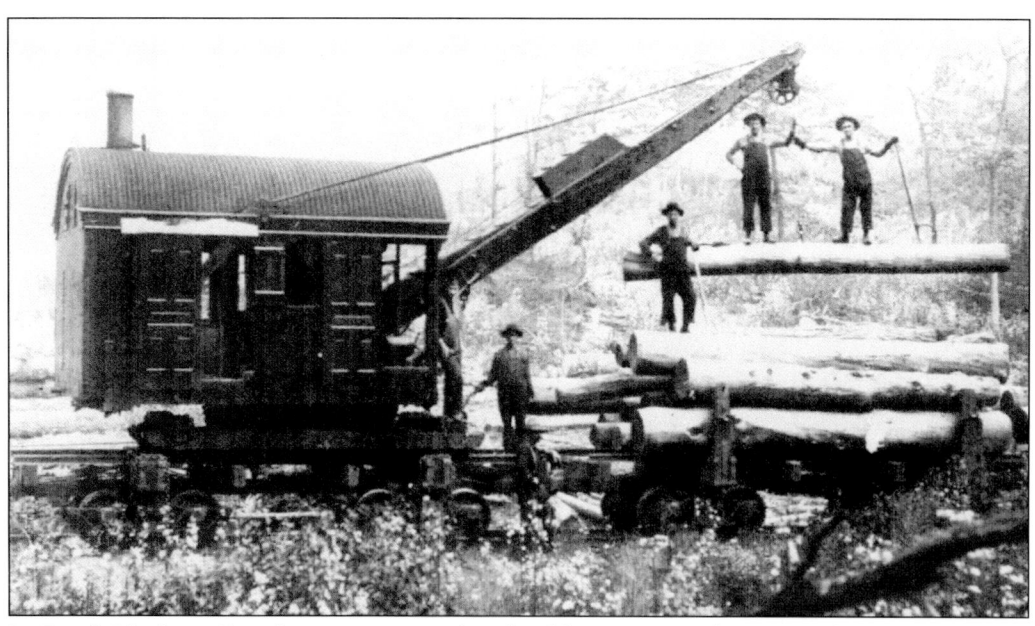

In Penfield, the railroad crane was used to load logs onto railway cars for transportation to the mills.

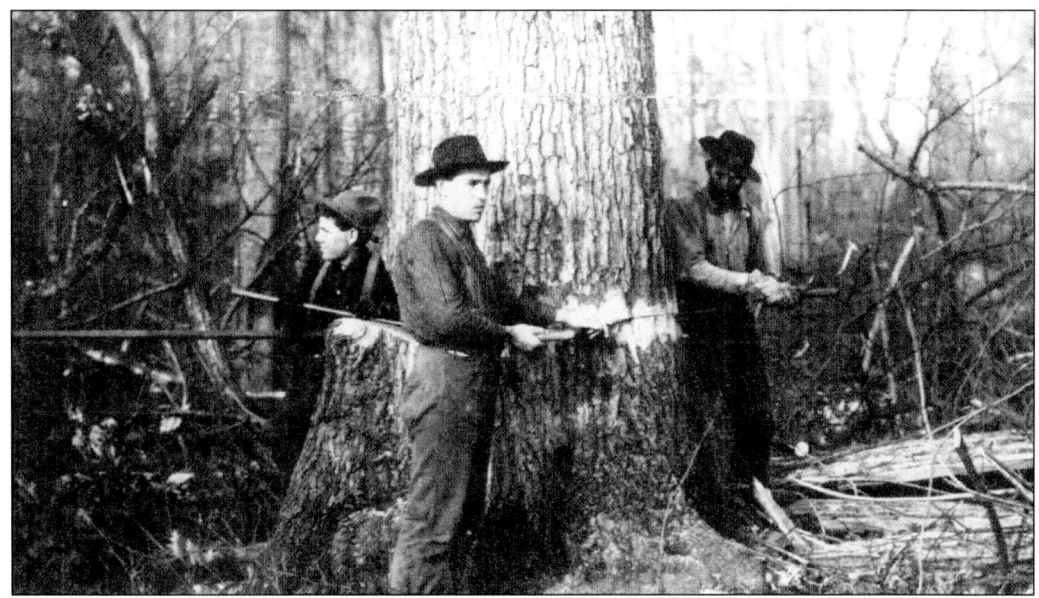
Men from the Penfield area use a crosscut saw to cut a very large tree for the lumber company.

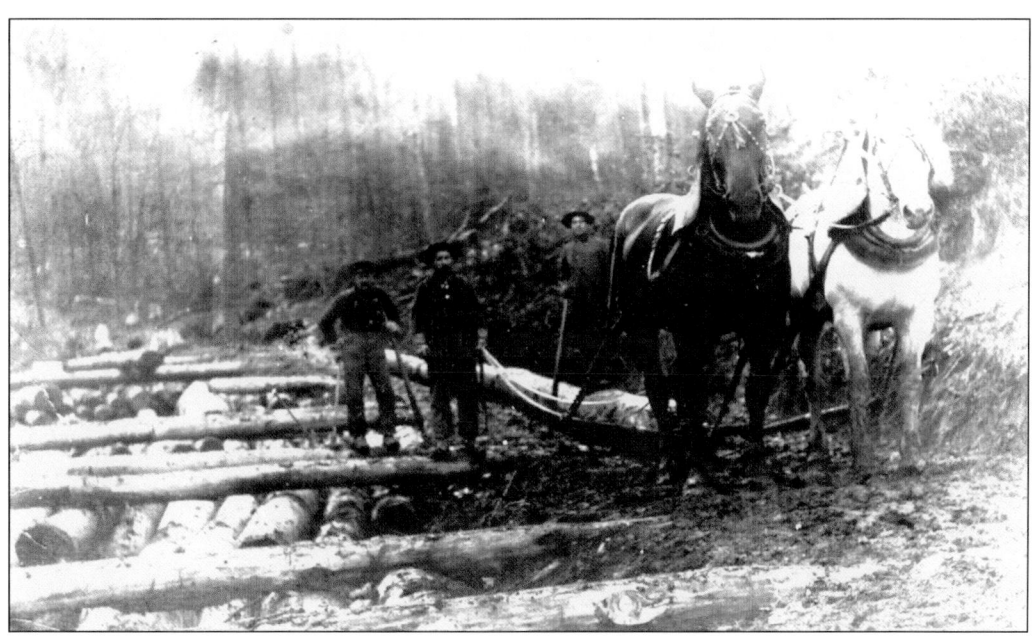
Horses were used to haul the logs out of the Penfield woods. The logs were then shipped to the mill.

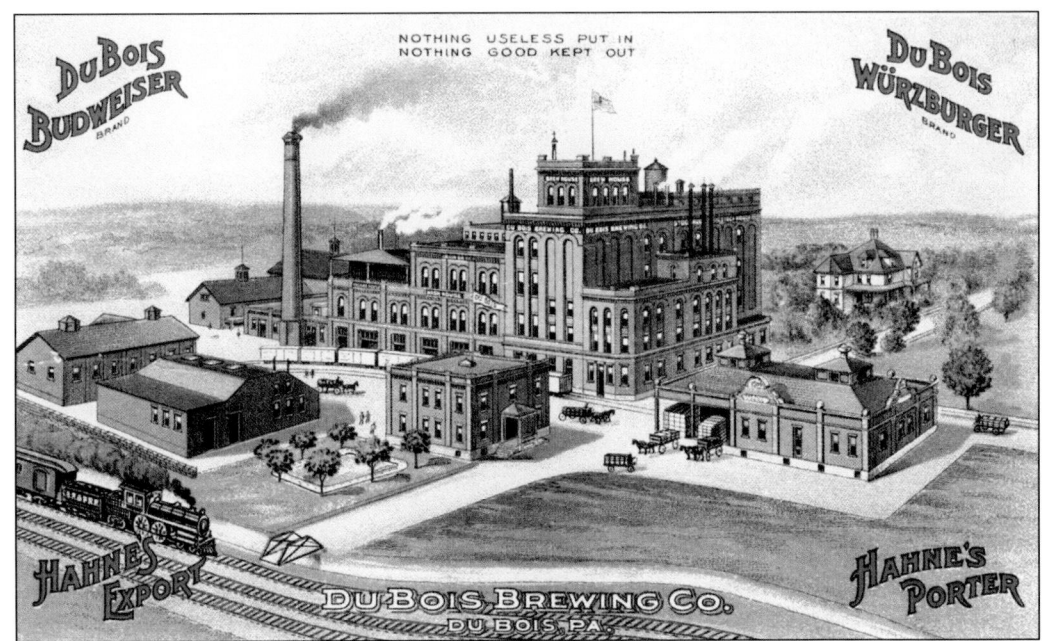

The DuBois Brewing Company was built in 1896 and was owned and operated by Frank Hahne, who was born in Germany. DuBois Budweiser beer was produced here until 1972, when the brewery was sold to a firm in Pittsburgh.

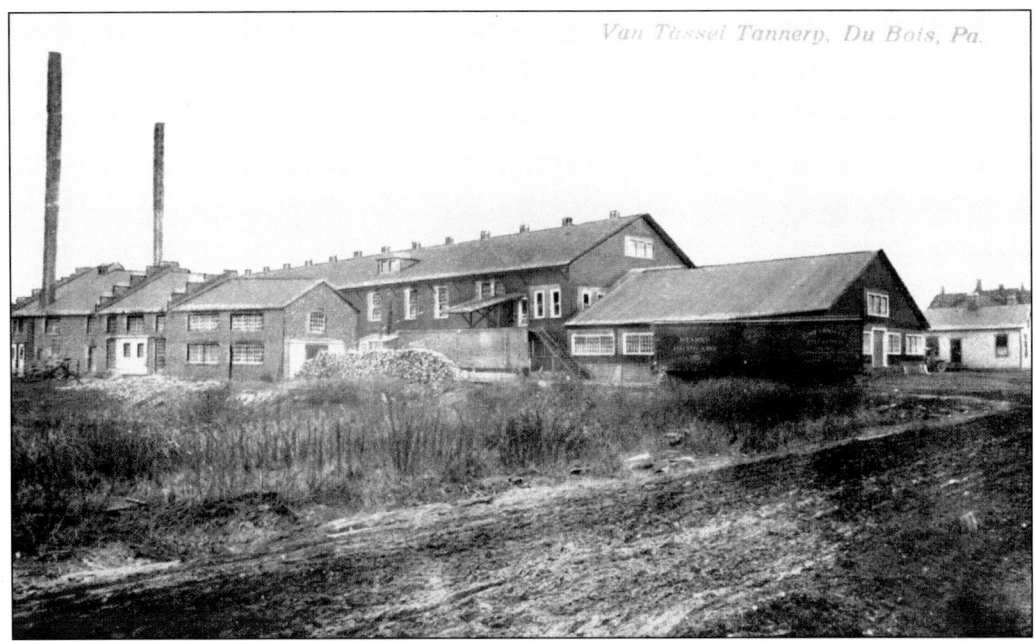

The Van Tassel Tannery in DuBois operated from 1889 to 1898, producing 1,000 tanned hides per week.

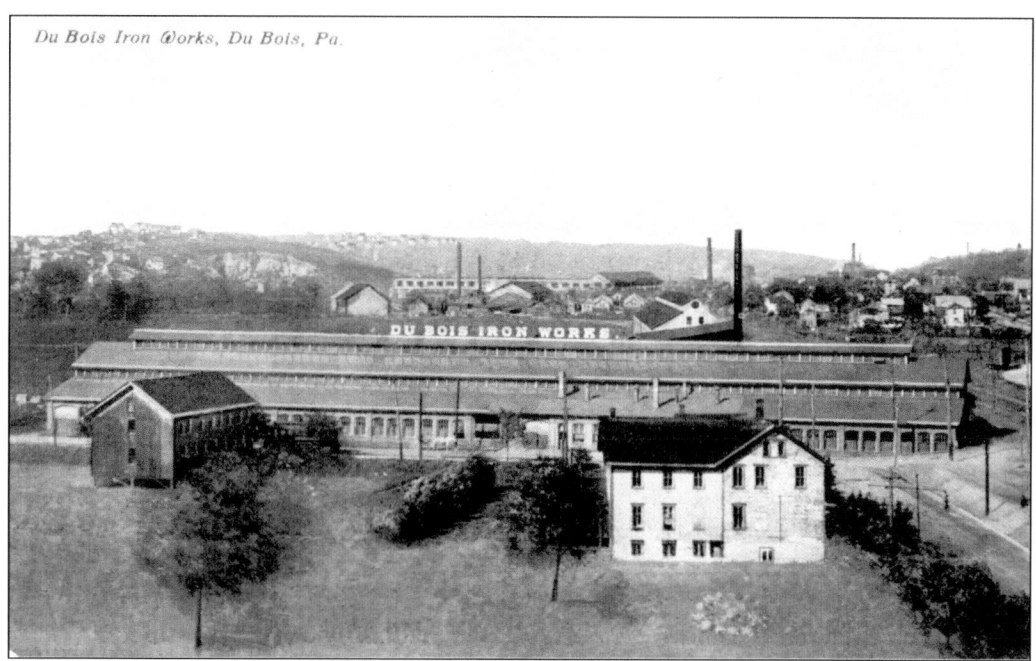

John DuBois founded the DuBois Iron Works in 1876. In 1947, it became the Pittsburgh DuBois division of the Rockwell Manufacturing Company. The building in the foreground was the Blue Moon Tavern. The smaller building was called the Pattern Shop for the iron works.

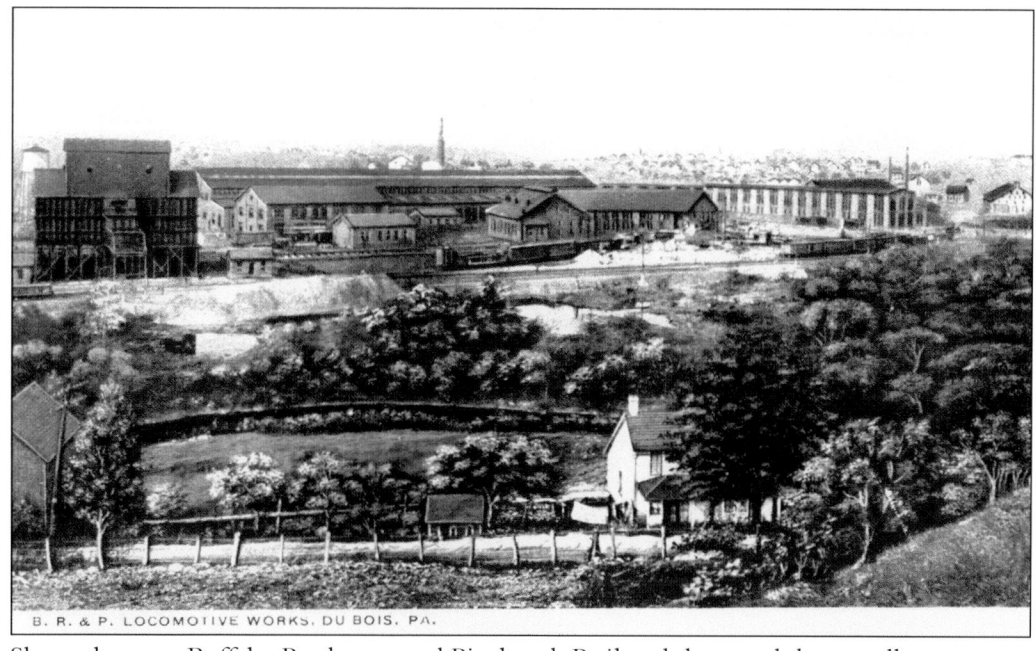

Shown here are Buffalo, Rochester, and Pittsburgh Railroad shops and the roundhouse.

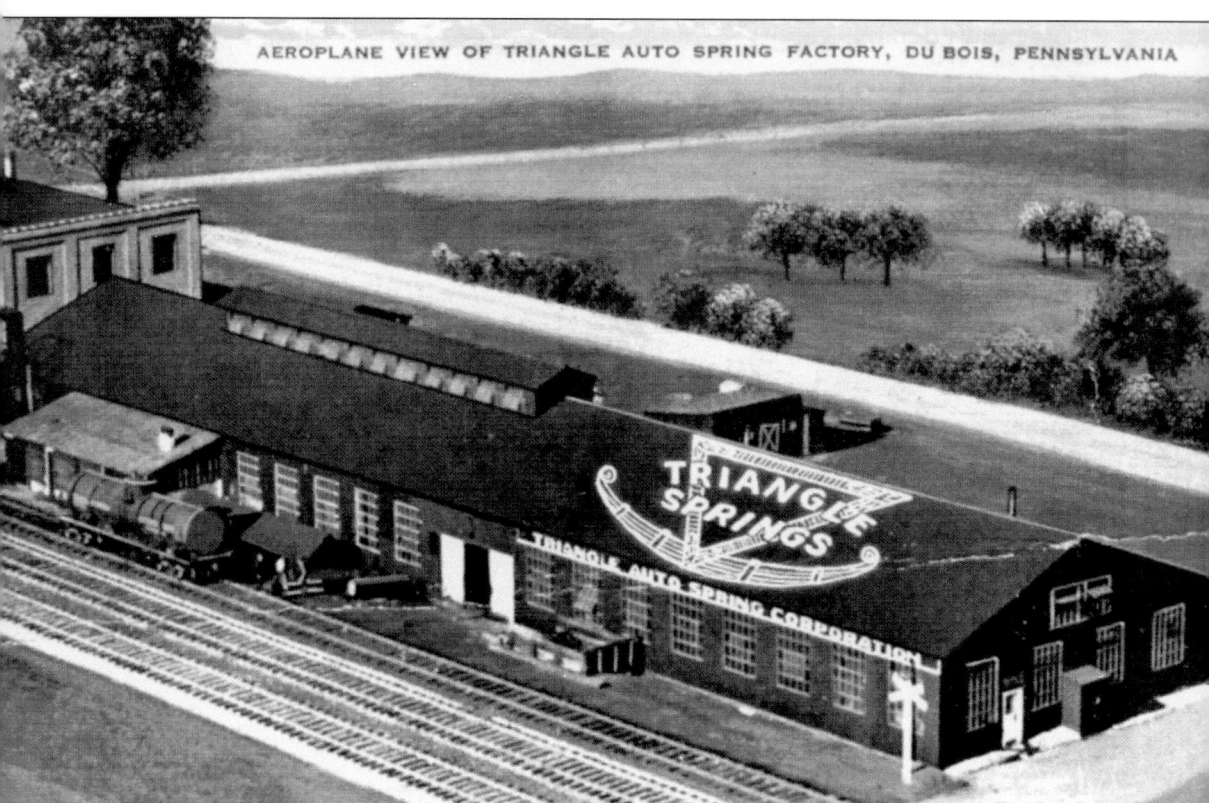

Fred Brown, J. Claire Dunlap, and Earl Oldknow founded the Triangle Auto Springs Company, which manufactured springs for automobiles and trucks. John Deardorf later developed a nationwide market for the business. Triangle Springs moved from Pittsburgh to DuBois in 1927. D. E. Hibner was plant manager.

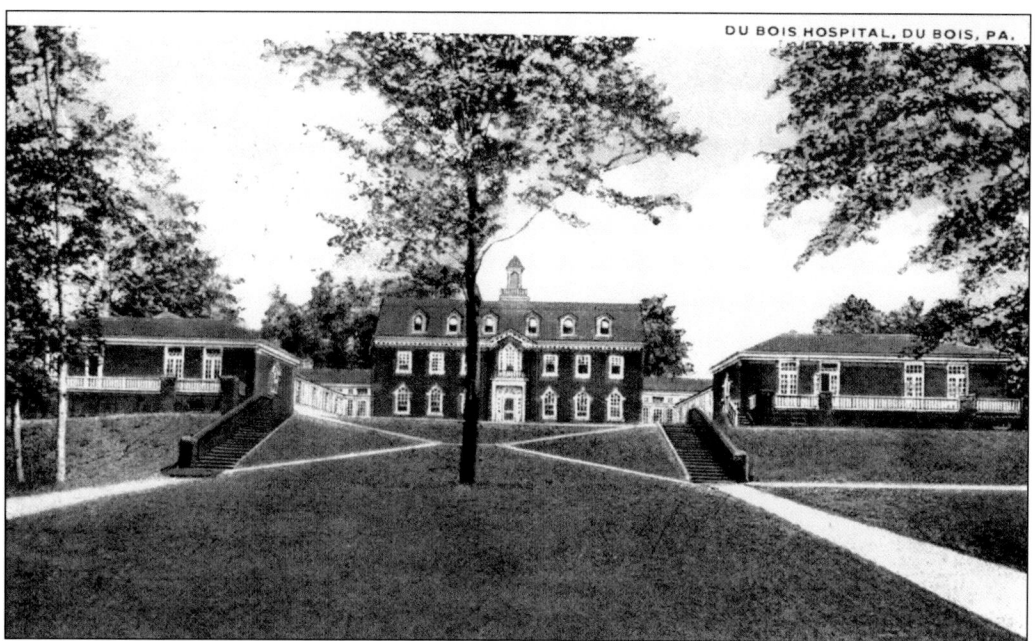

DuBois Hospital was founded in 1897, with Dr. Fugate and Dr. J. C. Sullivan serving as surgeons. The hospital was located on West Scribner Avenue and had 23 beds. The building soon became inadequate, and a new one was built on South Main Street. The hospital has expanded several times over the years.

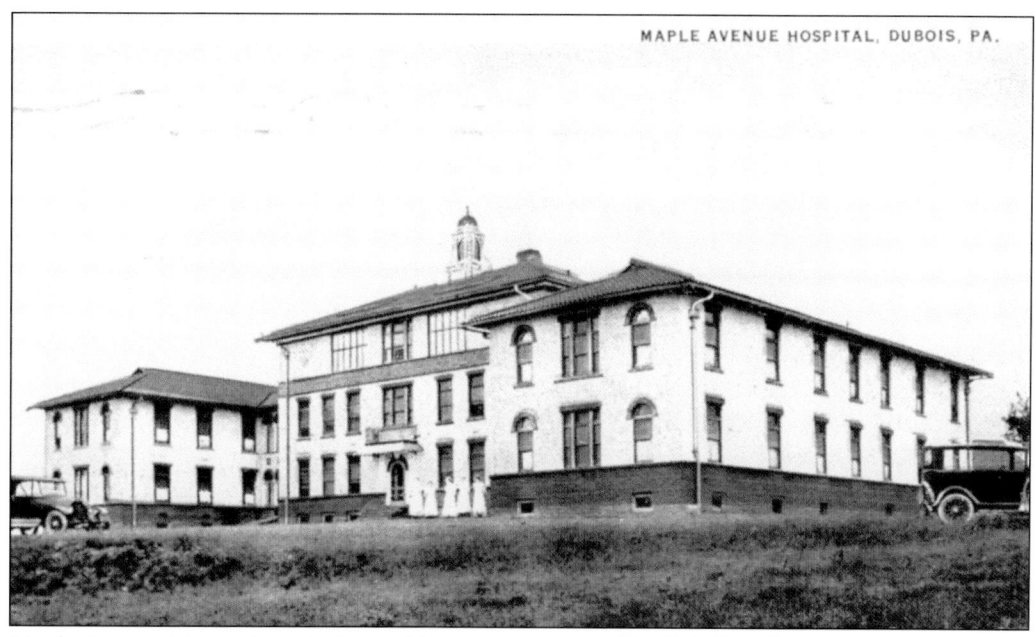

Maple Avenue Hospital was built in 1915 at a total cost of $41,200. The first patient was admitted in October 1918 for treatment of Spanish influenza. Doctors S. M. Davenport, Hillary, Booher, E. E. Hauck Sr., and Quinn served this 35-bed hospital.

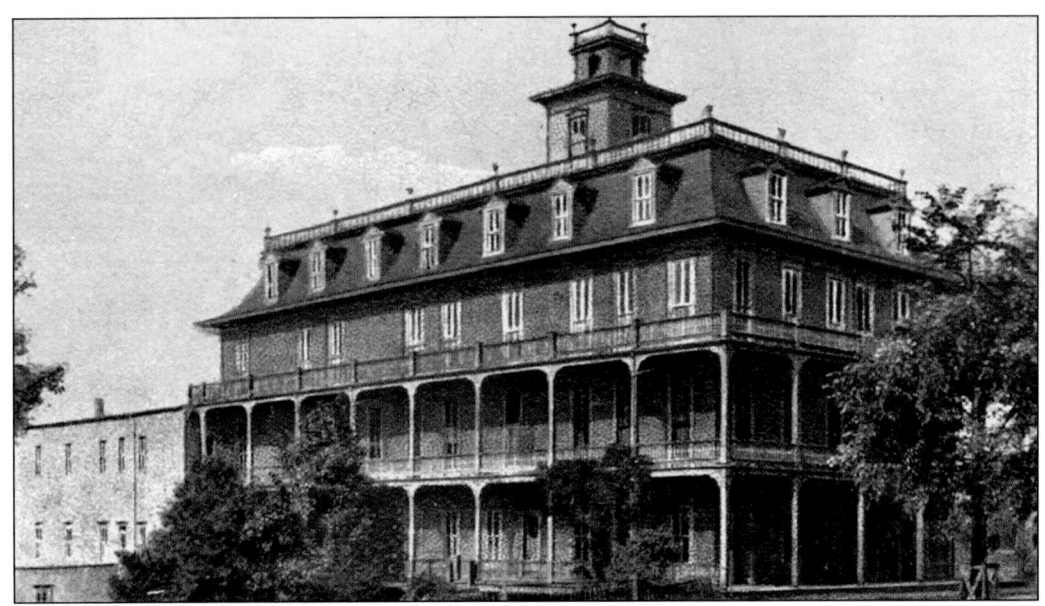

The DuBois House Hotel was in service during the lumbering days and was located between the present WCED radio station and the Best Western. The building was constructed by John DuBois in his early lumbering days, between 1874 and 1900. The first floor was occupied by his store, the second floor by his offices, and the third and fourth floors by the hotel. The building became the home of DuBois Business College in 1885. It was demolished shortly after World War II.

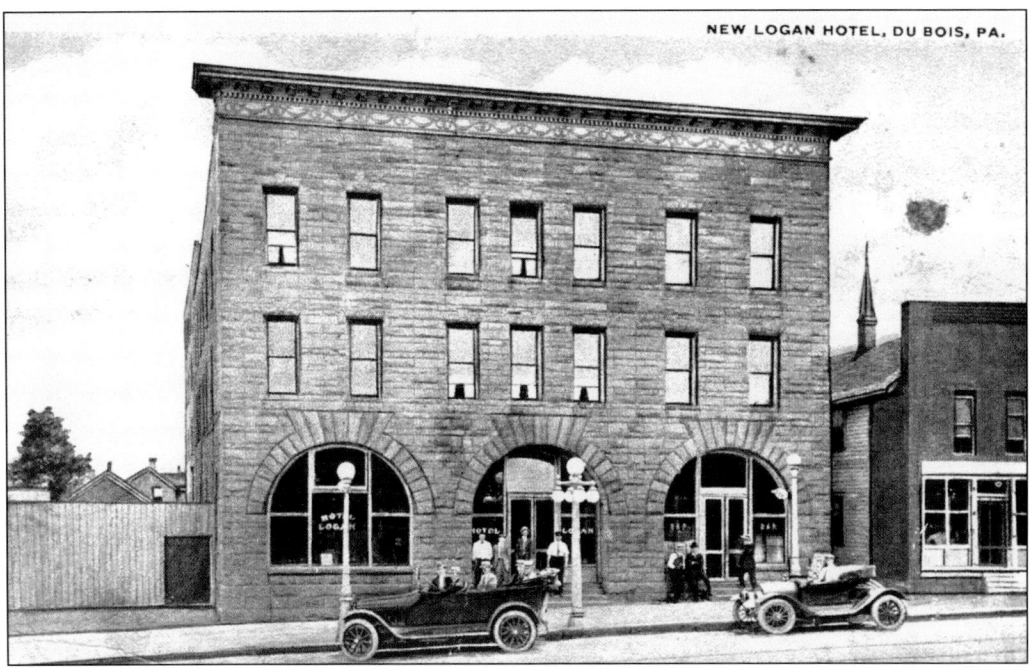

The Logan Hotel was built in the early 20th century by George and Tom Minns and was managed by George Sloppy. It gained prestige in the early 1920s, when a four-story addition was built. The hotel was destroyed by fire in the 1960s.

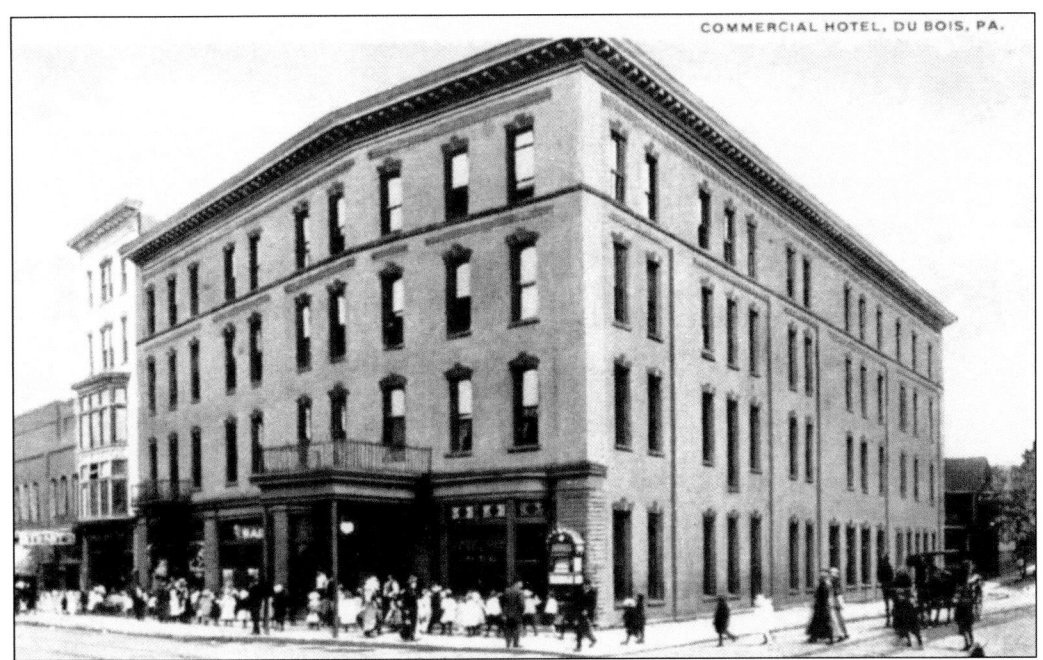

The Commercial Hotel was built in the 1890s and was a hub of activity. Its name was later changed to the Pershing Hotel. The Harris Theater was added later. The Harris DuBois Theater became part of the hotel in the mid-1930s

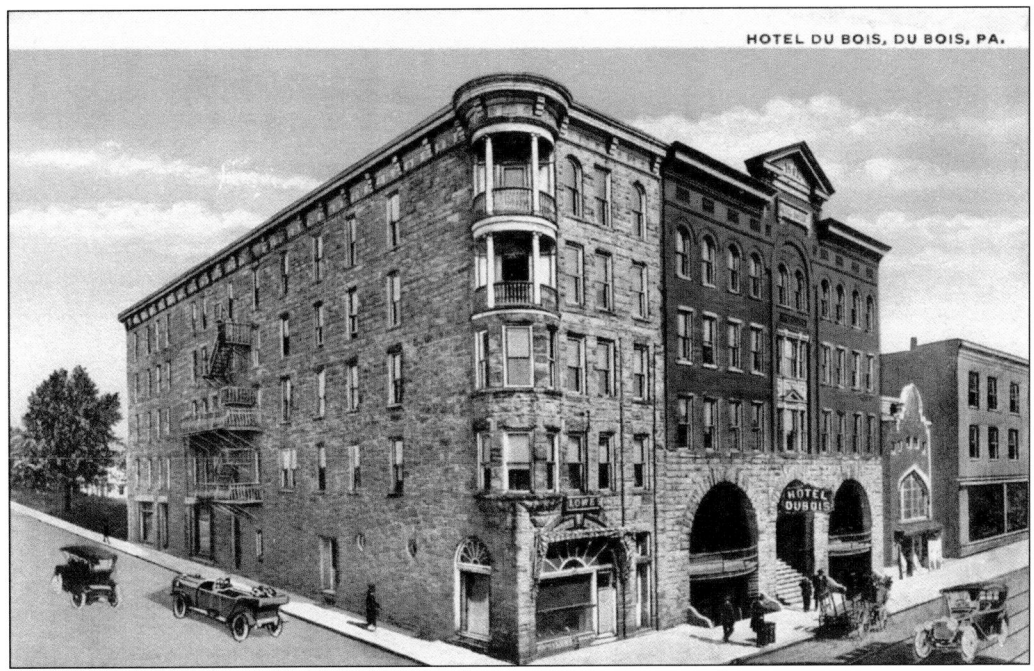

The early Courier Express newspaper building, located at the corner of West Long Avenue and High Street, was three stories high. Two more stories were added later. The Hotel DuBois was next door.

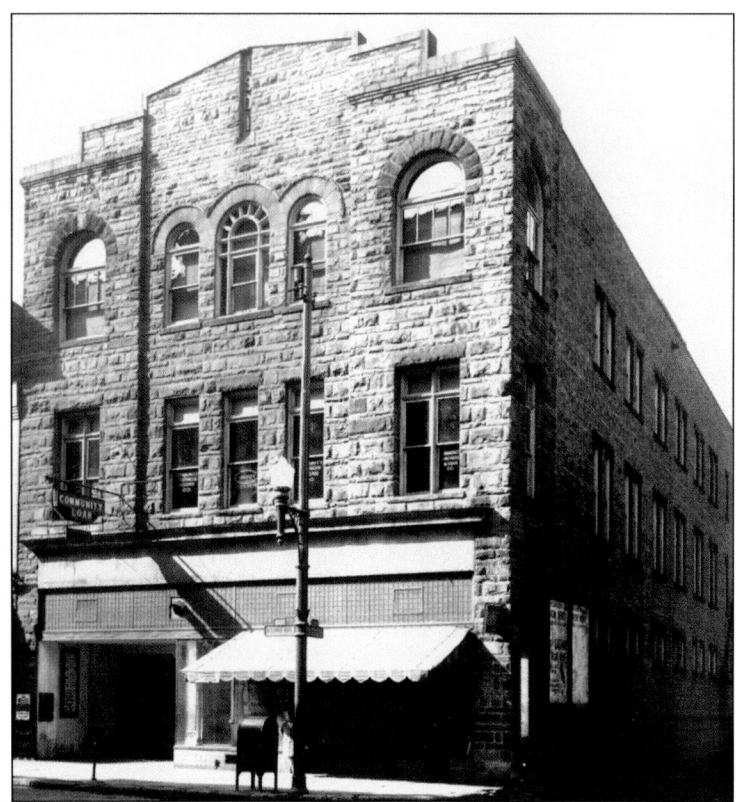

The first YMCA building was dedicated in 1901. It was located on West Long Avenue where St. Michael's Terrace is today. In the mid-1930s, the YMCA moved to a new facility on Scribner Avenue, which served thousands of people until its closing in 1979. Since 1981, the YMCA has been located on Parkway Drive.

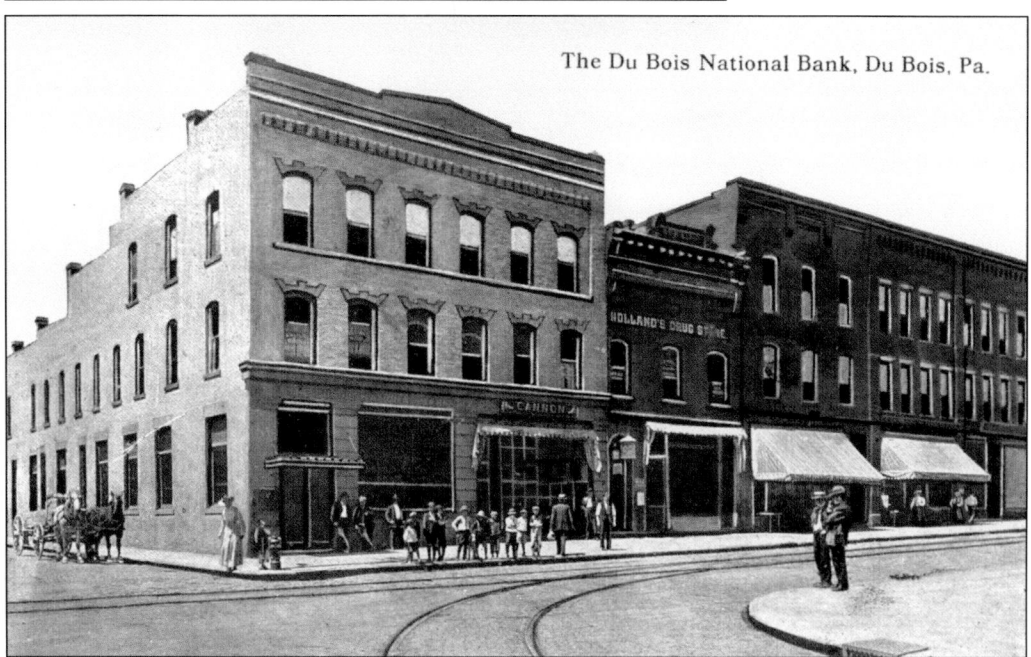

The DuBois business district was located at the corner of Long and Brady Streets. DuBois National Bank was on the corner, followed by Con Allen's shoe store, Blankfeld Jewelry, and Brown's Boot Shop. The area was organized by John E. DuBois and S. C. Bond on November 21, 1889.

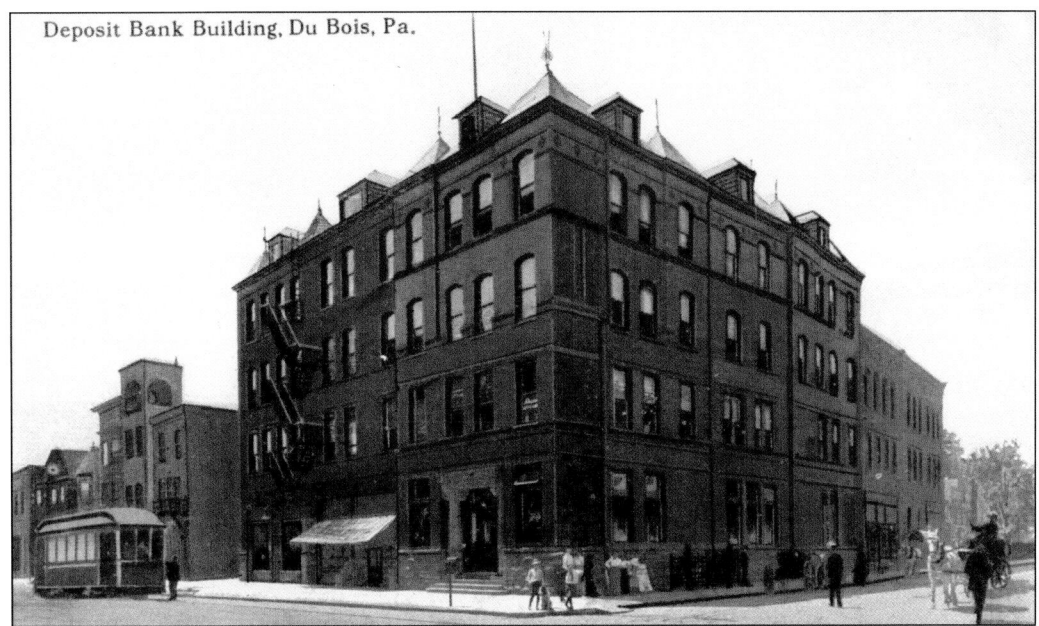

The Deposit National Bank building is located on the corner of Brady Street and East Long Avenue in DuBois. It is the oldest existing bank in town. The first building was constructed in 1880. After it was destroyed by the 1888 fire, a new building was constructed in January 1889. The Harbison furniture store was located next to the bank.

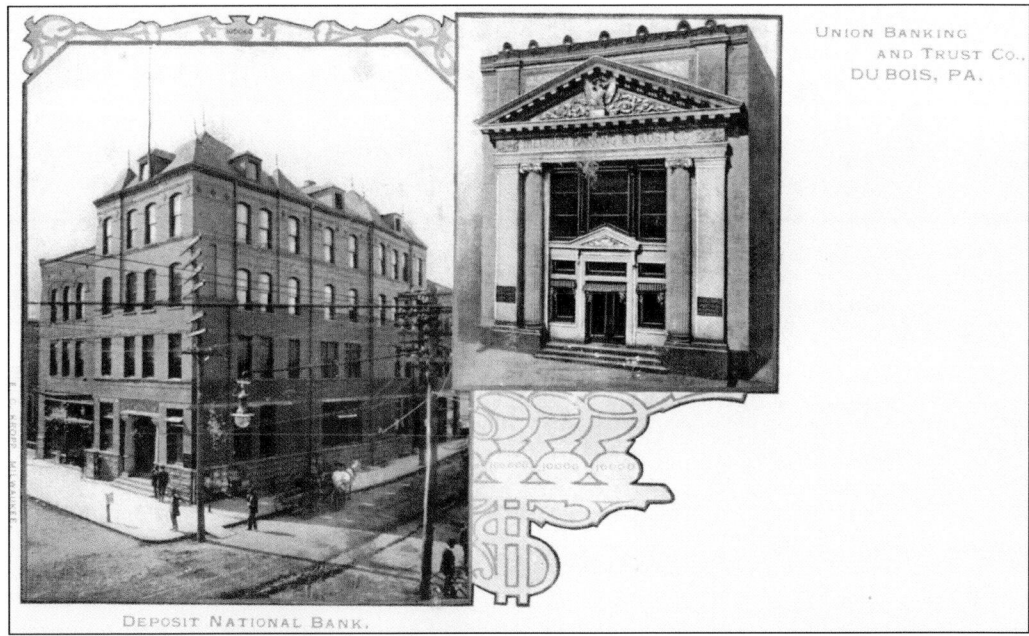

The Deposit National Bank and Union Banking and Trust Company are shown here.

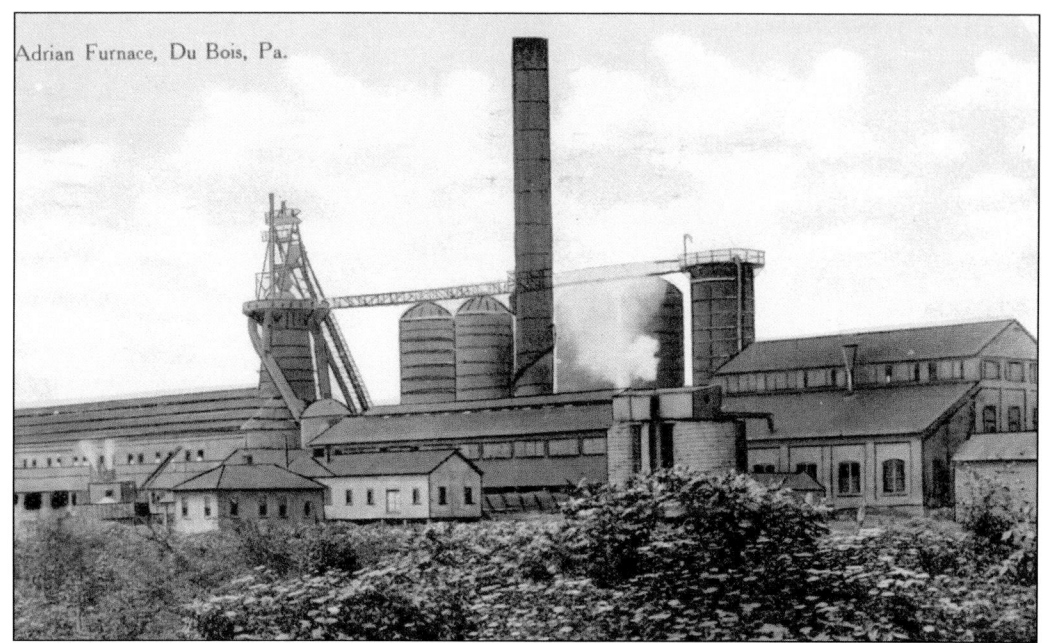

The Adrian Furnace Company was another business located in DuBois. Construction of the building began in 1902, and on August 8, 1903, the million-dollar plant was ready for operation. The Rochester and Pittsburgh Coal and Iron Company operated it until 1904, when the charter was granted to the Adrian Furnace Company.

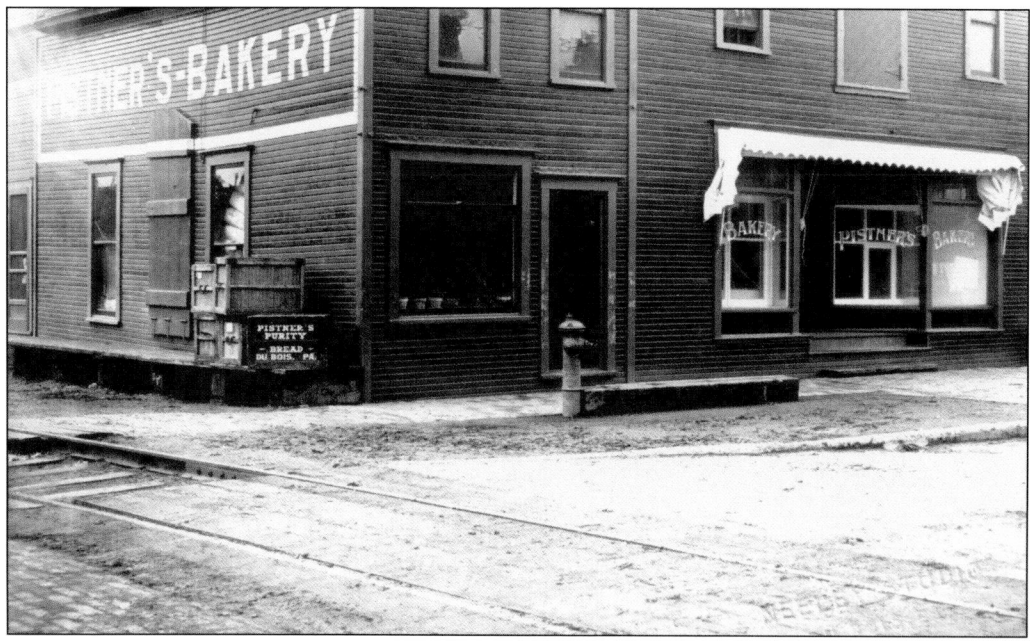

The Pistner Bakery, opened in 1913, was located on West Washington Avenue until c. 1950. The building was then occupied by Wayland Feed and Farm Supply. The building is now the home of Now and Then Antiques.

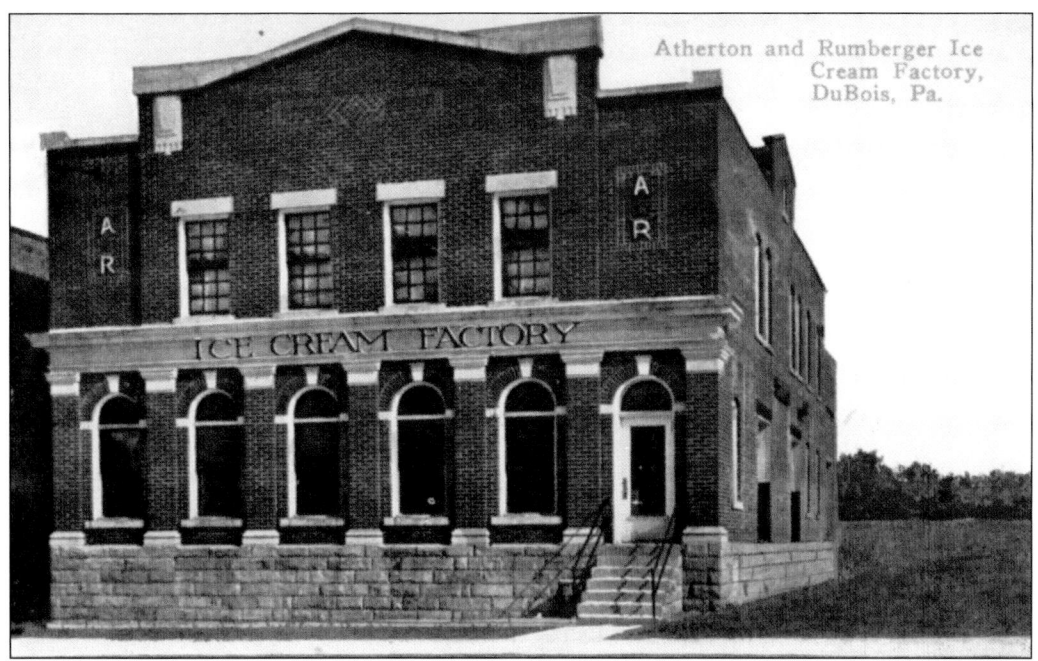

The Atherton and Rumbarger Ice Cream Factory opened on Jared Street in 1910 and operated until 1929.

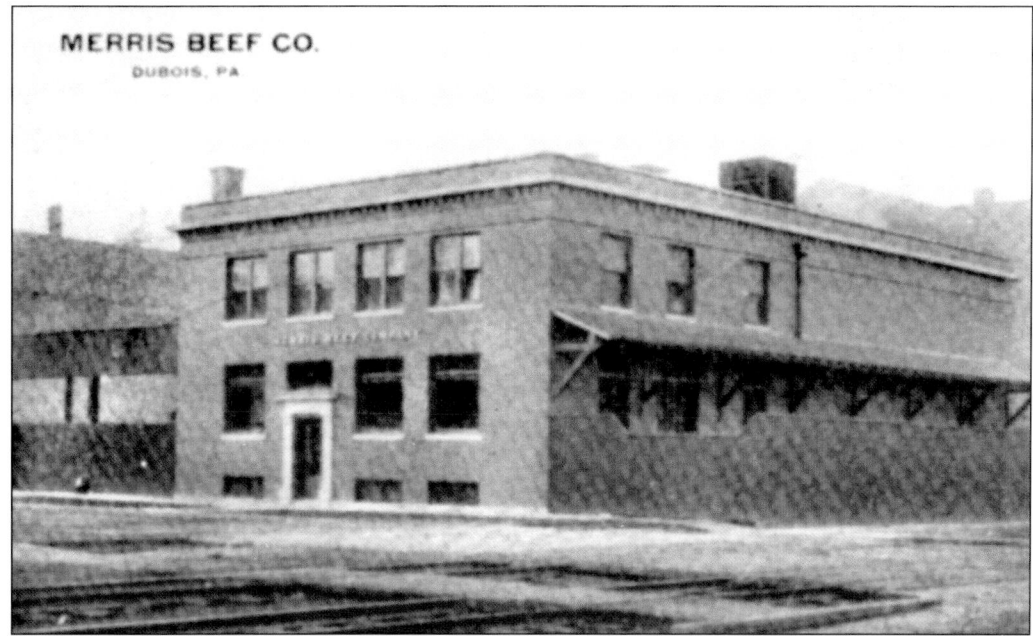

The Merris Beef Company, located on West Washington Avenue, was owned by Eugene and Howard I. Merris. They sold wholesale dressed meat in the early 20th century. The building later housed Larkin Plumbing and Heating.

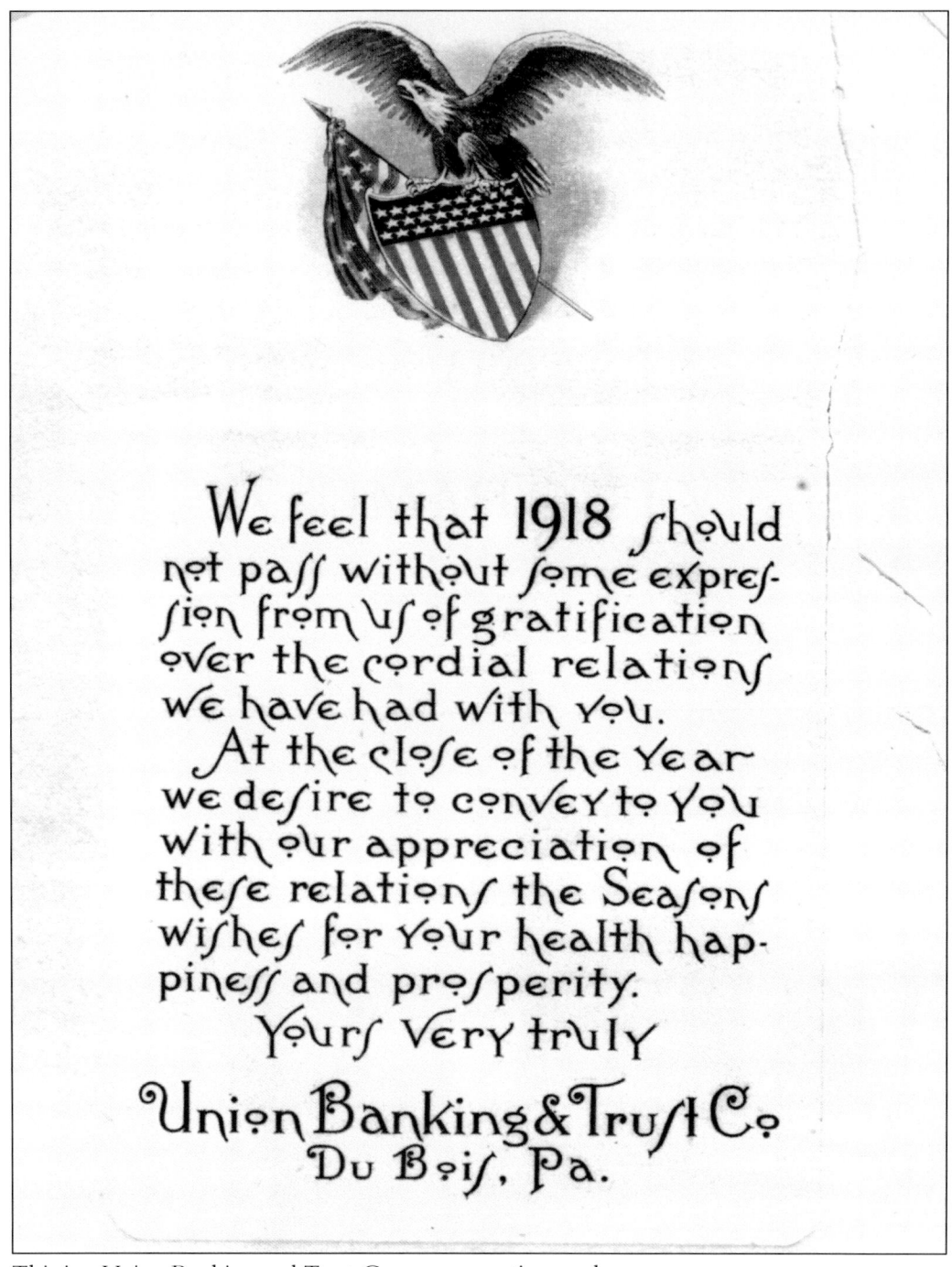

This is a Union Banking and Trust Company greeting card.

Five
COMMUNITY

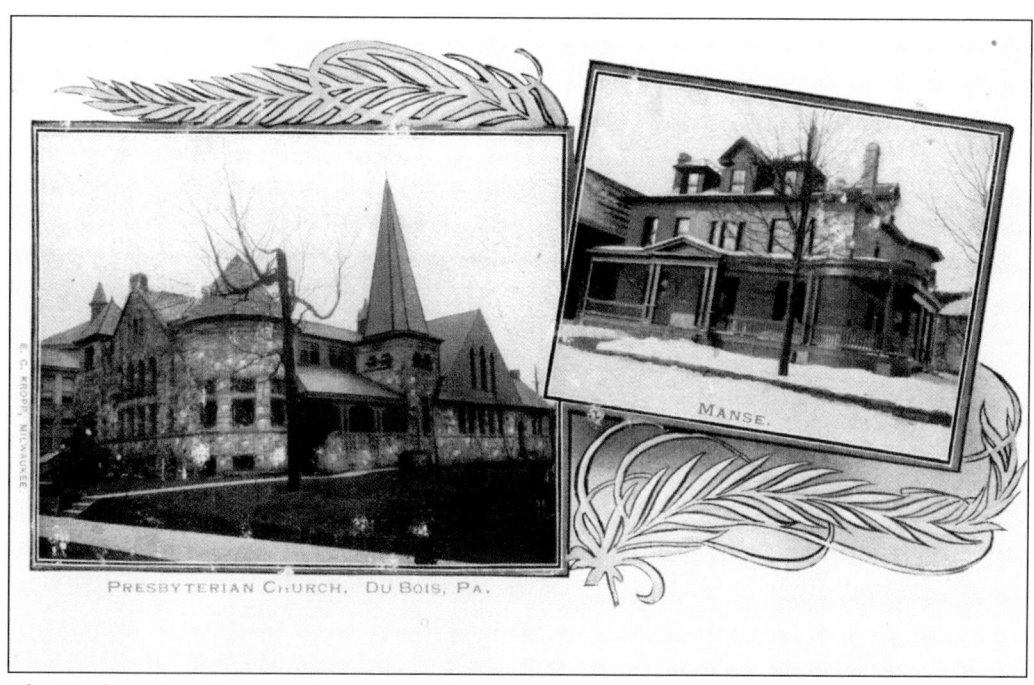

The Presbyterian church and manse are shown here.

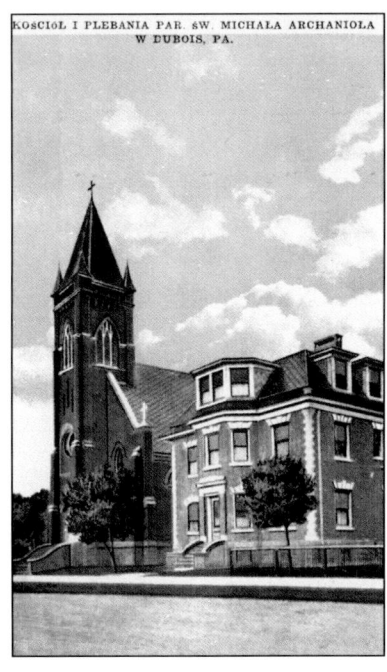

St. Michael's Polish Catholic Church was established in 1909, and the church building and rectory were dedicated on May 30, 1912, by Bishop Fitz Maurice. The church was founded to serve the Polish and Czechoslovakian immigrants who came to this area to work in the lumber mills and coal mines. Joseph Rajs was the first pastor.

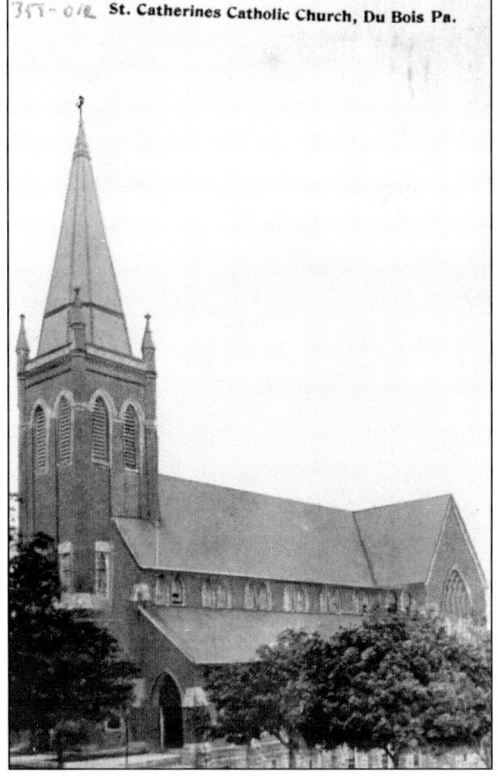

The original St. Catherine of Siena Church was a wooden structure located on State Street, across the street from the present church. A large new brick church, with a steeple visible to the entire town of DuBois, was completed in 1893. A major fire destroyed the upper portion of the building in 1909, but it was soon rebuilt and is still in use today.

St. Joseph's Lithuanian Catholic Church was established in September 1893 with Adam Kiewiseg as pastor. The first church and rectory were built in 1894. The church was closed for two years in 1922 and 1923. Then, in 1924, a new church was constructed under the leadership of Michael Urbanos, who served there for 53 years. The basement of the new church served as a school until the old building could be remodeled for the school. The last class graduated in 1972.

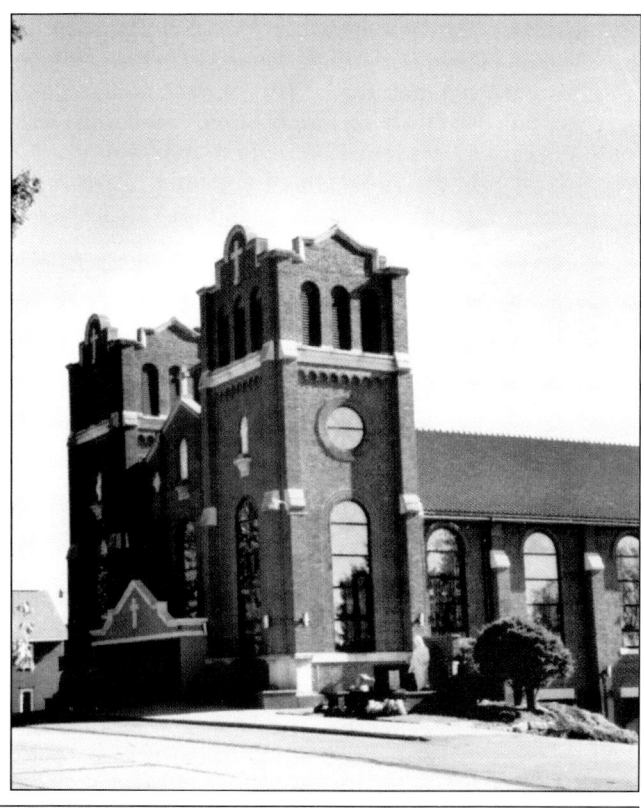

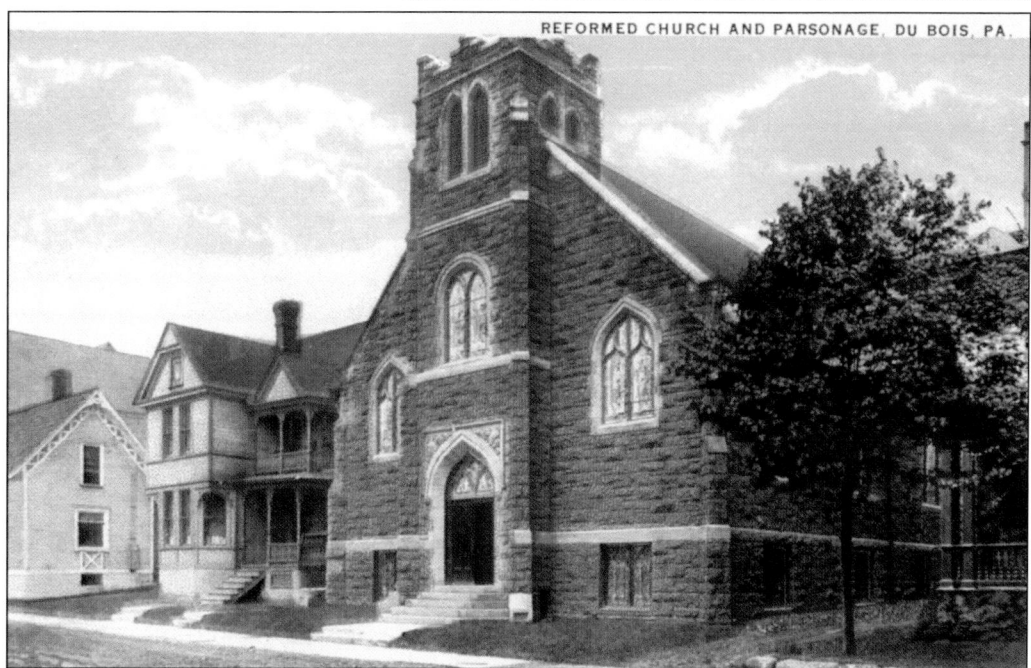

In 1880, members of "Old Mother Trinity" Church organized St. Peter's Reformed Church. One of the early pastors was Rev. R. E. Crum. The building suffered damage during the great fire of 1888, and a new stone church was built and dedicated in 1913.

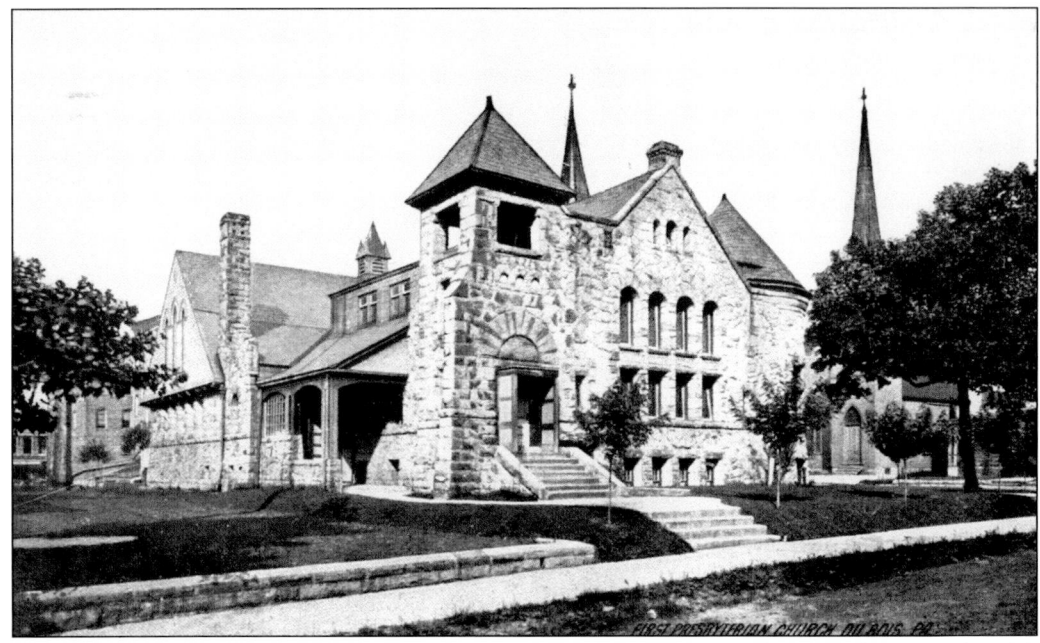

The First United Presbyterian Church of DuBois was formed in 1876 by a small group of Welsh immigrants and was called Bethany Presbyterian Church. In 1885, the name Bethany was dropped. The church is located on the corner of Scribner and High Streets in DuBois.

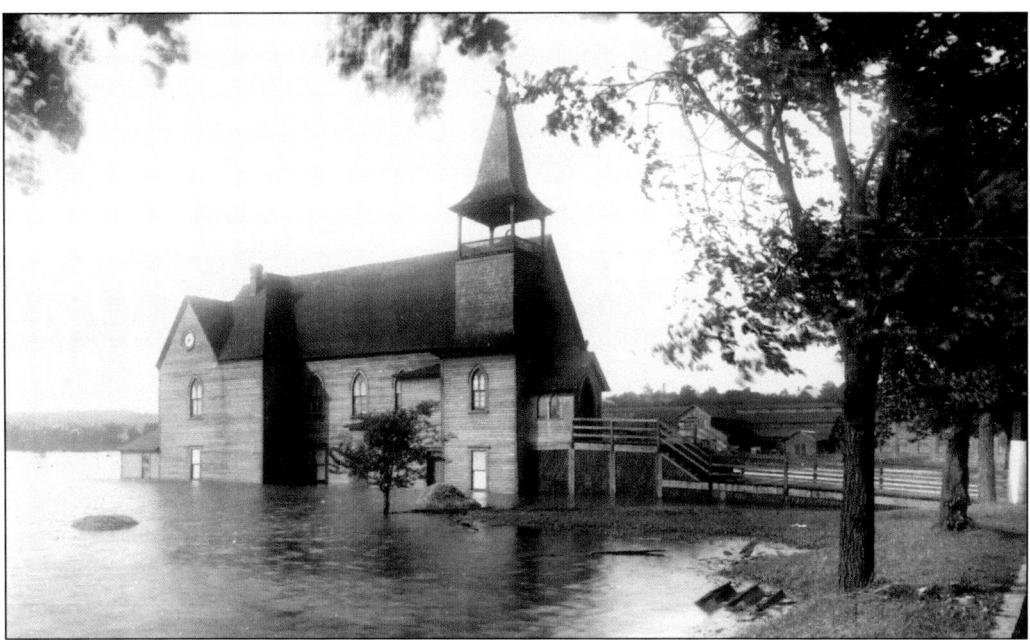

The Episcopal Church of Our Savior, located in DuBois, was organized in 1882 by founder George Vosburg as a Sunday school. The first service was held in the DuBois school. The new church building opened on Easter of 1884 on Plank Road, now Liberty Boulevard. After the flood of 1936, the old church was torn down, and the new stone church was built on the opposite side of Liberty Boulevard.

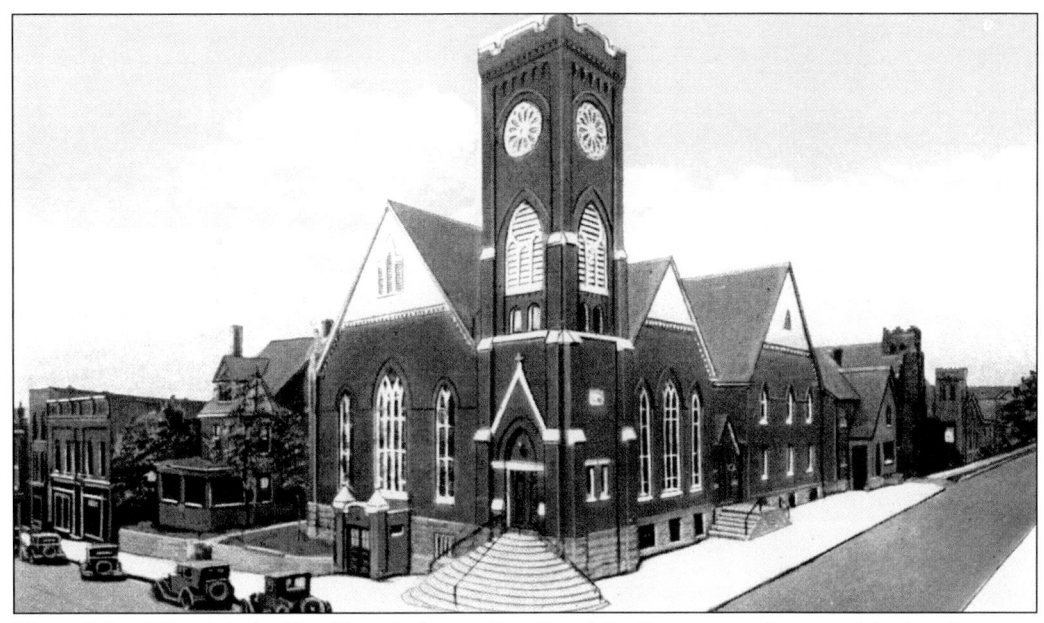

The original First Methodist Church, located on Franklin Street, was destroyed during the great fire on June 18, 1888. The present structure was built in 1889 on the corner of Long Avenue and High Street. Major remodeling and additions took place in 1928, 1959, 1970, and 2003.

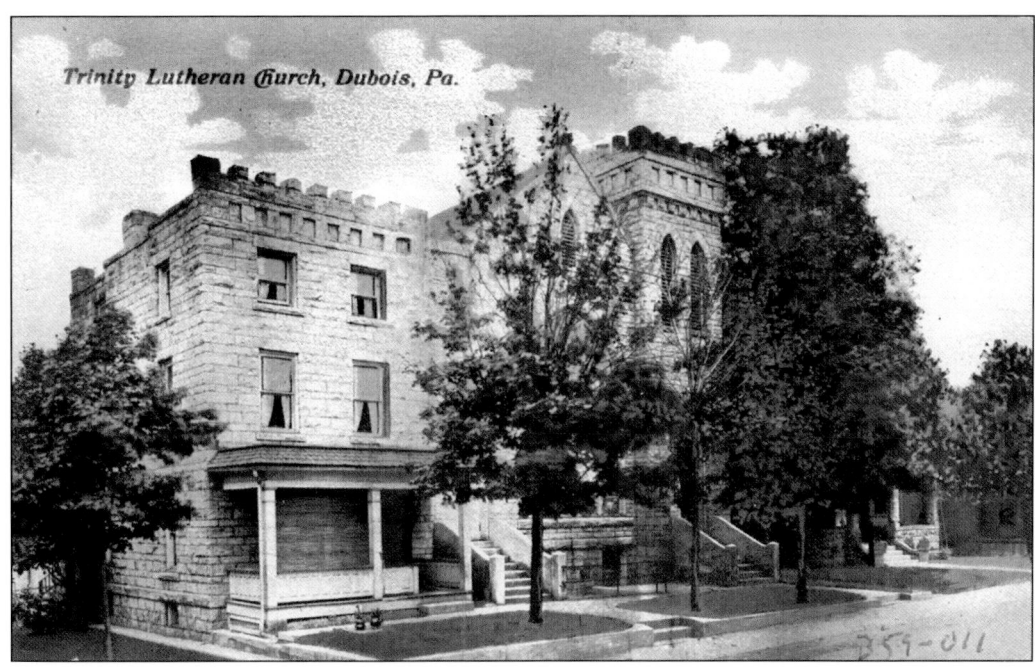

The Trinity Lutheran Church in DuBois opened in 1909 in the basement of the building. The church building, which was constructed at a cost of $26,000, was completed and dedicated in 1914. The stone for the church was taken from the Gocella Stone Quarry in Falls Creek.

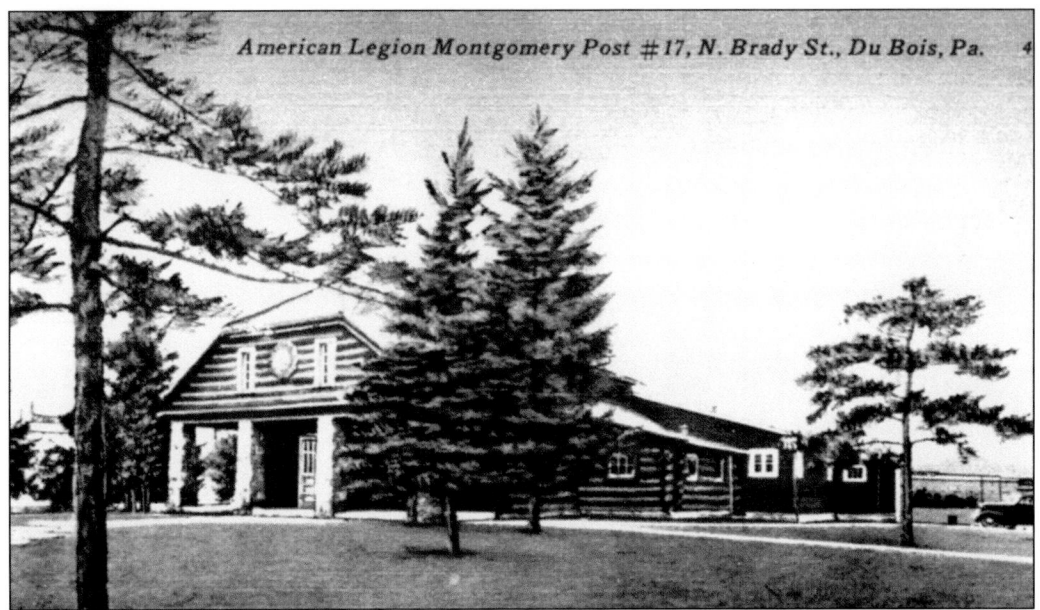

The American Legion Montgomery Post No. 17, known as the Hut, opened in 1931.

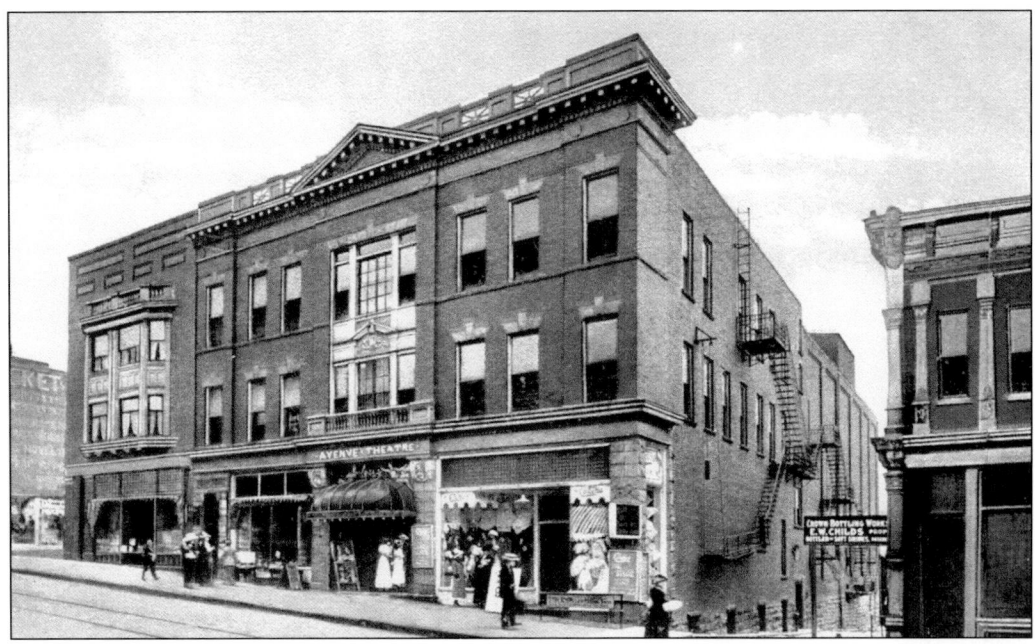

The Avenue Theater, built by a partnership known as Patton and Way, opened on September 2, 1902. Its first attraction was *The Messenger Boy*, a large production headed by Frank Deshon and performed by a company of 50 people. In 1929, the theater showed its first talking movie, *The Follies of 1929*.

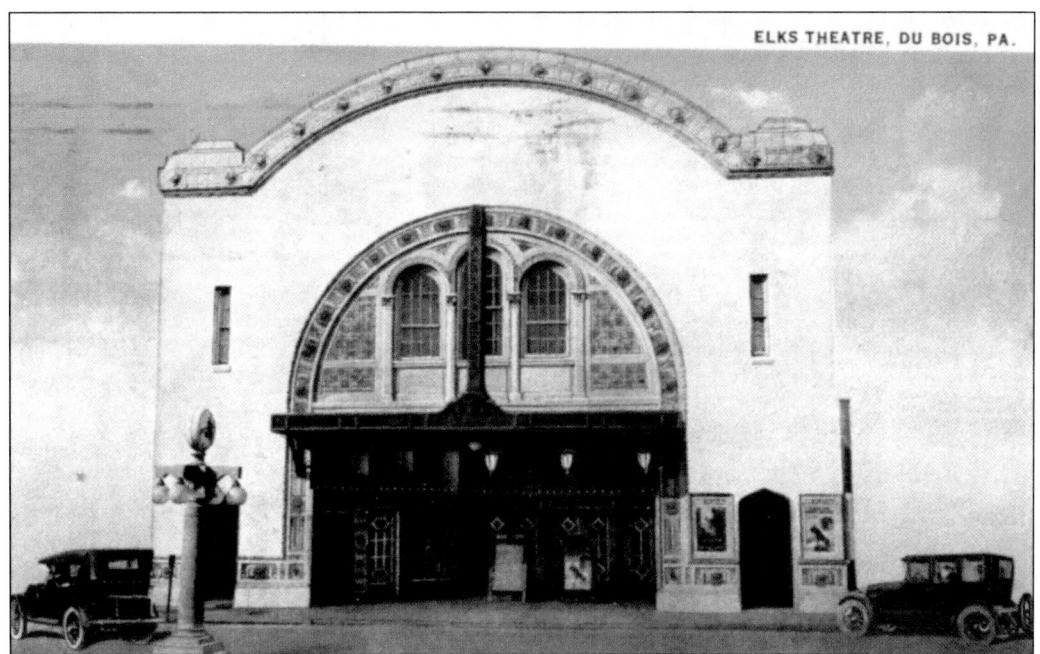

The Elk's Theater was constructed and opened in 1923. Patton and Way leased the theater in 1925 and continued to operate it until November 1944.

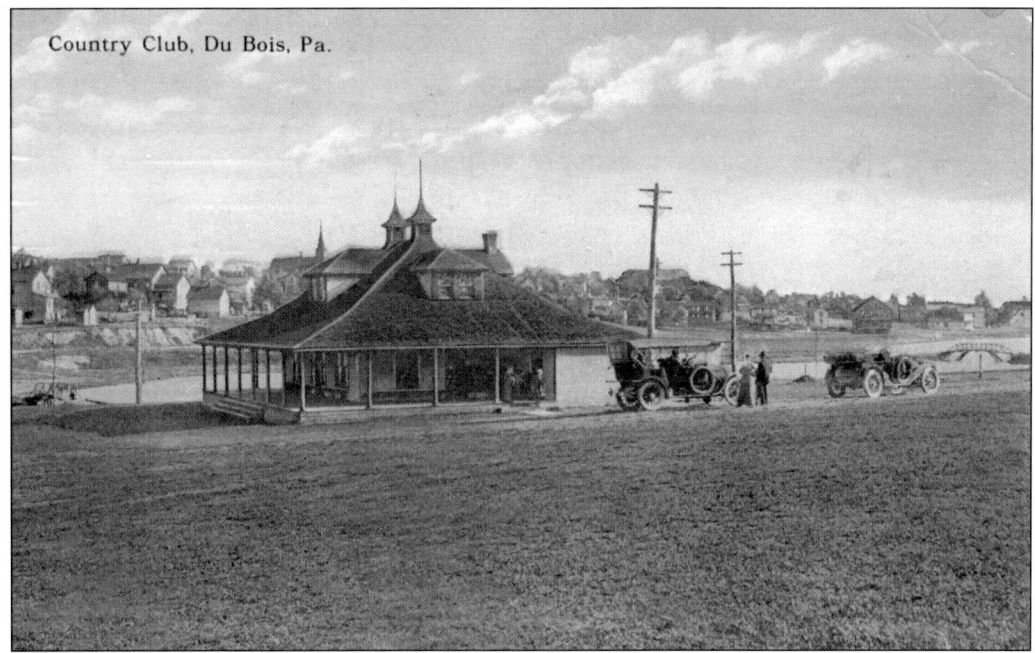

The DuBois Country Club, shown here in 1913, was formed in 1903. The frame structure was built without a basement, insulation, or heat, and was used only in the summer. The dues were $50 per year.

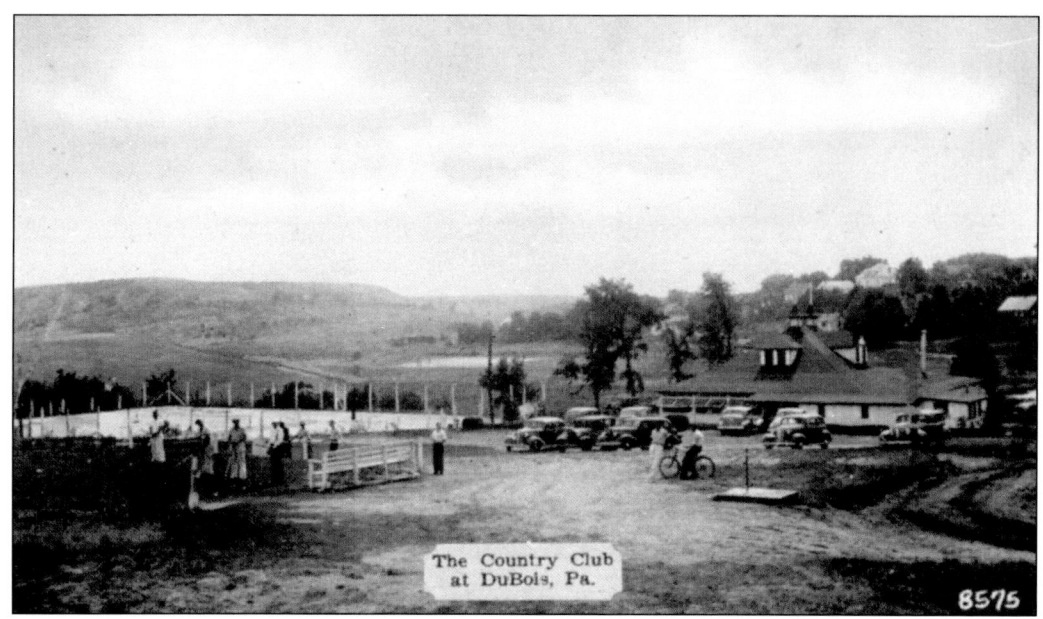
The DuBois Country Club is seen here in 1938.

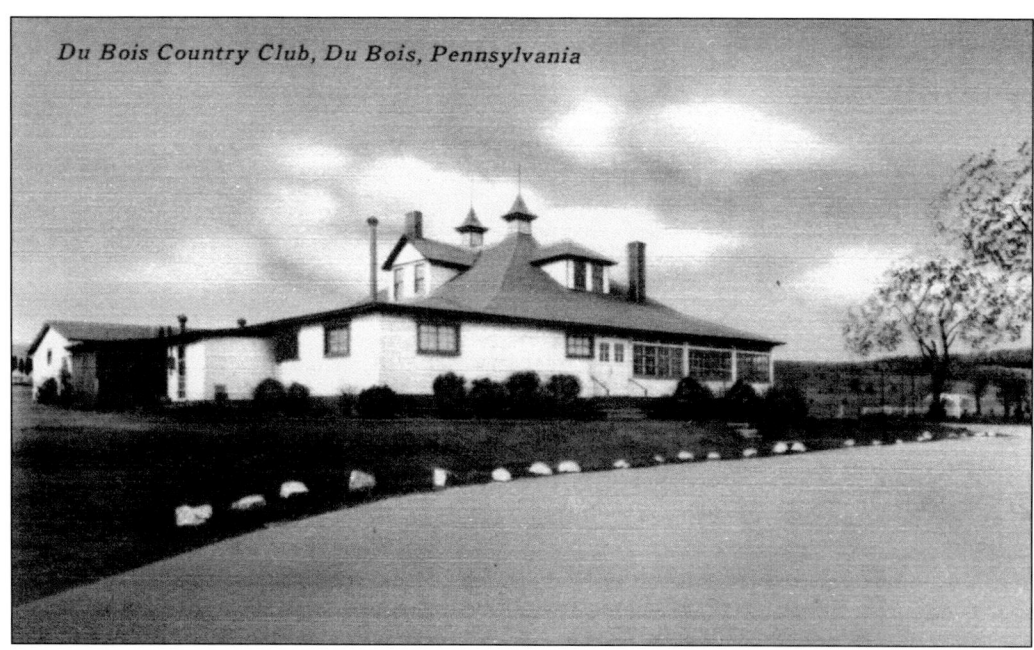
This photograph of the DuBois Country Club was taken in 1945.

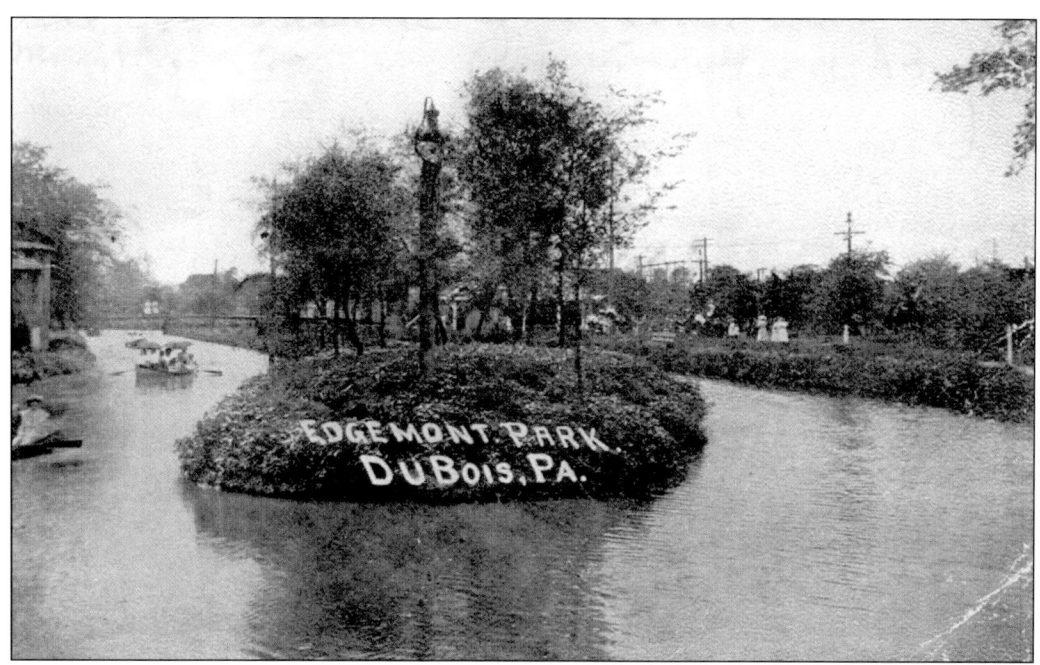
Edgemont Park is seen here.

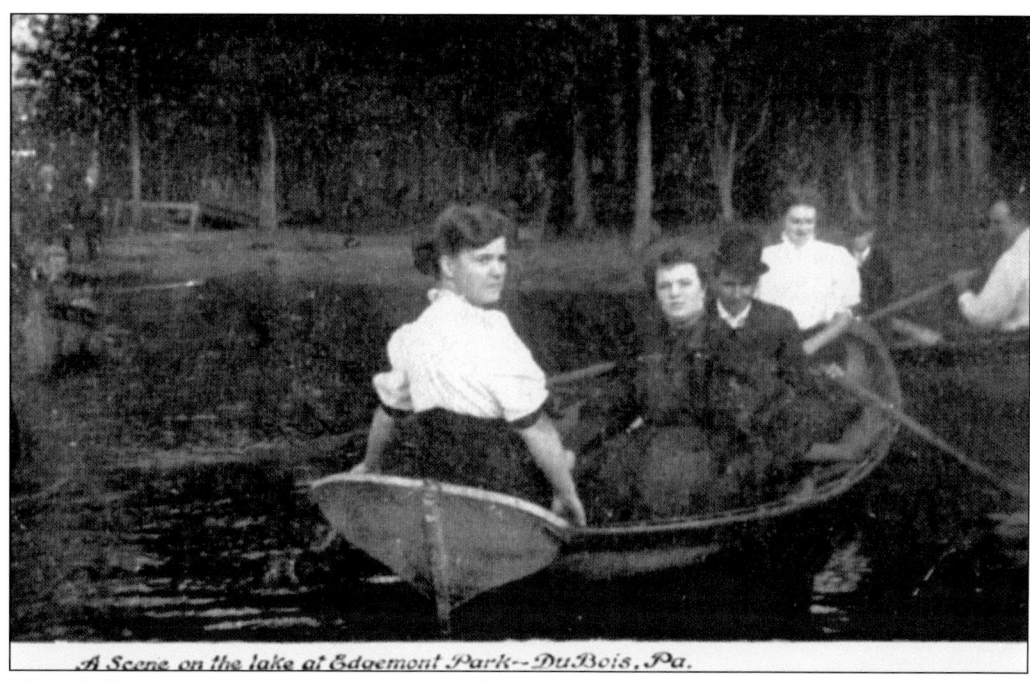
These ladies are enjoying a canoe ride at Edgemont Park, which was located between DuBois and Falls Creek.

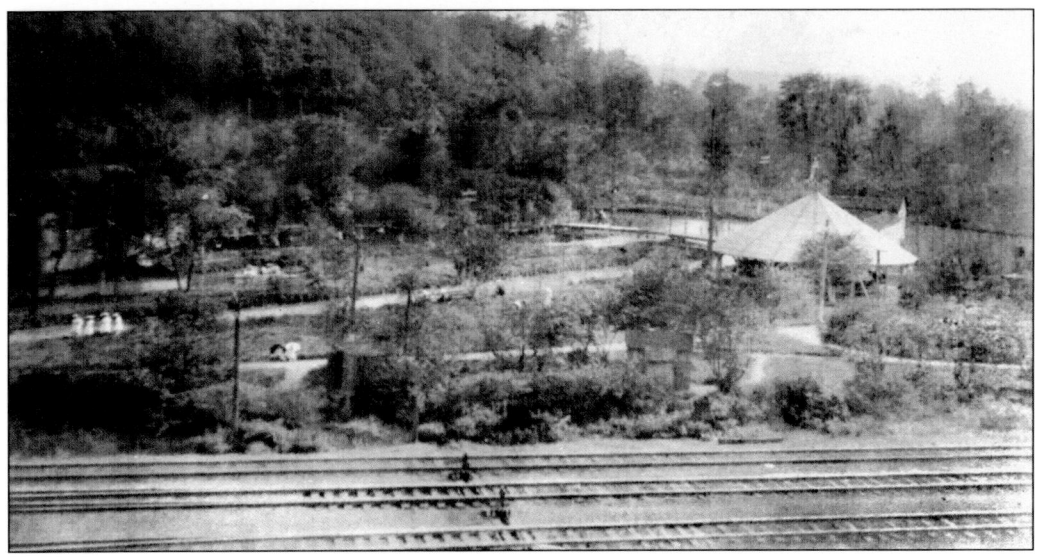

Edgemont Park was located near what is now called Larkeytown. Visible in this image are the BR&P railroad tracks, walkways, band shell, and boating area.

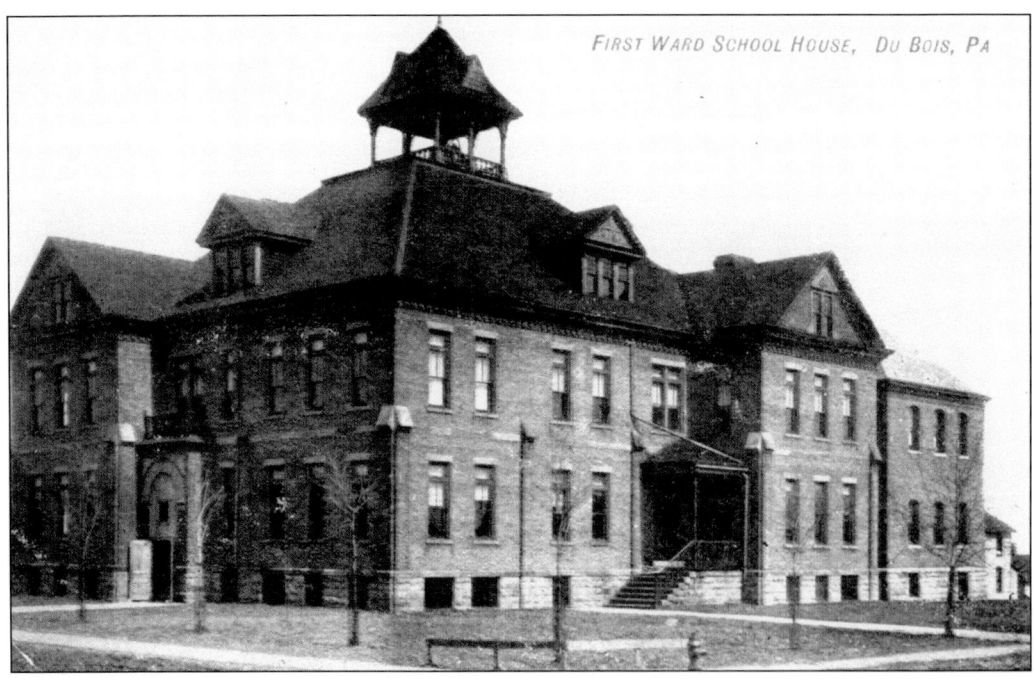

The first ward school in DuBois, the Hubert Street Elementary School, was built in 1892, and an addition was built in 1902. The school closed in December 1976.

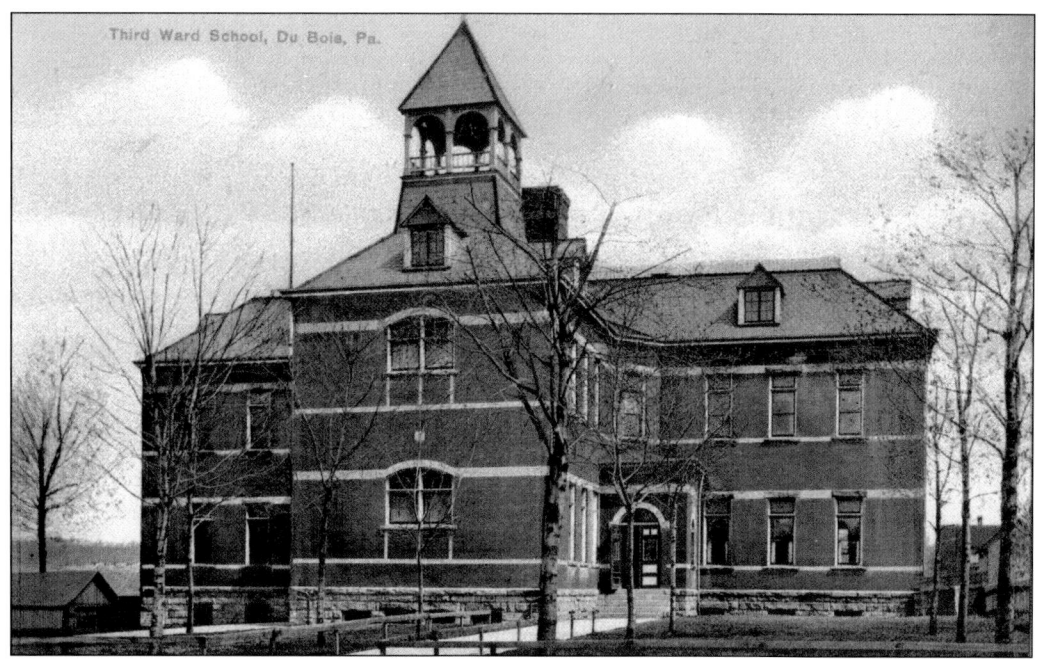

The DuBois Second Avenue grade school was built in 1902, and an addition was added in 1909. The school closed in December 1976.

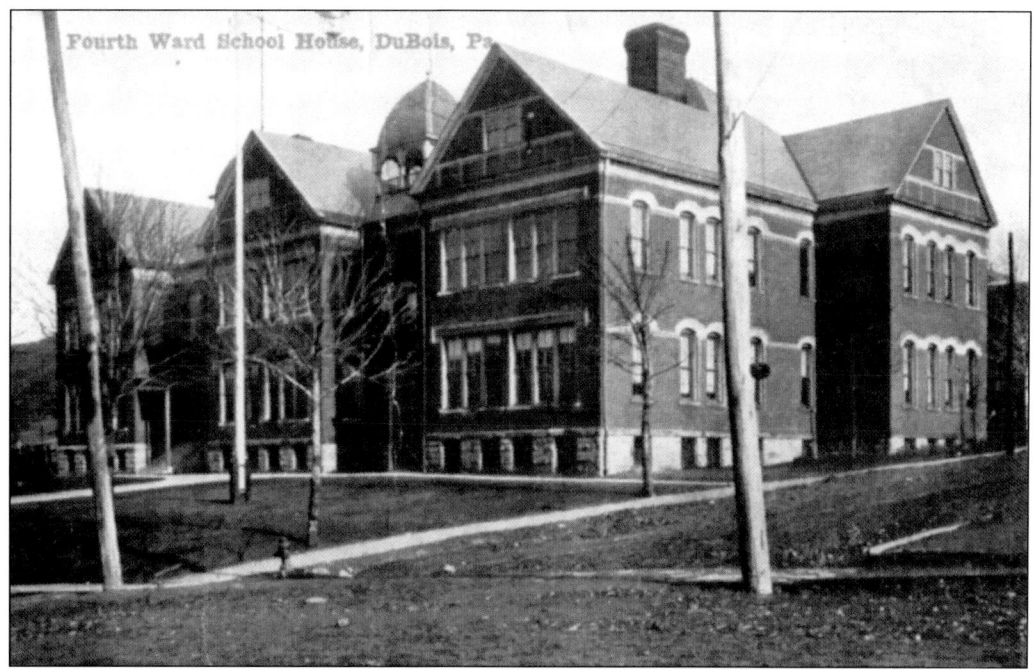

The Olive Avenue grade school was built in 1892. Additions were built in 1895 and 1907. The school closed in February 1976.

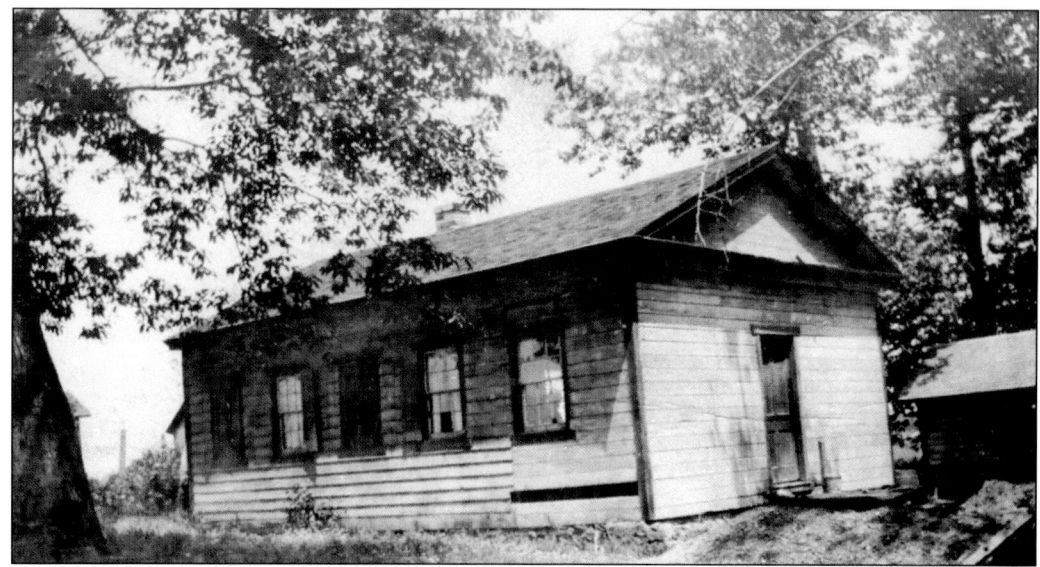

Chestnut Grove School was located in Bloom Township. It was converted for other uses when the era of one-room schoolhouses ended.

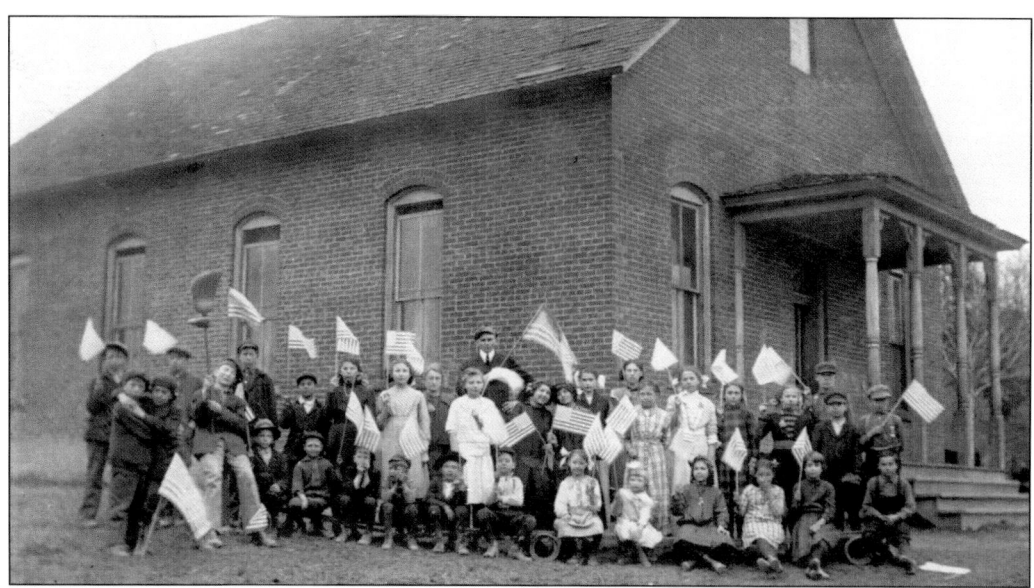

Pine Grove School on Kilmer Road was one of a number of small schools in Sandy Township. Oklahoma Elementary School, built in 1956, put an end to the one-room schoolhouses.

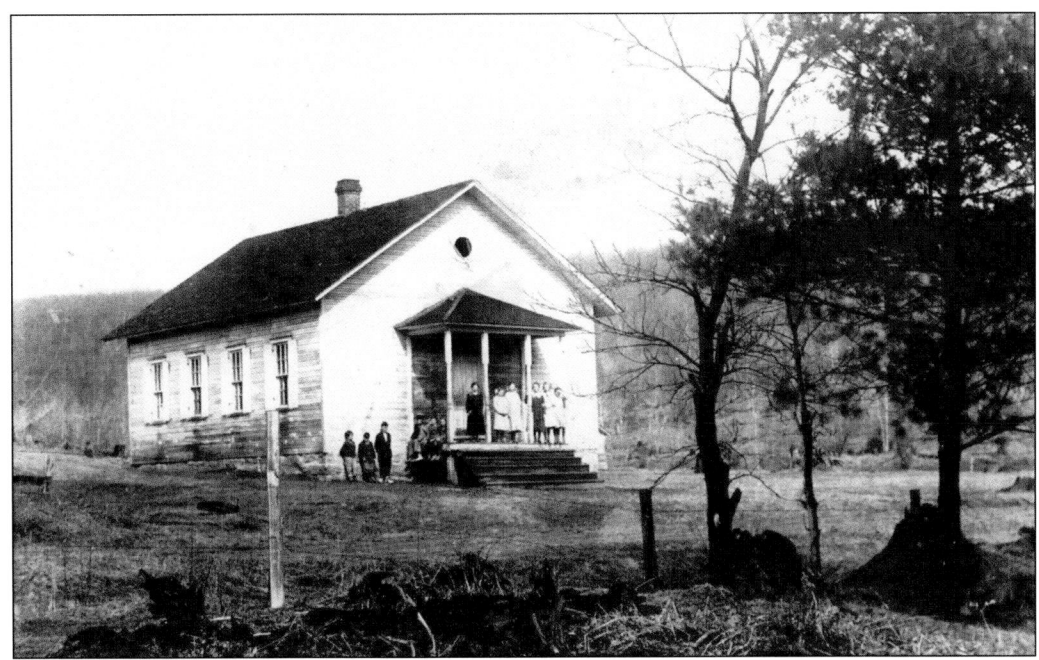
Brown School, located on Mountain Run Road in Sabula, was one of a number of small schools that became obsolete in 1956.

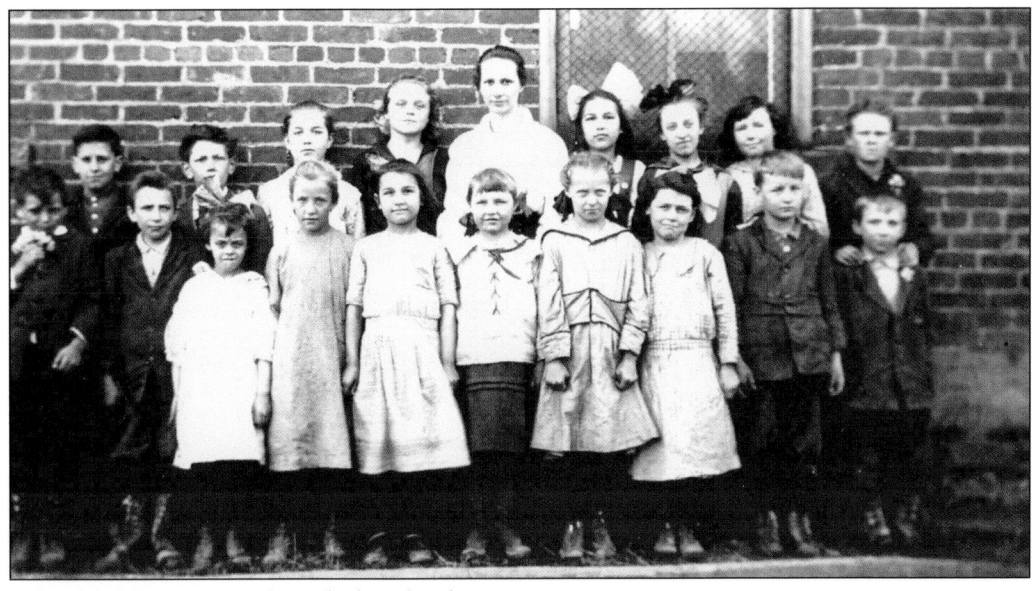
Schoolchildren pose at the Sabula School.

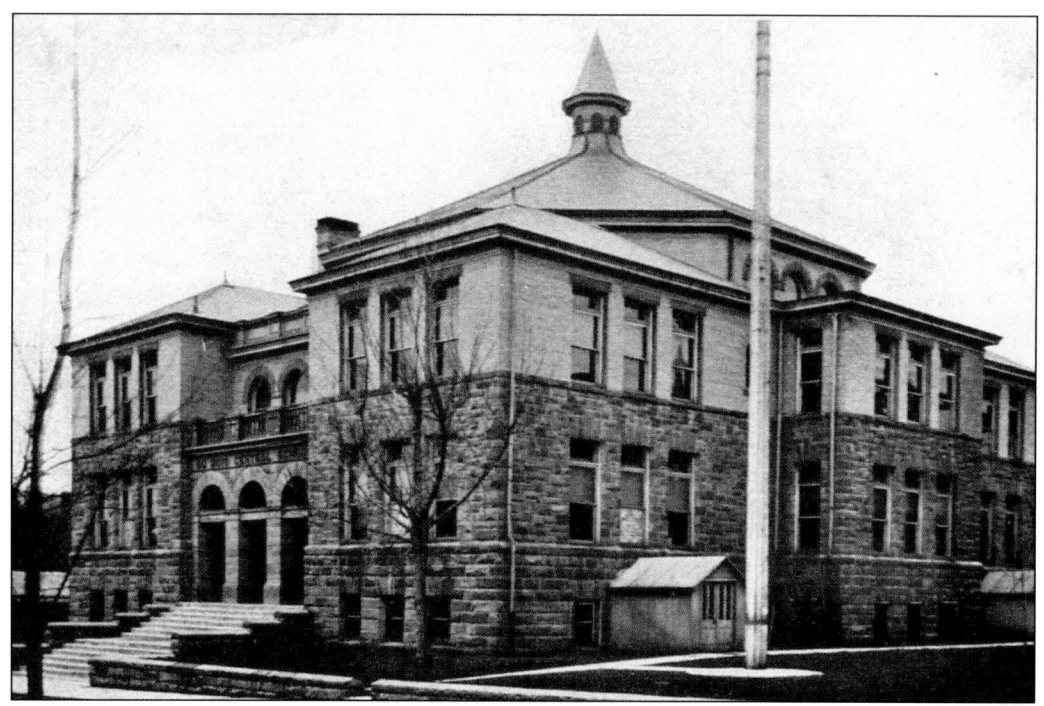

The Central School of DuBois was located on Scribner Avenue and was built in 1901 at the cost of $58,970. It was used as a junior high until *c.* 1964.

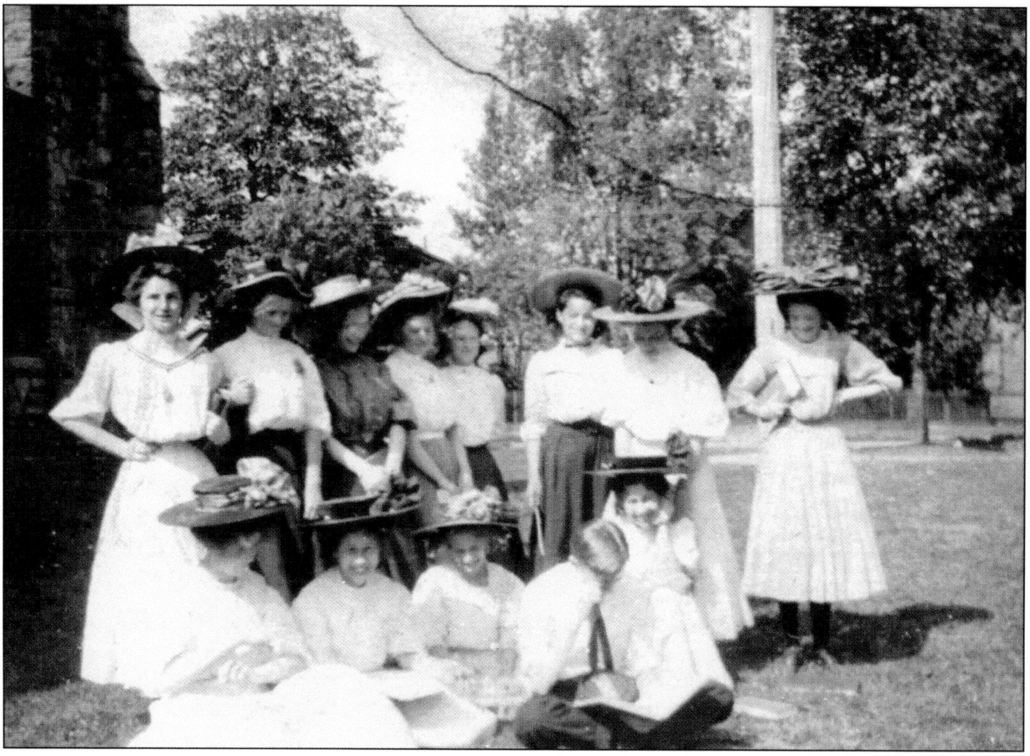

This is the DuBois High School class of 1909.

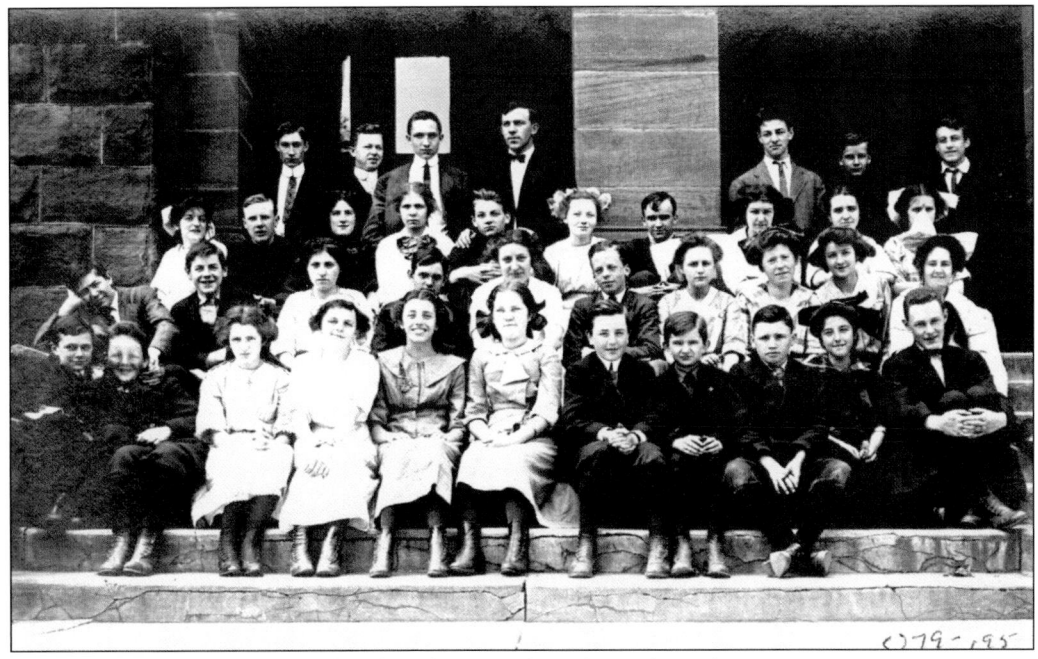
A Central School class posed for this photograph in the early 20th century.

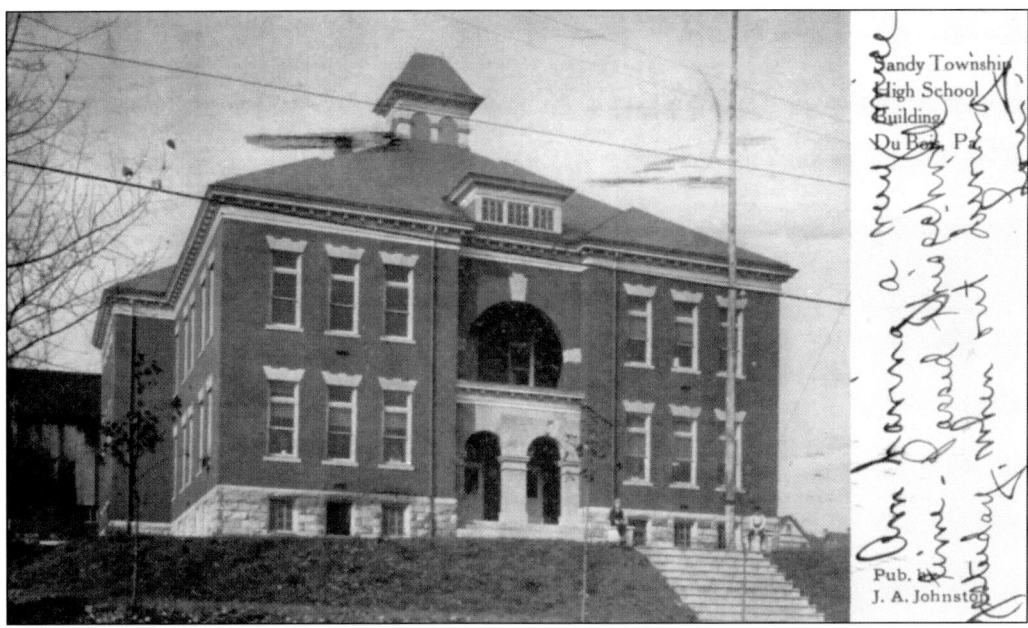
Sandy High School was built in 1920 and housed grades 9 through 12. Until 1936, grades seven and eight were located in a small school building, which is partially pictured on the left side of the postcard, called the Portable School or the "Chicken Coop." In 1958, Sandy High School became an elementary school. It closed in December 1976.

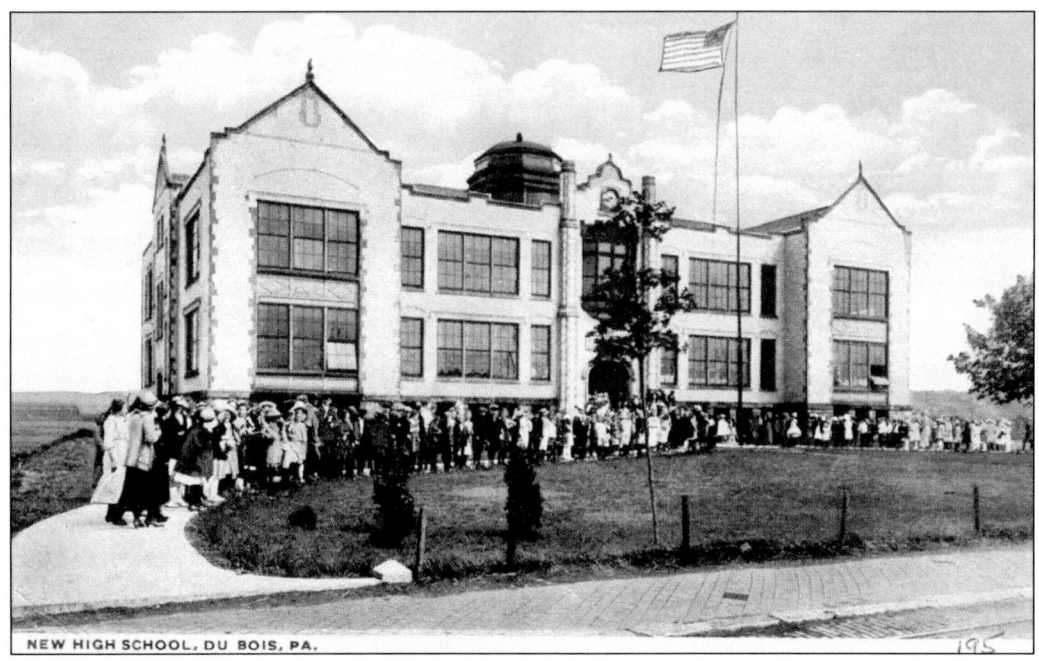

Construction of the new DuBois High School on Liberty Boulevard began in 1909, and the new building opened on February 20, 1911. This school was used as a high school until 1964, when it became the junior high school. It was closed and removed in 1995.

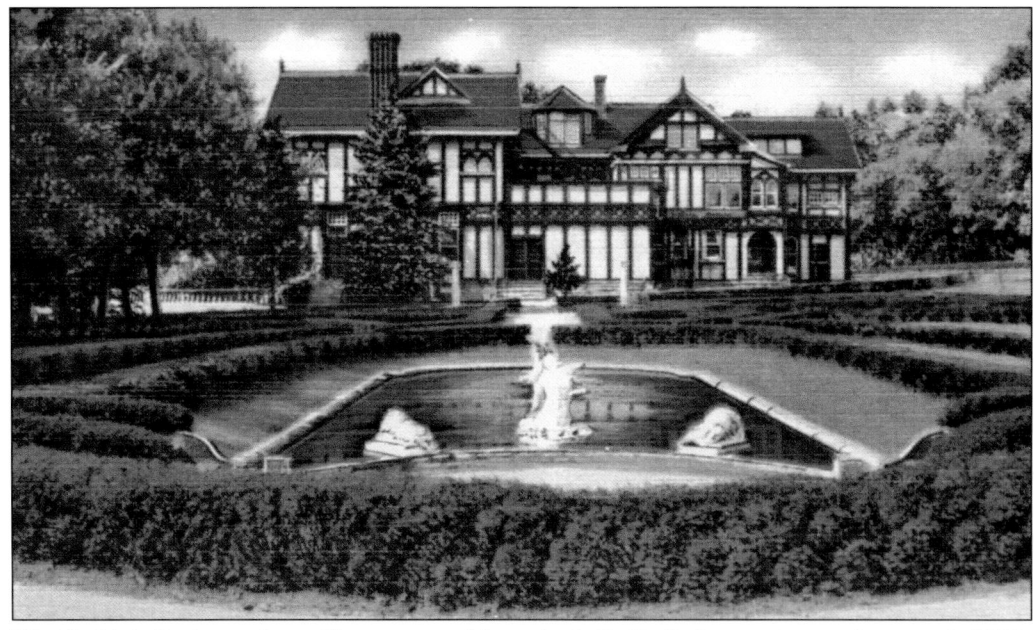

The DuBois Undergraduate Center moved into the J. E. DuBois mansion on January 3, 1938.

Six

RAILROADS

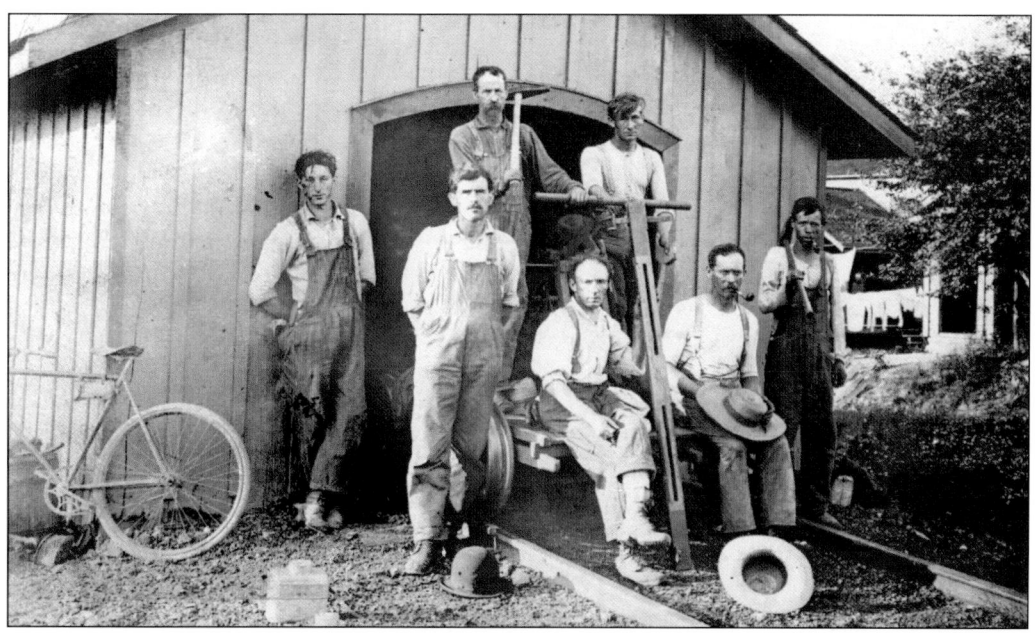

A group of railroad workers sit on a paddy car, which was used to transport the workers to sections of the railroad that needed repairs.

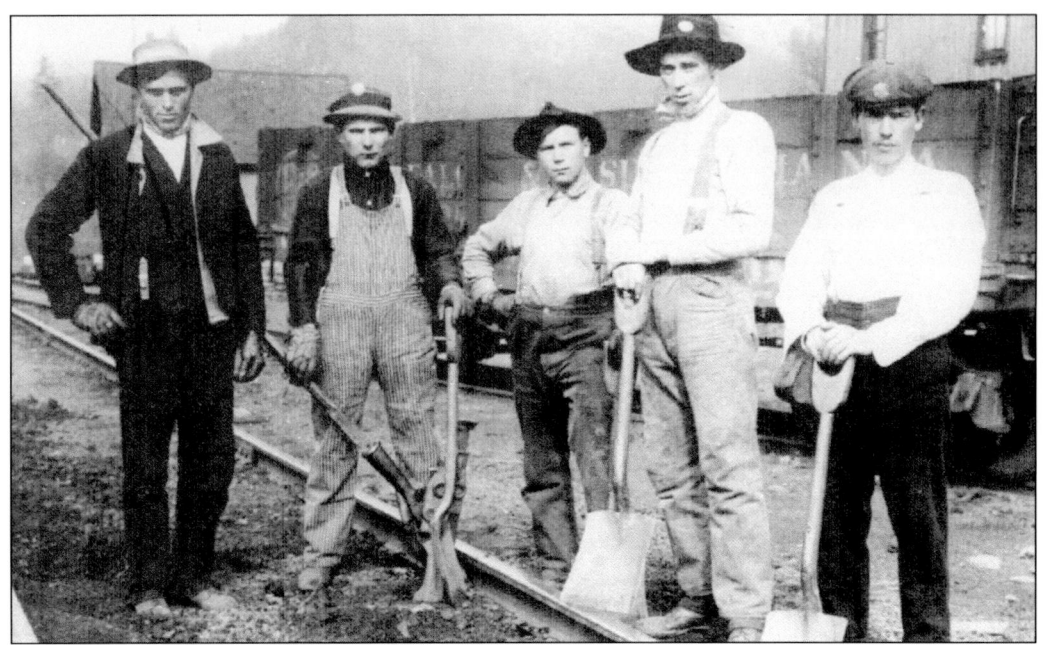
The men working along the railroad were called Gandy Dancers. A coal car is in the background of this image.

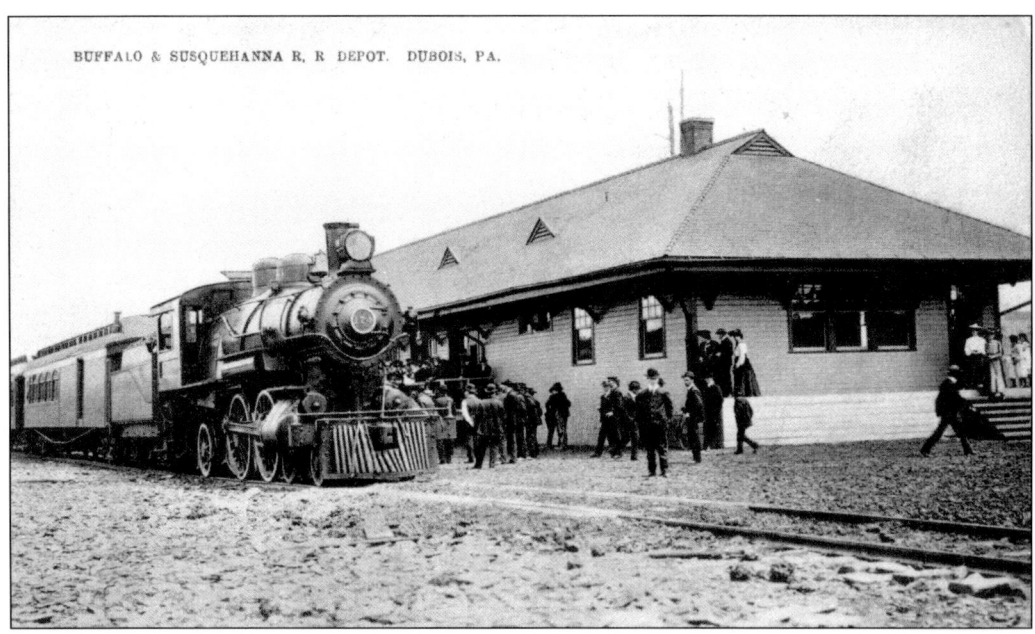
The Buffalo and Susquehanna Railroad Depot in DuBois was created by the Goodyear brothers of Buffalo.

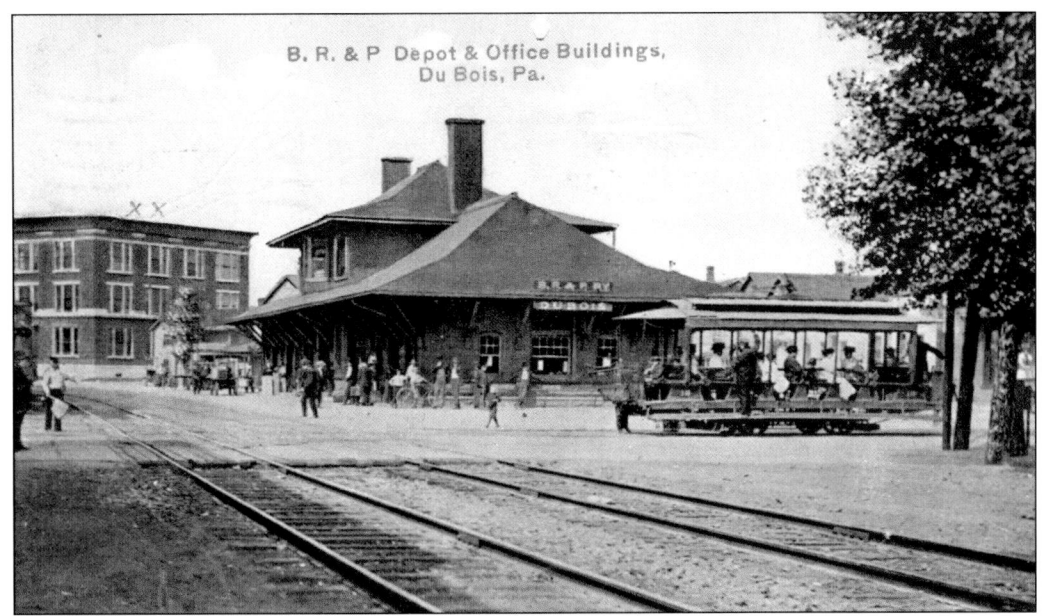

A trolley car is pictured at the Buffalo, Rochester, and Pittsburgh Railroad station, which was located on West Long Avenue in DuBois.

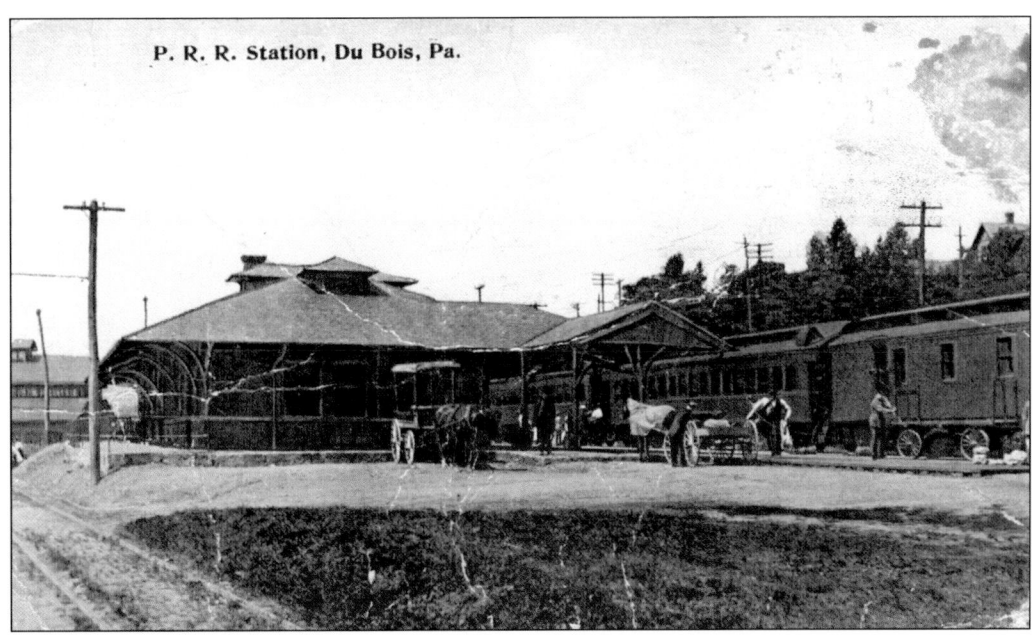

This BR&P train waits at the station, ready to load both passengers and freight.

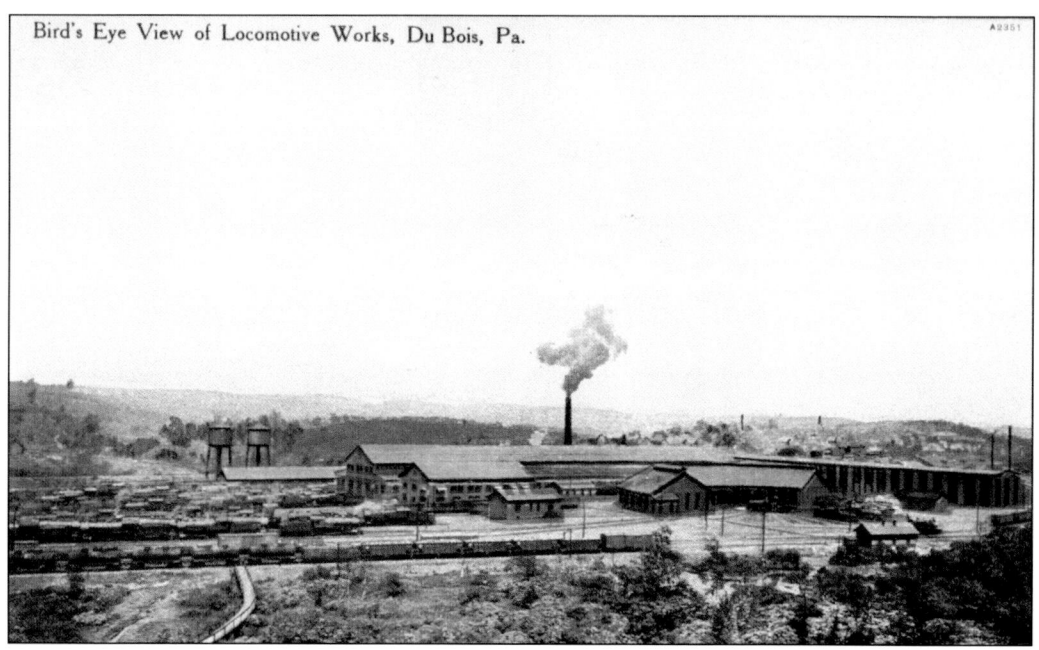

The Locomotive Works in DuBois consisted of a heavy repair shop and an engine house. The locomotive repair shop was constructed of brick and steel. The Locomotive Works was located at the northern boundary of the city and covered approximately 35 acres.

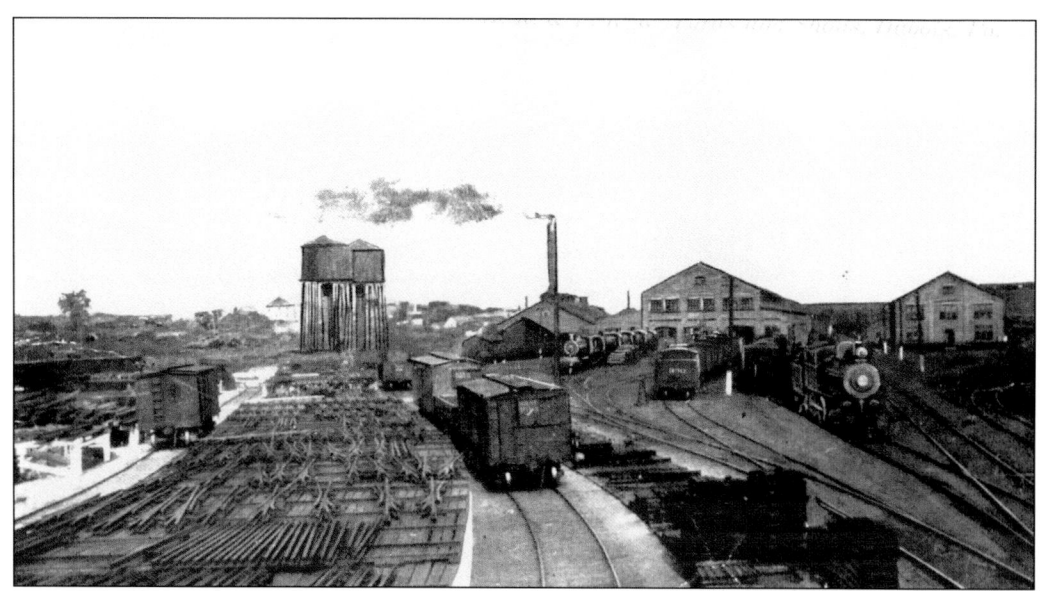

Pictured here are the BR&P railroad shops.

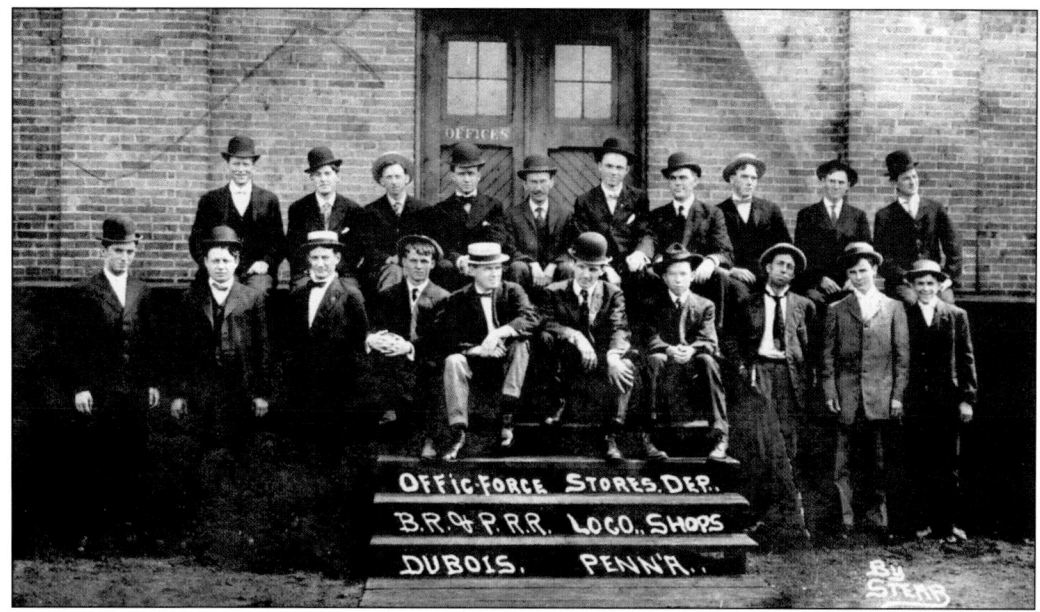
The office force of the Buffalo, Rochester, and Pittsburgh Railroad is shown here.

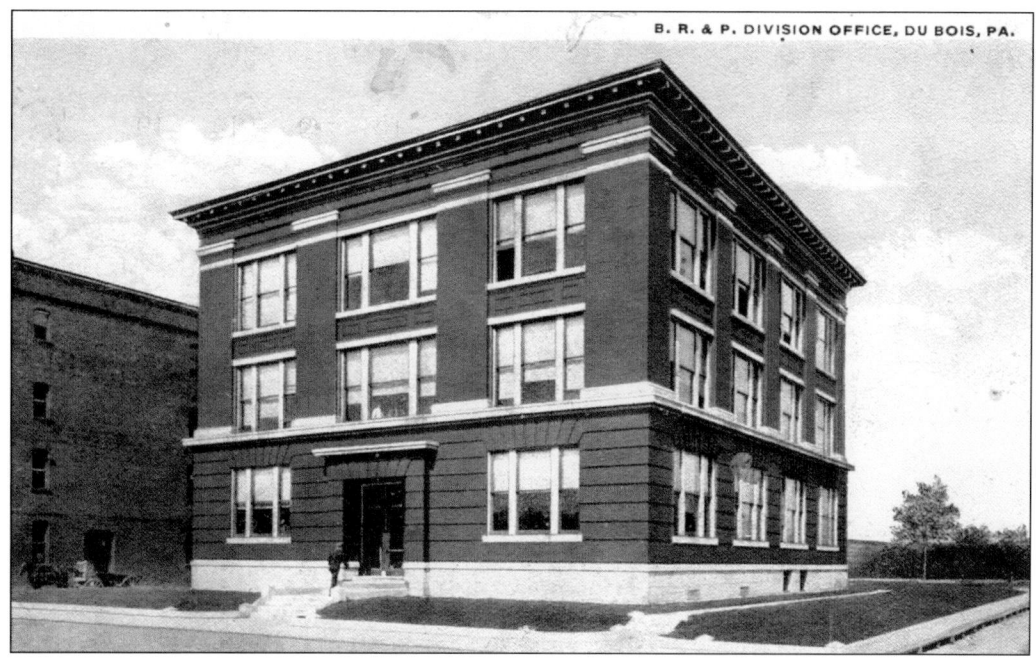
This is the BR&P business building.

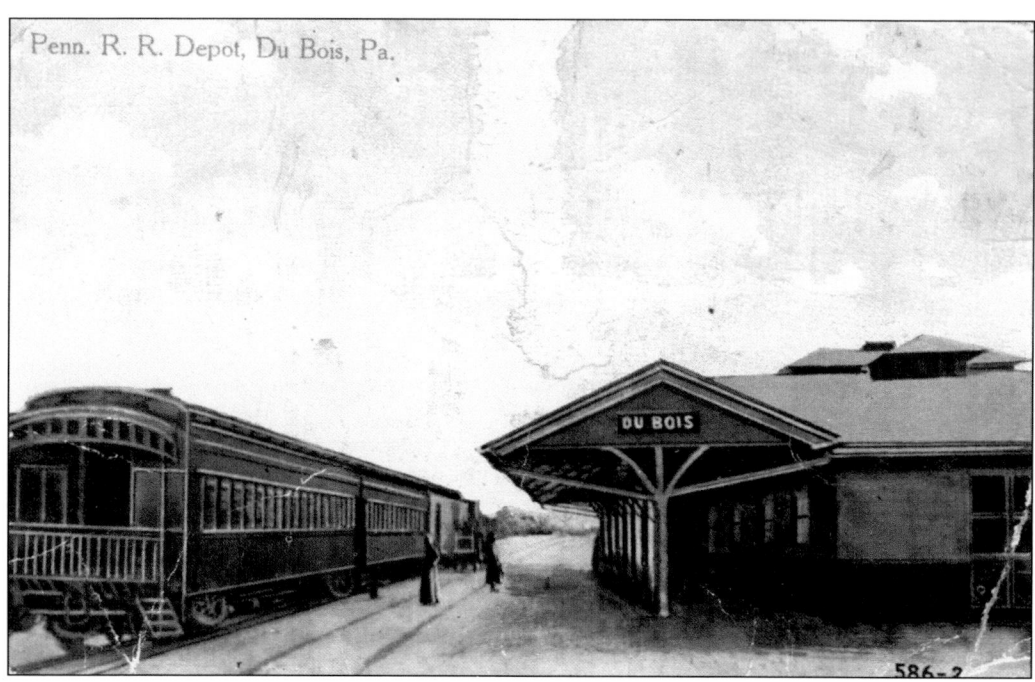

The Pennsylvania Railroad station is shown here.

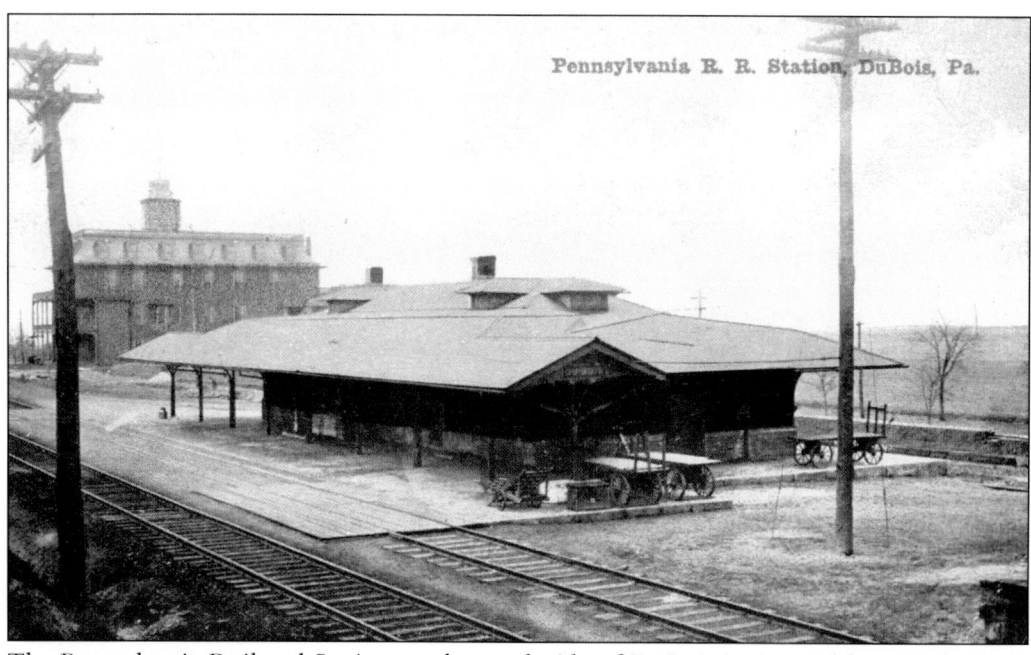

The Pennsylvania Railroad Station on the north side of DuBois is pictured here in the early 20th century. The DuBois House Hotel, which later became the DuBois Business College, can be seen in the background.

Seven
Brady Township and Falls Creek

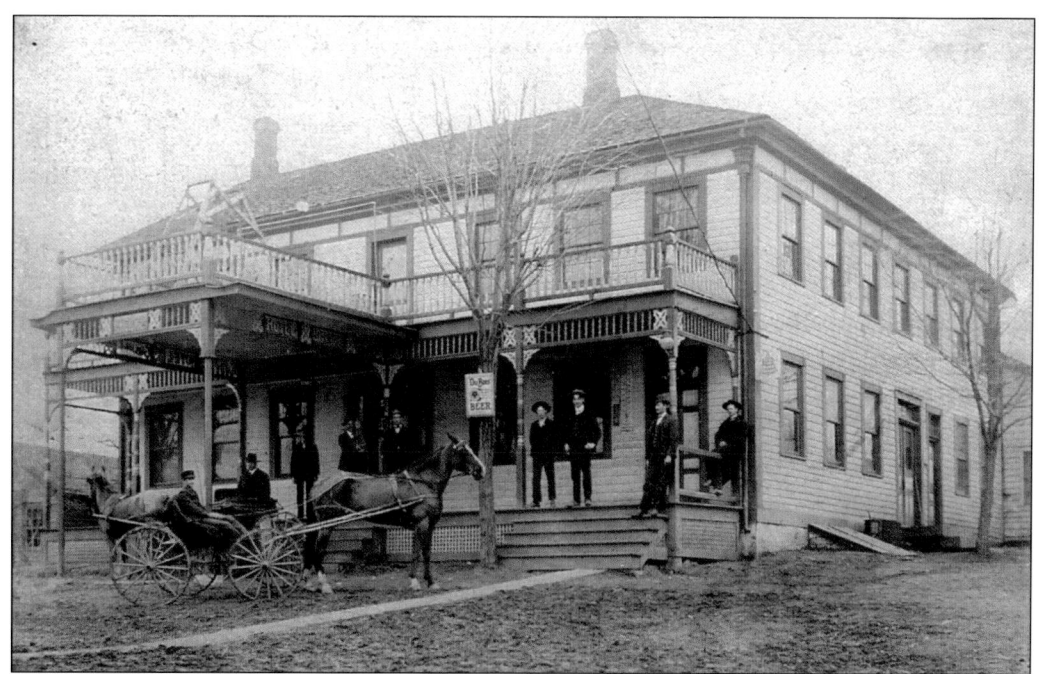

Robert W. Moore built the Merchants Hotel in Luthersburg in 1853 and sold it in 1865. Located at the crossroads of Routes 322 and 410, the hotel was later known as the Carlisle Hotel and, still later, the Golden Yoke.

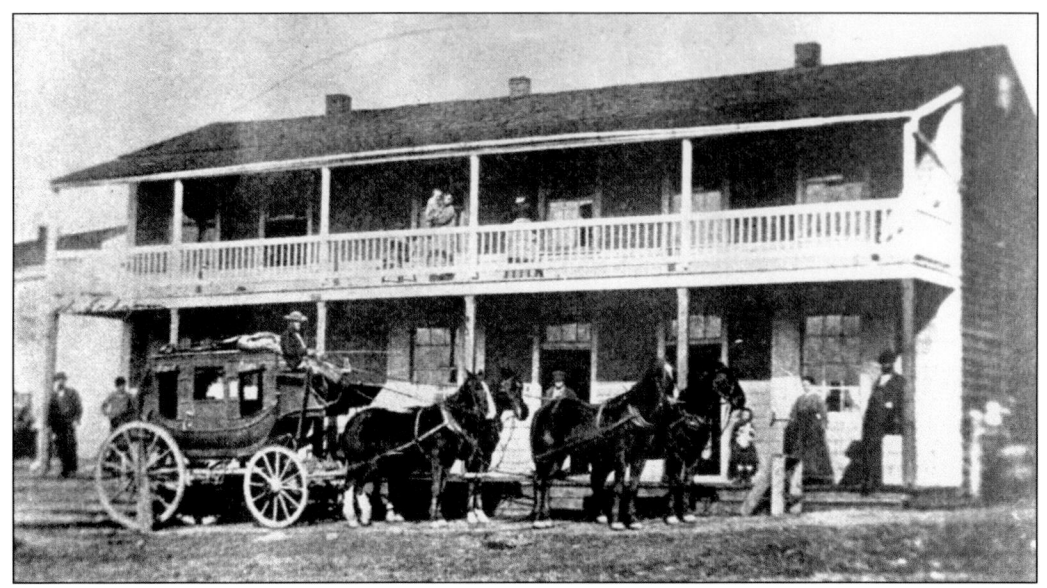

Shown here is the Schwen Hotel in Luthersburg. Pictured, from left to right, are William Schwen, Dr. William A. Means, Annie Schwen Butler and her unidentified daughter, William Schwen, Lizzie Weaver, Walter Schwen, and Conney Long. The carriage driver is unidentified.

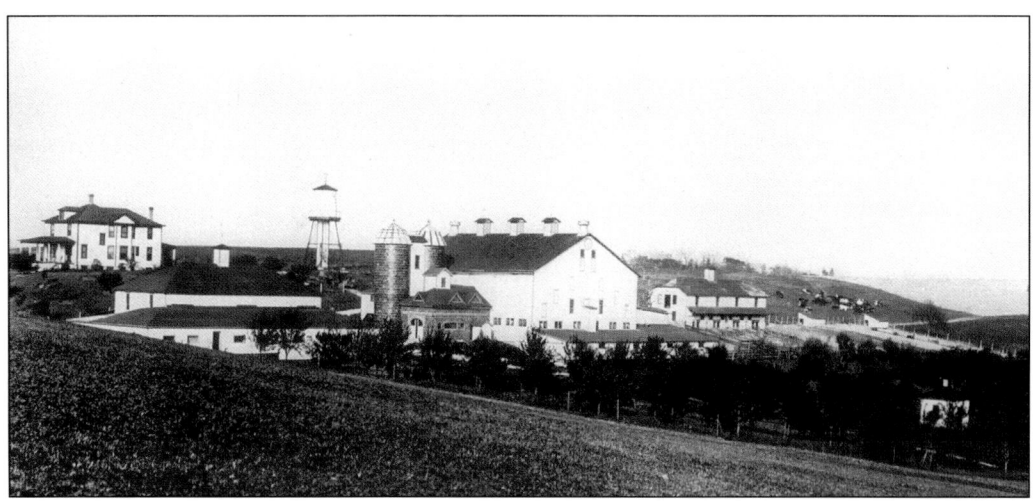

The DuBois Brewery Farm was located on route 322 in Luthersburg. John H. Hayes managed the farm from 1912 to 1925. The farm grew buckwheat and other grains that were used in the brewing of beer in the DuBois Brewery.

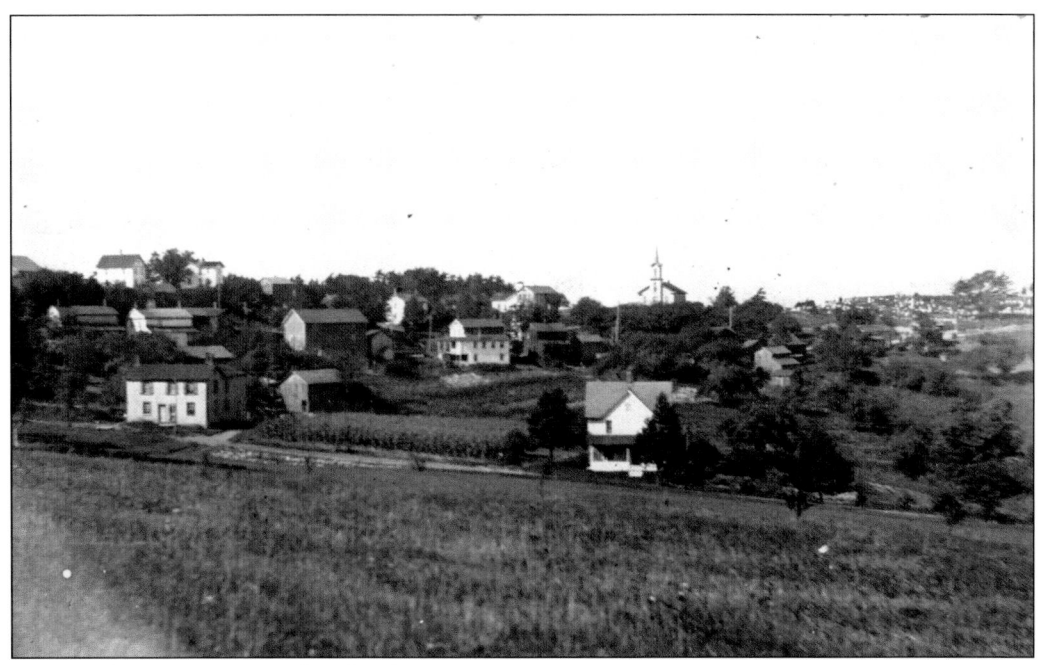
This is a bird's-eye view of Luthersburg.

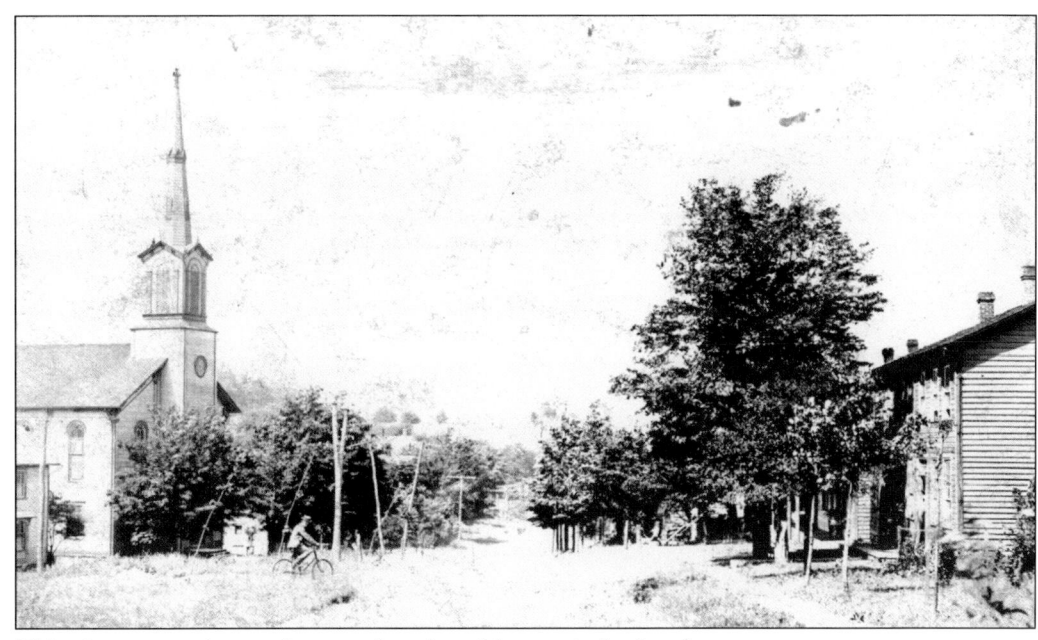
This picturesque image shows a church and houses in Luthersburg.

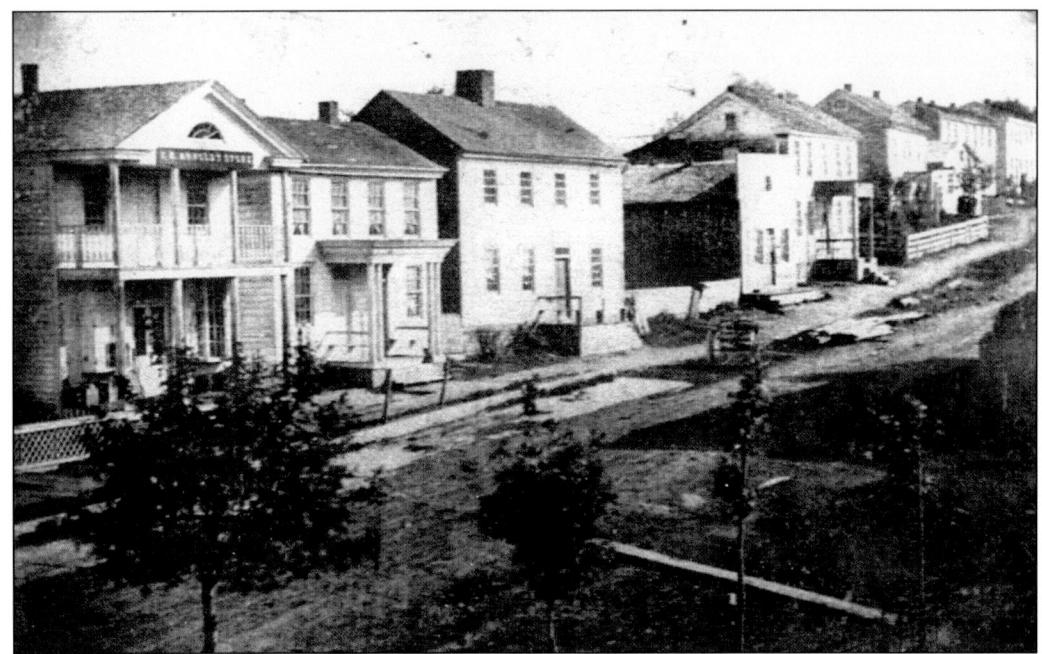
Luthersburg's Main Street is shown in the late 1880s. Most of the buildings burned in the fire of 1889.

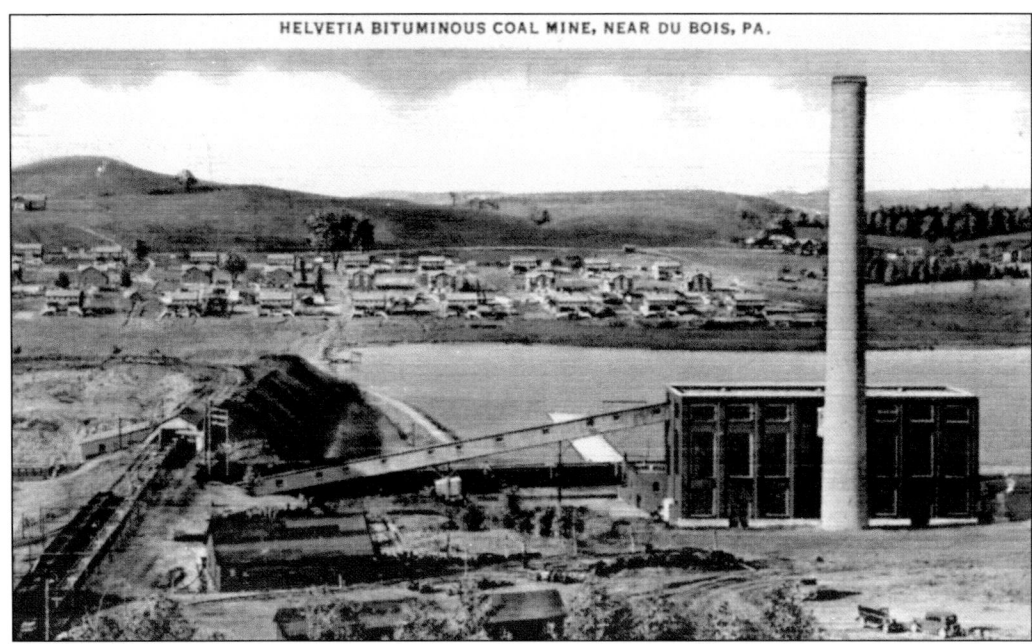
Adrian Iselin opened the Helvetia Mine in the early 1890s. Iselin also built a town of company houses for the miners to live in as long as the mine prospered. The Helvetia mine closed in 1954.

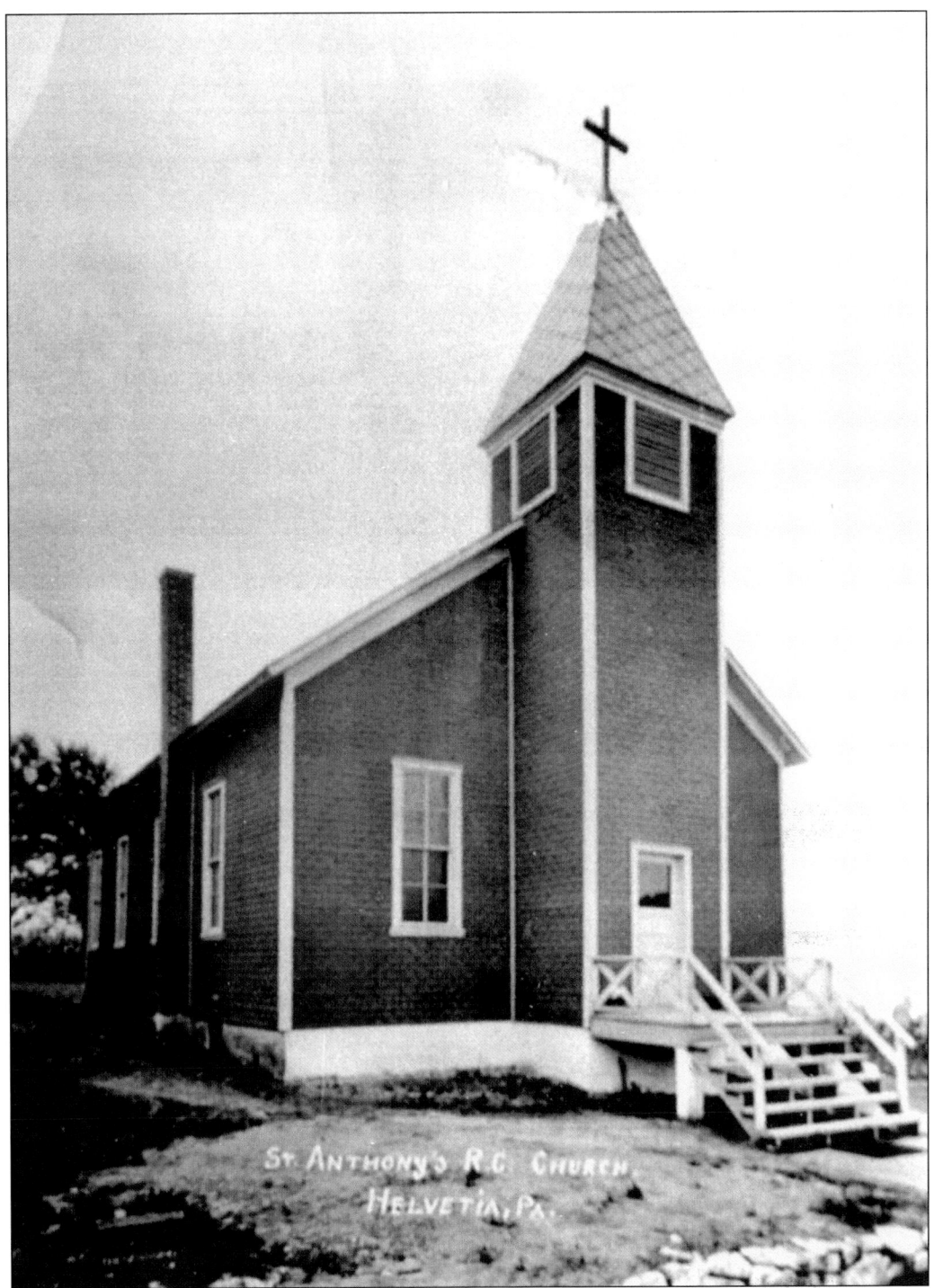

St. Anthony Catholic Church of Helvetia was built before the beginning of the 20th century. For most of its existence, the church was served by Father Urbonas, who later became Monsignor Urbonas of St. Joseph Parish in DuBois. St. Anthony Catholic Church burned down on March 12, 1955. Fortunately, all of the records of St. Anthony's were retained by St. Joseph Parish.

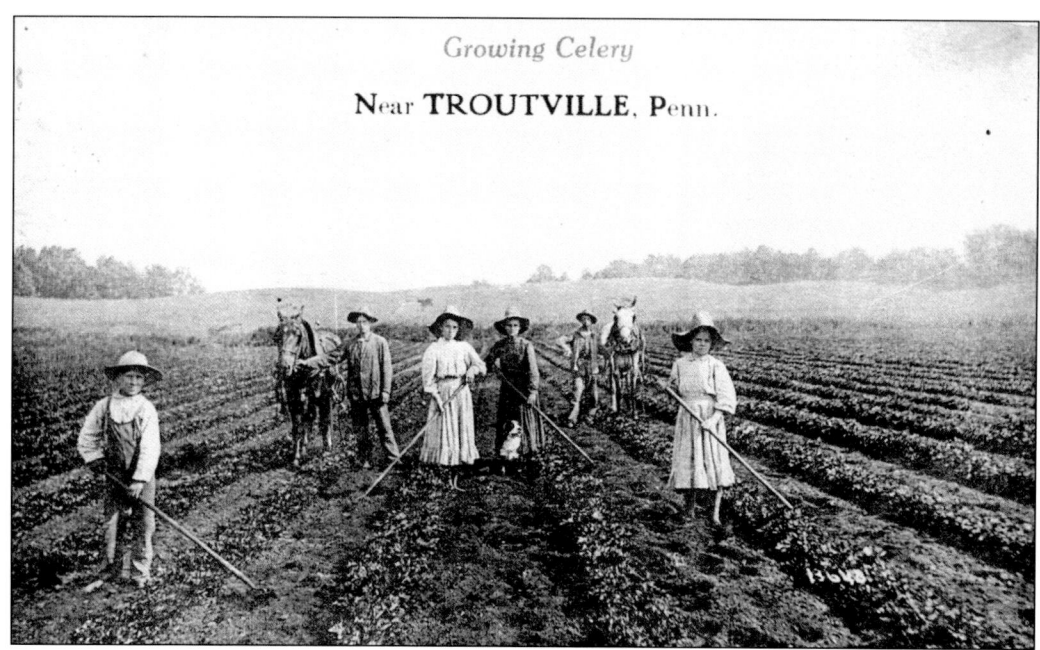
This image of celery growing was captured near Troutville.

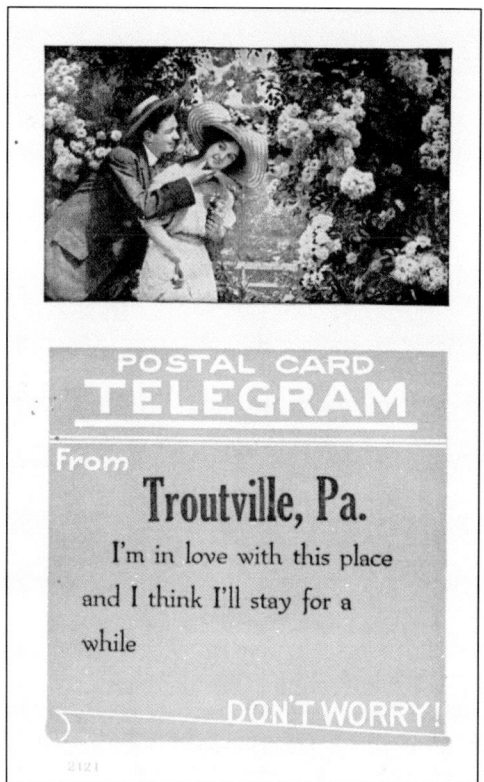
This greeting card is from Troutville.

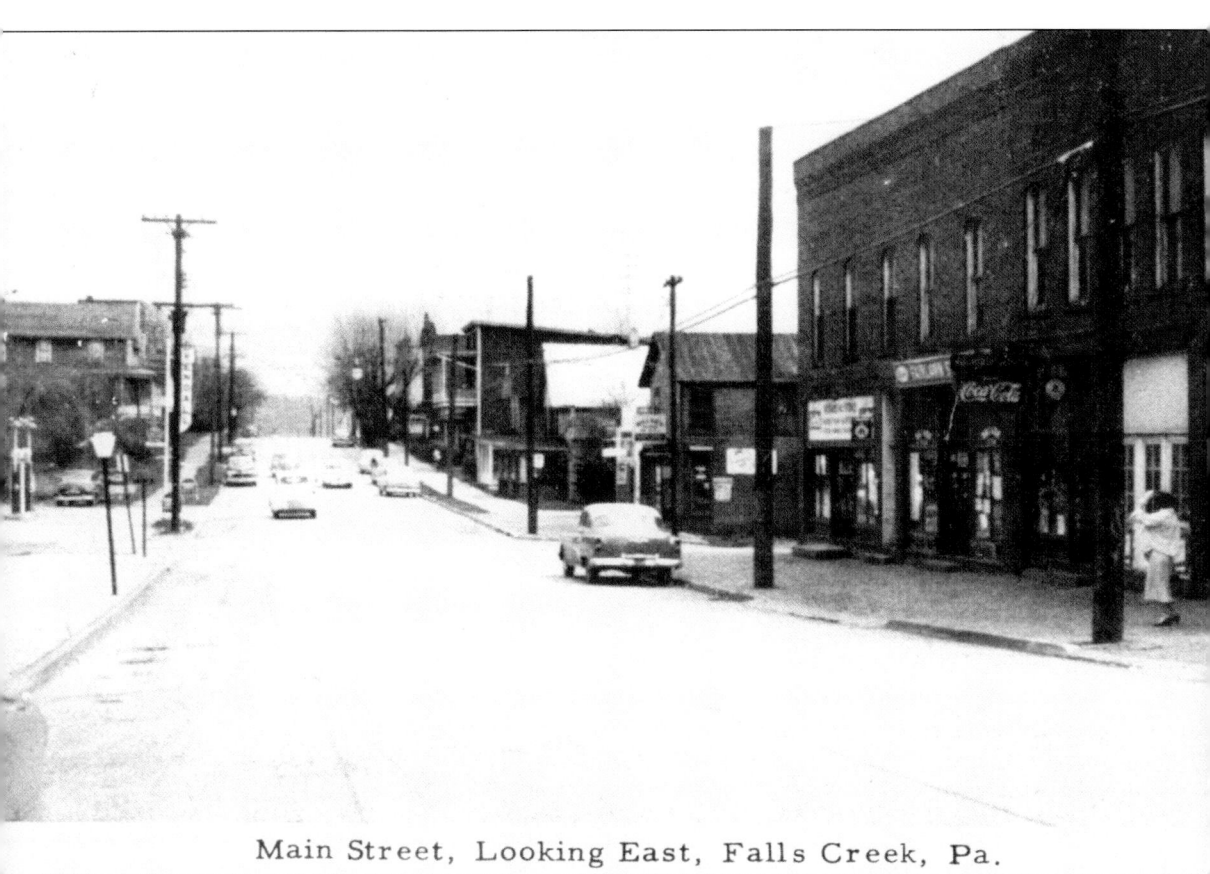

Main Street, Looking East, Falls Creek, Pa.

This postcard shows Main Street in Falls Creek, looking east. The Pennzoil gas station can be seen on the corner of First and Main Streets. Today, this building is the Falls Creek post office.

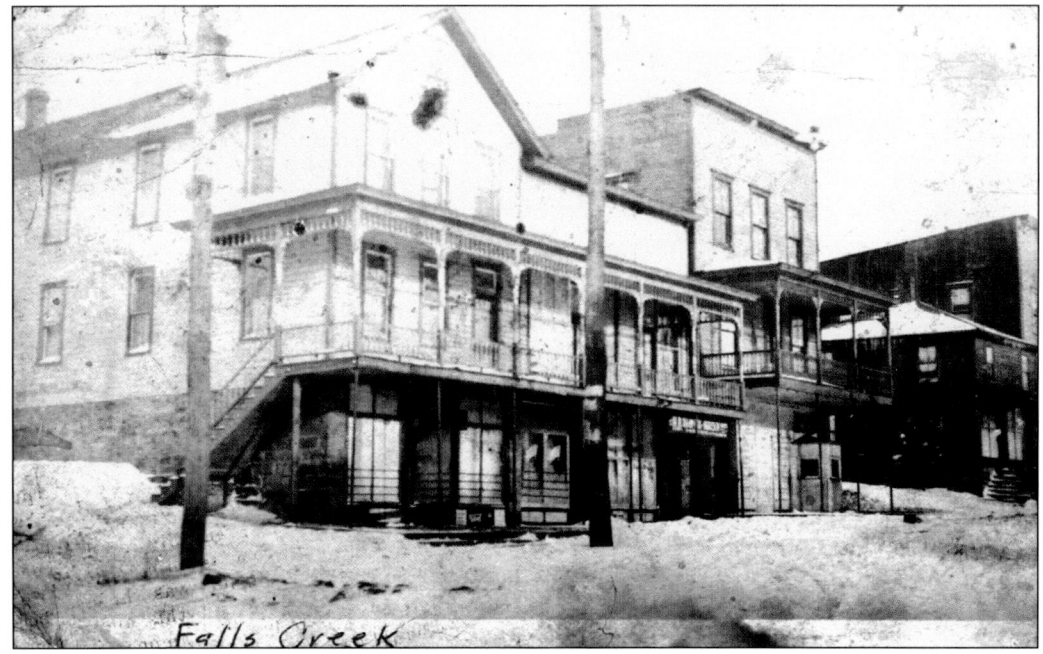

This is Main Street in Falls Creek as viewed from the top of Station Hill, looking toward the center of town.

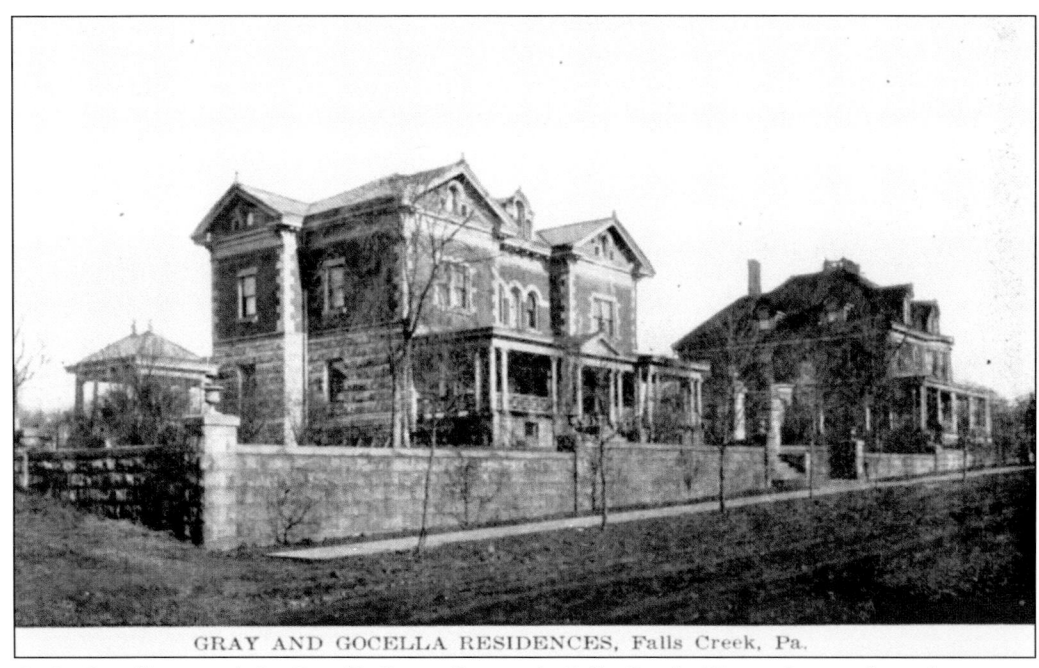

GRAY AND GOCELLA RESIDENCES, Falls Creek, Pa.

G. A. Gocella owned the Gocella Stone Quarry in Falls Creek. He used stone from the quarry to build his grand stone mansion on Jefferson Avenue in the early 1890s. The Gray mansion is located next door and was owned by Ralph Gray.

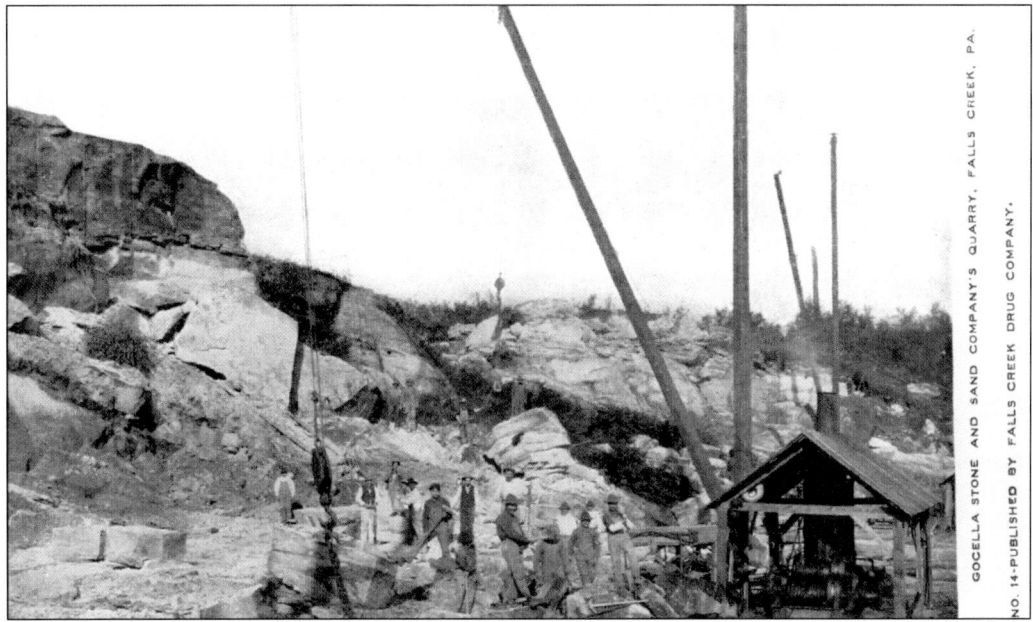

The Gocella Stone Quarry and Sand Company furnished stone that was used to build many building and bridges. The Gocella mansion, now owned by the Eagles Club, and the great stone bridge over the river at Harrisburg both stand as monuments to Gocella.

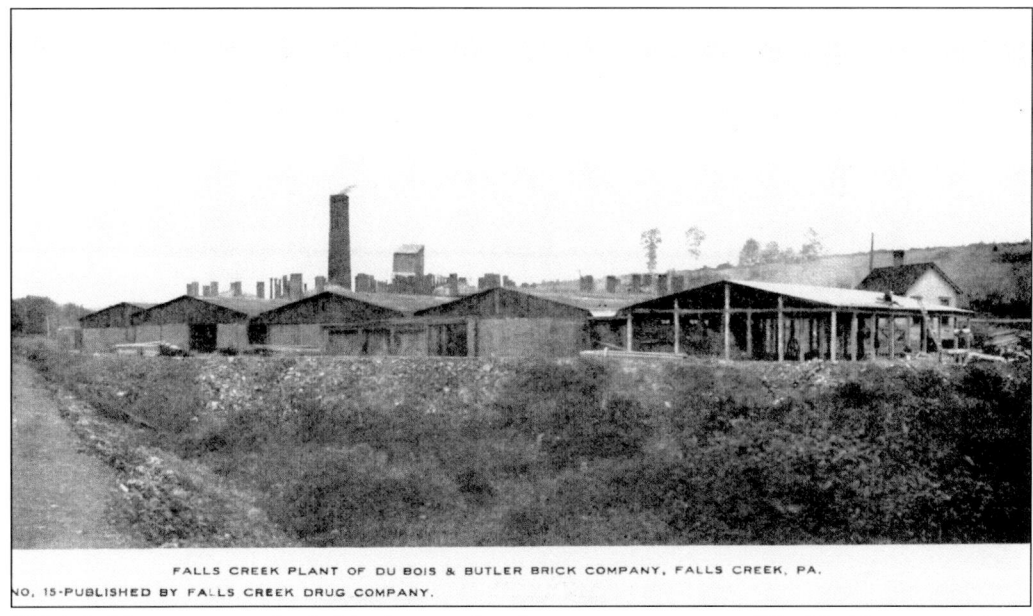

Uriah J. Matson opened a brick plant under the company name of R. M. Matson and Son. Located on Route 950 near Reynoldsville, the plant was later bought by the DuBois and Butler Brick Company. Today it is owned by Allegheny Powder Metallurgy.

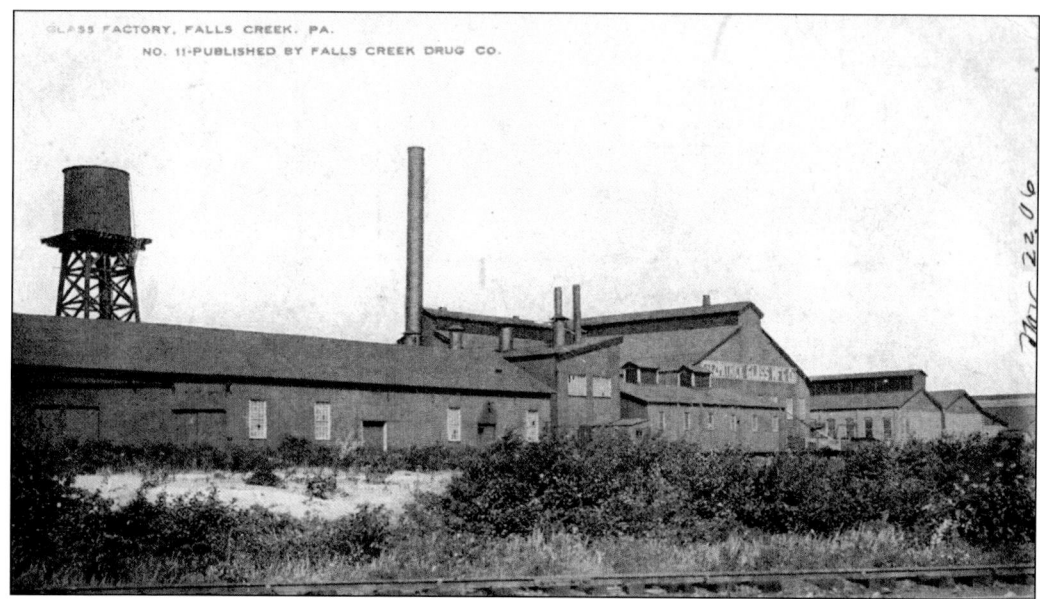

The Fitzpatrick Glass Company manufactured glass in Falls Creek. This building later housed the Jackson China Company.

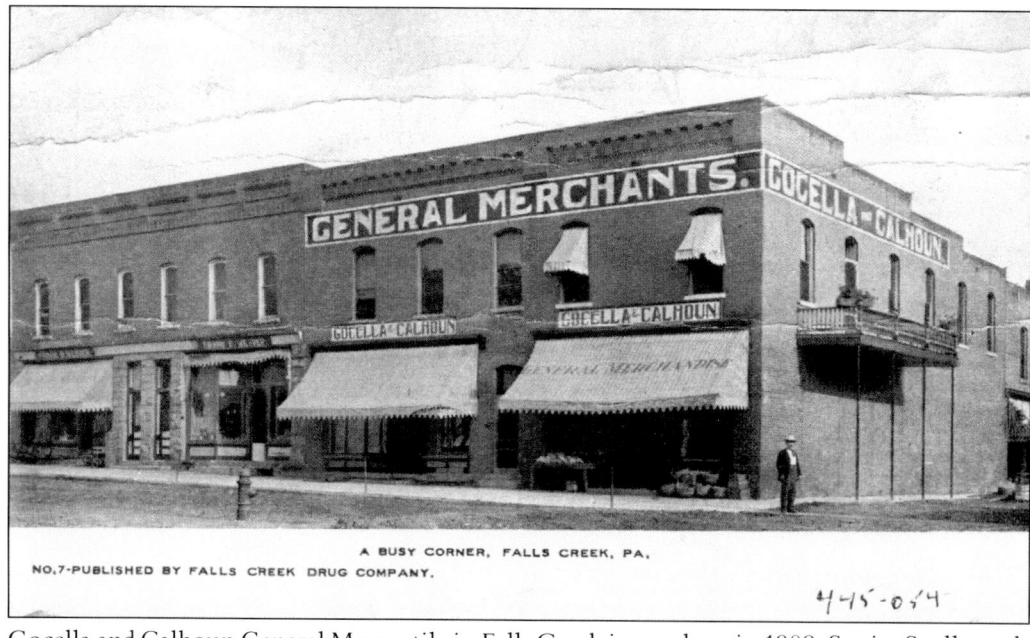

Gocella and Calhoun General Mercantile in Falls Creek is seen here in 1908. Squire Snell stands on the corner, and Weaver's hardware store is on the left.

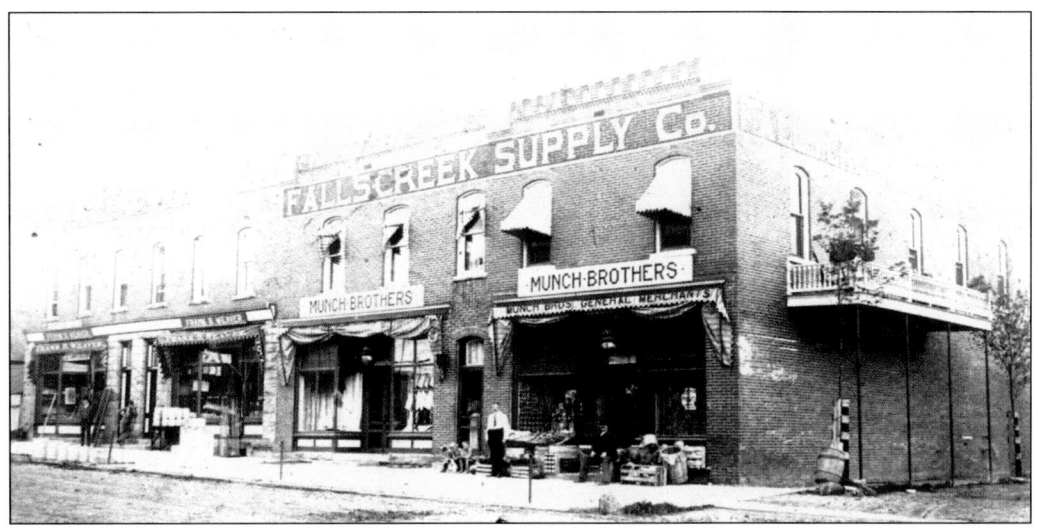

The Falls Creek Supply Company was owned and operated by the Munch Brothers, who were general merchants. The building later housed the Schaffner furniture store until it burned in the late 1970s.

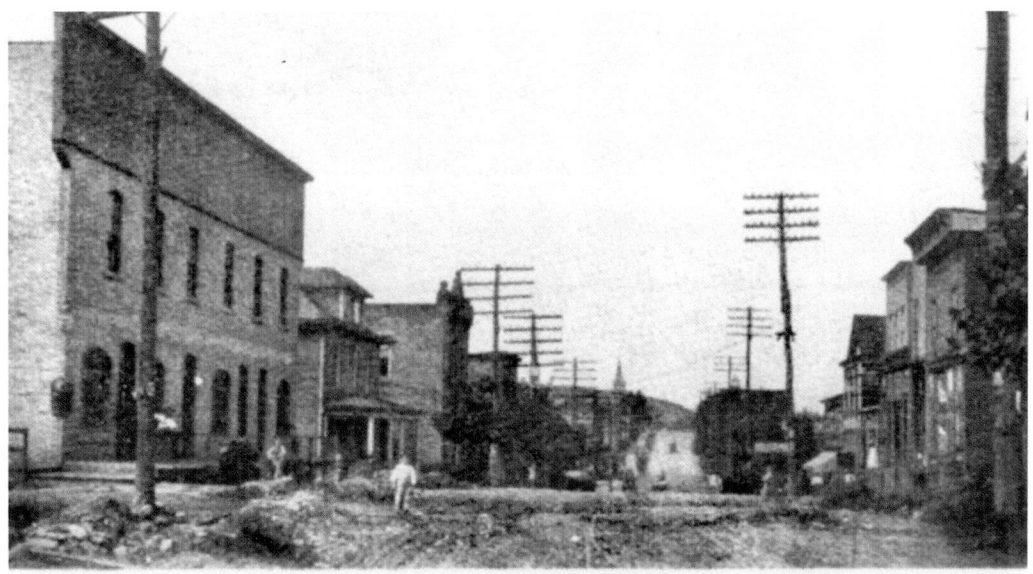

This image of Main Street in Falls Creek looks toward downtown from Station Hill. A hotel can be seen on the left, and the third building on the left is the home of the *Falls Creek Herald*. The steeple of the Presbyterian church is visible in the background.

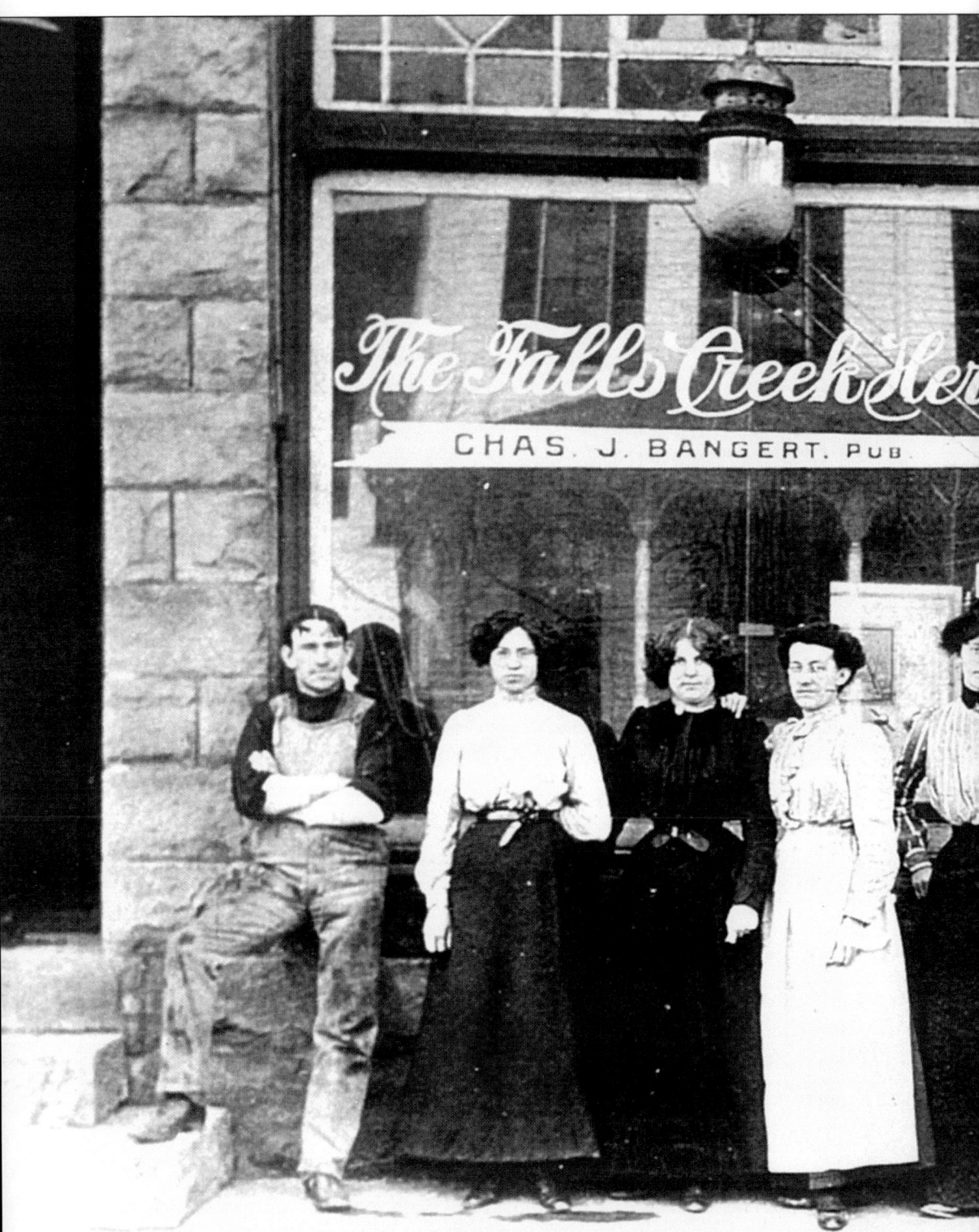

The *Falls Creek Herald* was established in 1891 by Charles J. Bangert. After four fires damaged his newspaper

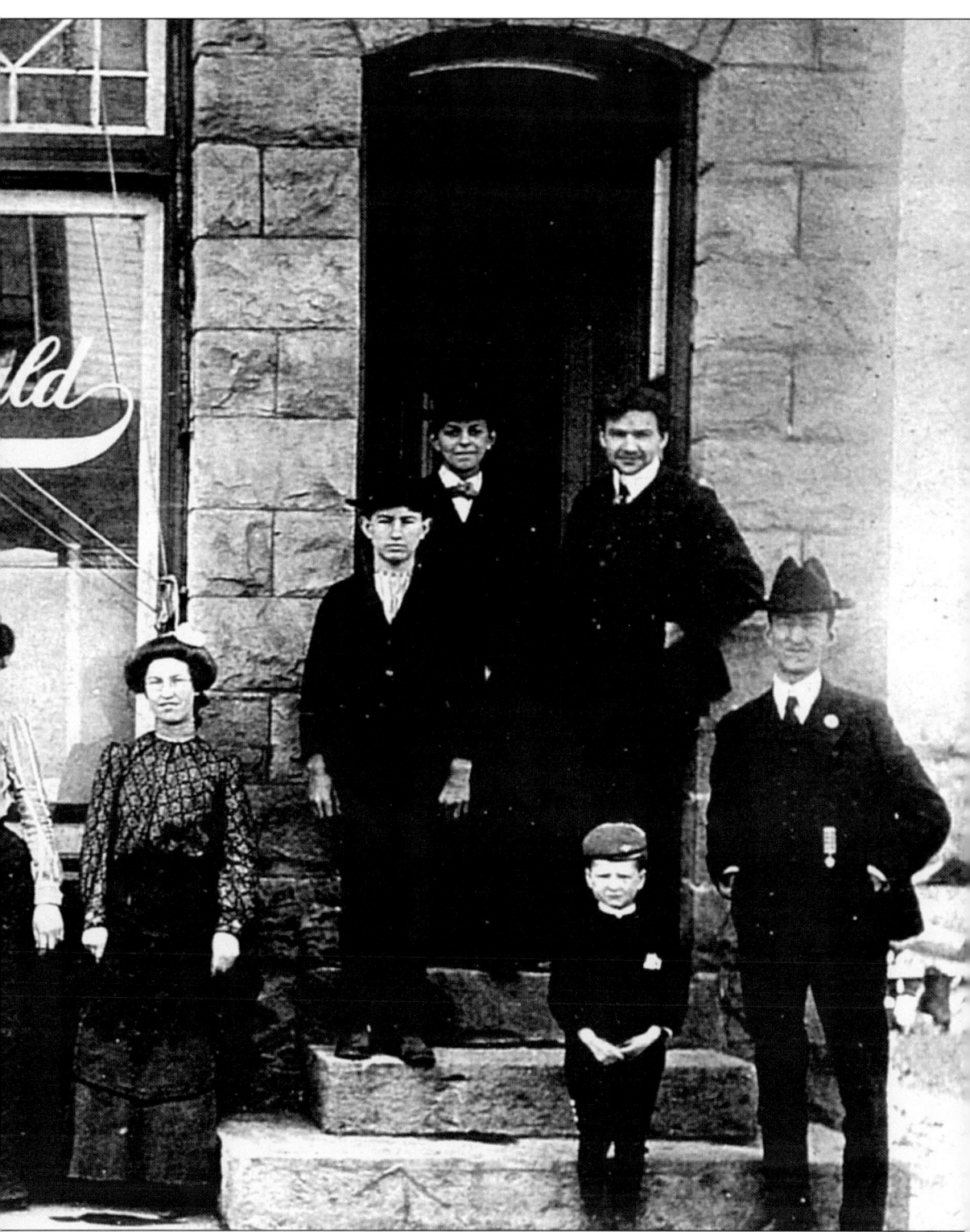

business, Bangert built this brick and stone building. It was later used as the Falls Creek Bank.

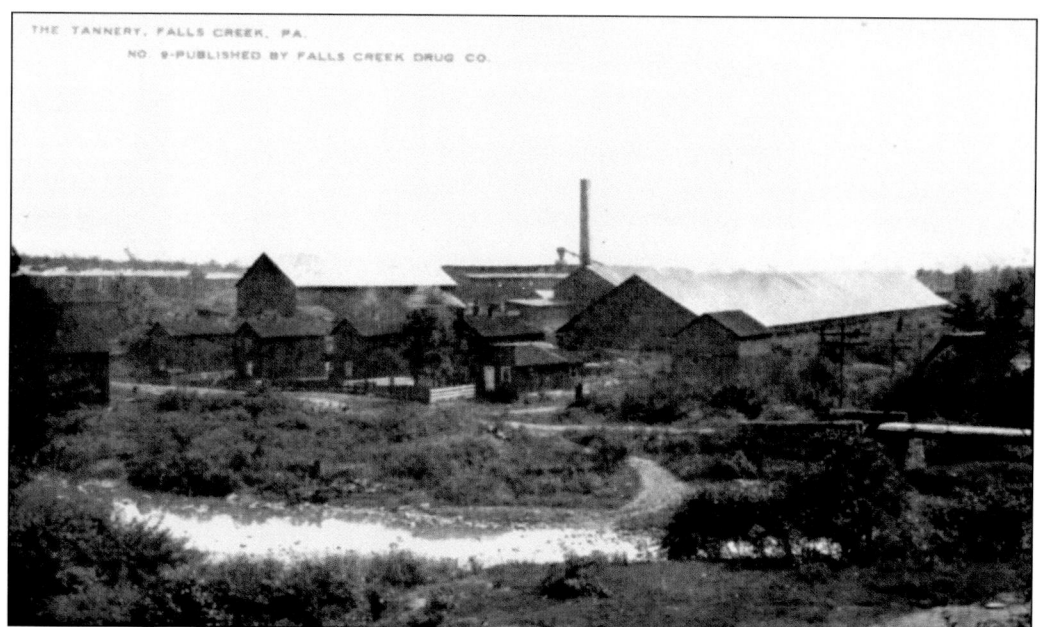

Thomas E. Procter built a tannery and company houses in Falls Creek in 1891. The tannery was one of the largest in the area and produced leather for shoe soles.

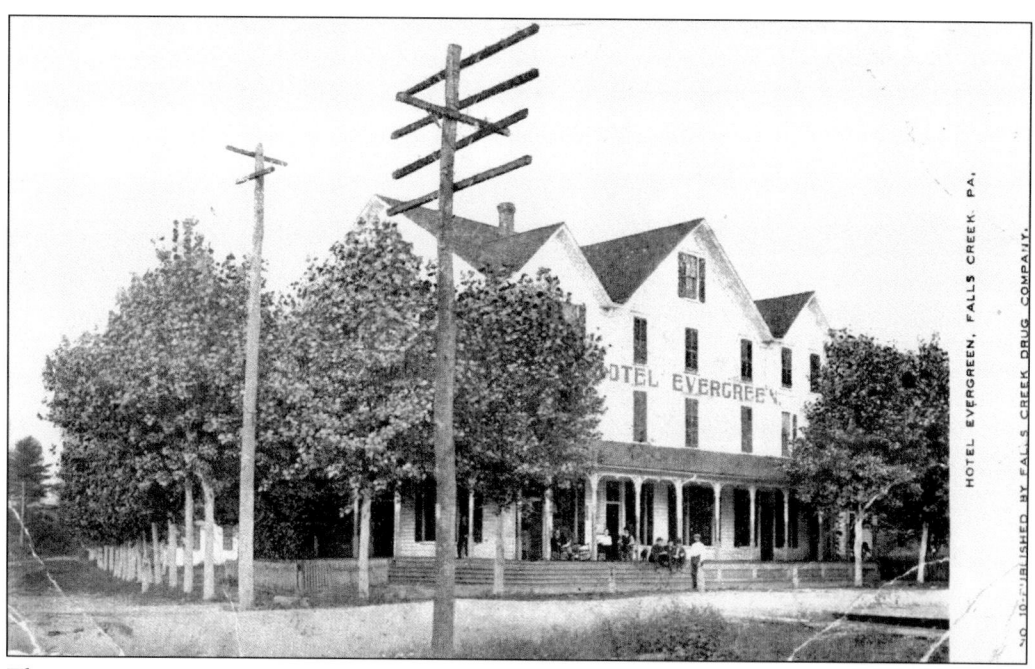

The Evergreen Hotel in Falls Creek was located on Jefferson Avenue near the railroad. It was later the carrier rooming house.

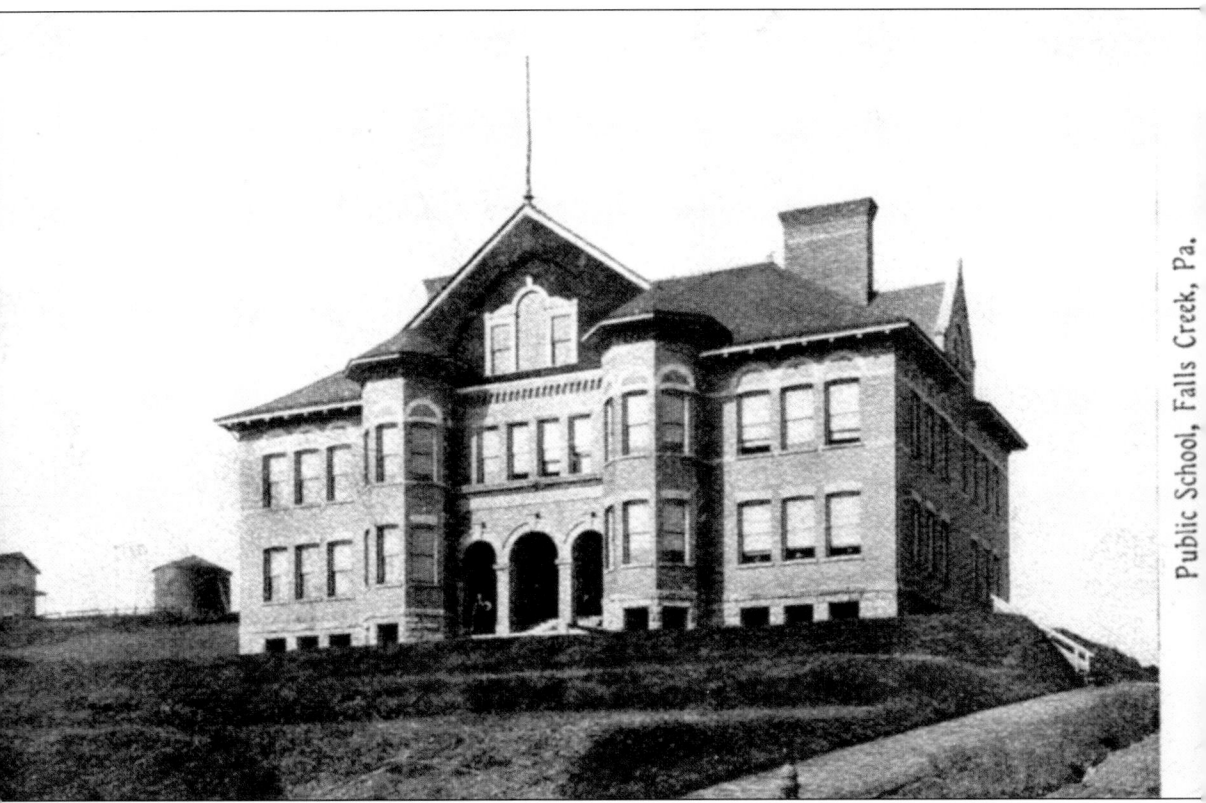

The Falls Creek School was built and opened in 1902. The 13-room building was located on Taylor Avenue and served both grade school and high school students. The school closed its doors in the early 1960s.

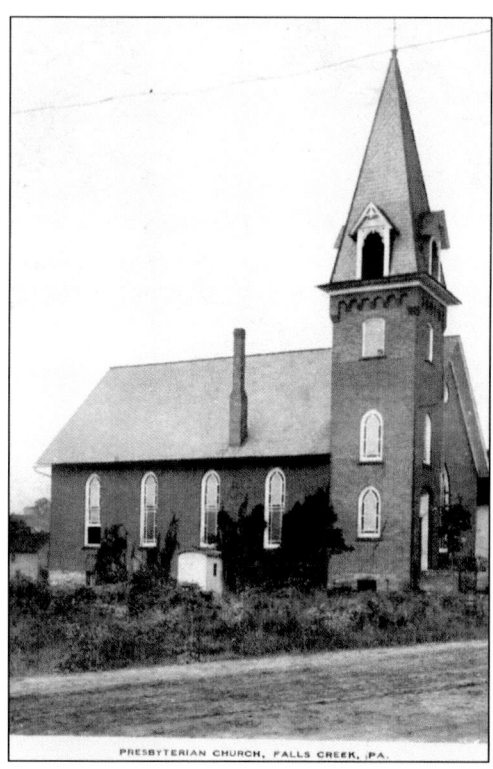

The Presbyterian Church in Falls Creek was started in 1890 in the Evergreen Schoolhouse. The first church burned in 1893, and a new church was started in 1894. Church services were held in the basement of the new building until the main sanctuary was completed in 1895. A large bell was placed in the belfry in 1900.

The cornerstone of the Falls Creek Catholic Church was laid in 1901. The building was dedicated in 1902, with Monsignor McGiveny serving as its first pastor. The church was temporarily closed during World War II, but it was repaired in 1947–1948 and reopened with 200 parishioners.

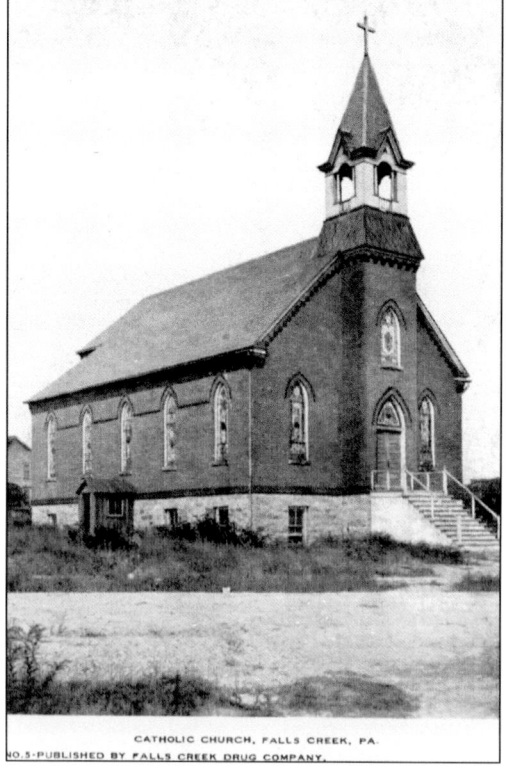

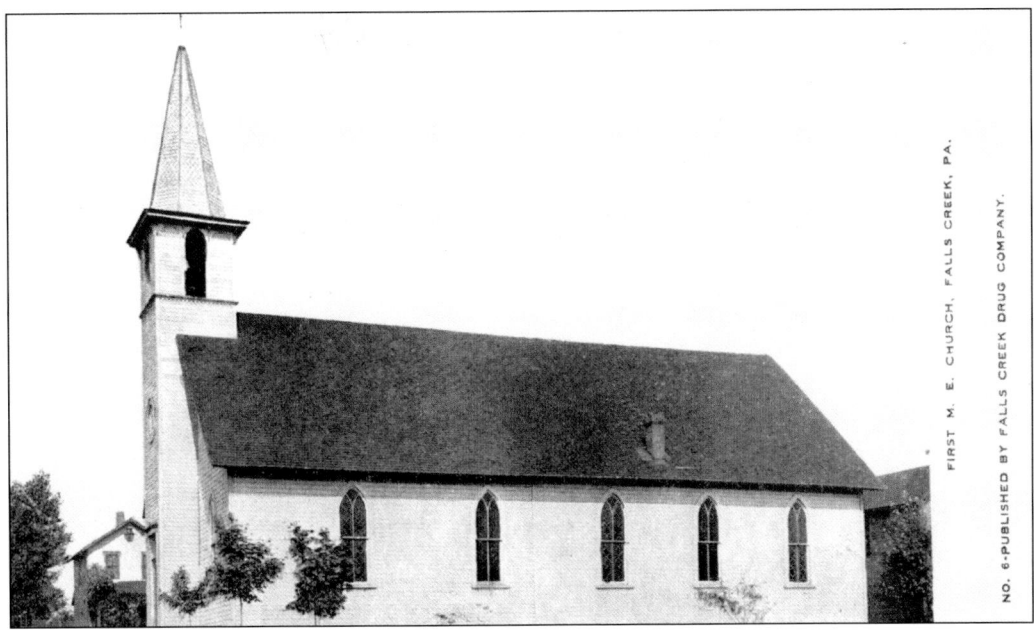

The United Methodist Church building in Falls Creek was begun in 1890, and the church was dedicated in 1891. When more room was needed, an addition was built on the west side of the church. The basement rooms were added in 1980.

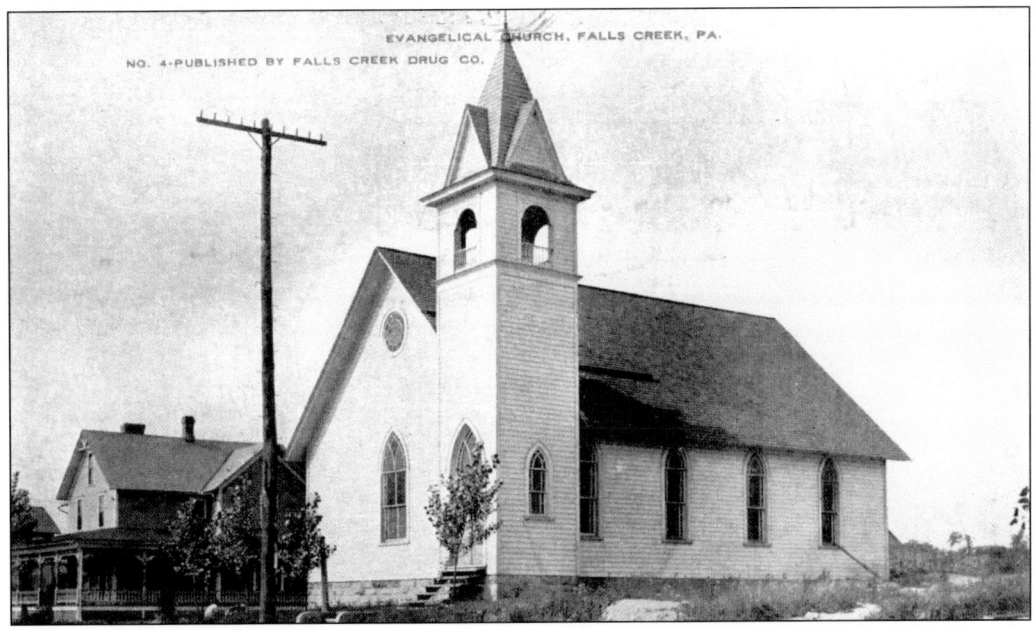

The Evangelical church in Falls Creek was built on the corner of Main and Second Streets. The church burned down along with the Fuller Building and was rebuilt. When the population changed and fewer members attended the church, the building became a community center. It was later made into Willar's Market.

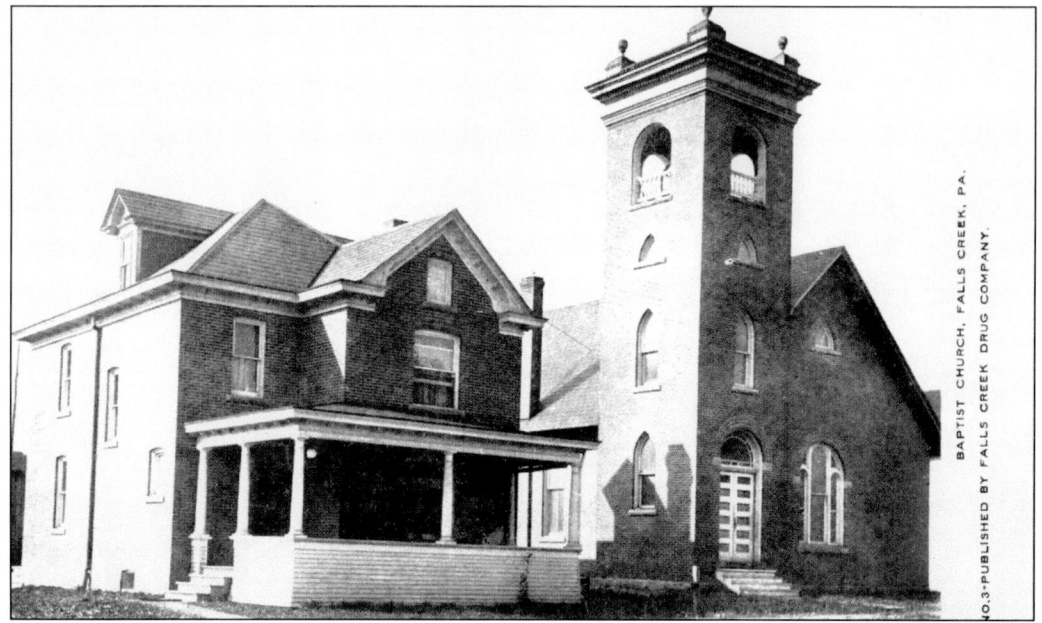

The Falls Creek Baptist Church was organized in 1901, and the building was erected in 1905. In 1942, the Christian and Missionary Church was organized and began holding services in this building.

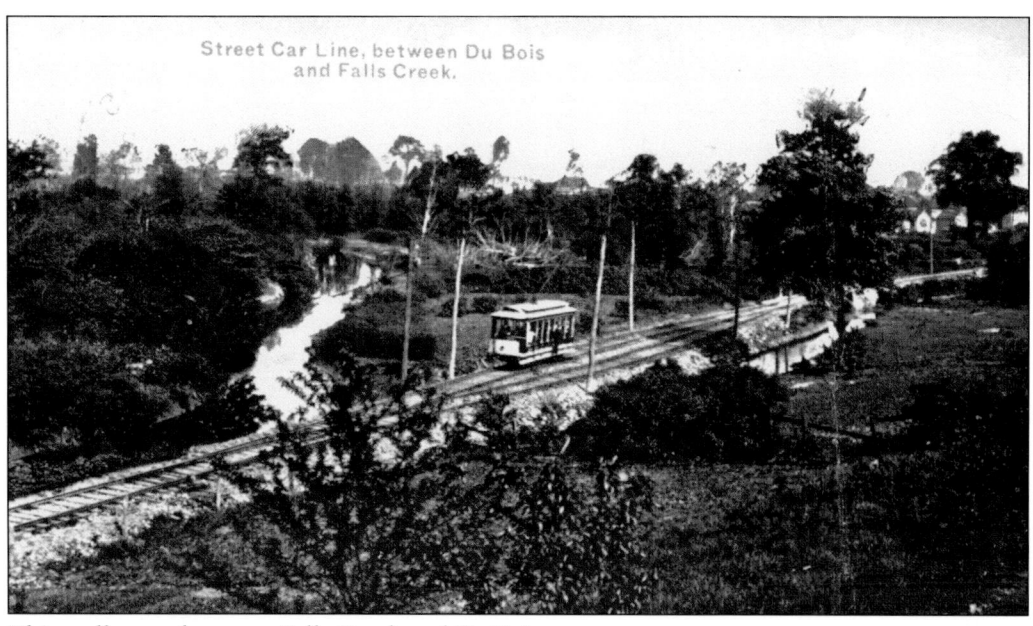

This trolley ran between Falls Creek and DuBois.

Eight
Sabula and Penfield

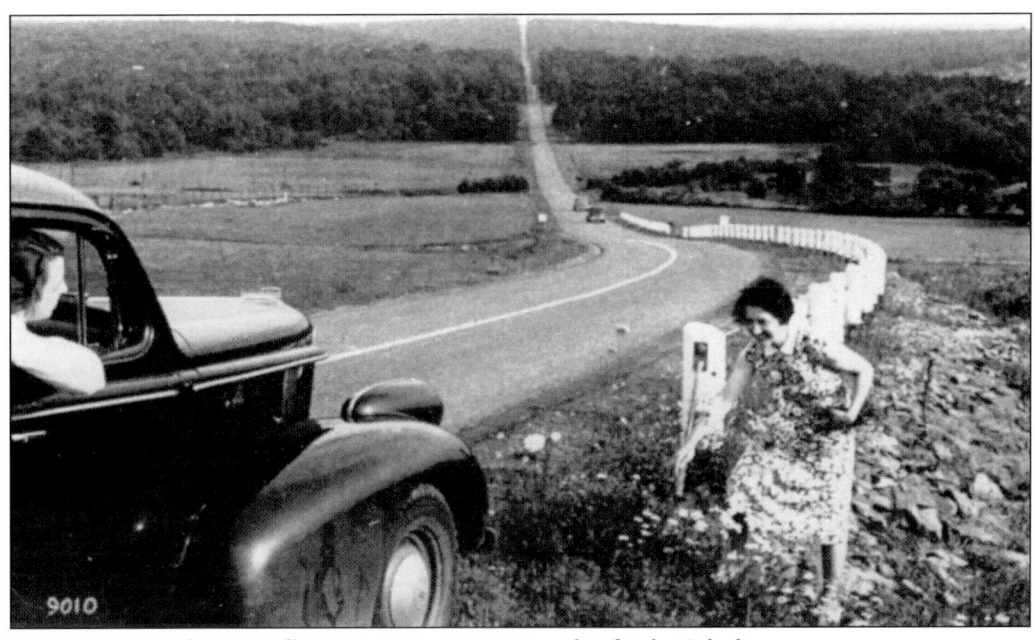
Two women pick spring flowers on Route 255 north of Lake Sabula.

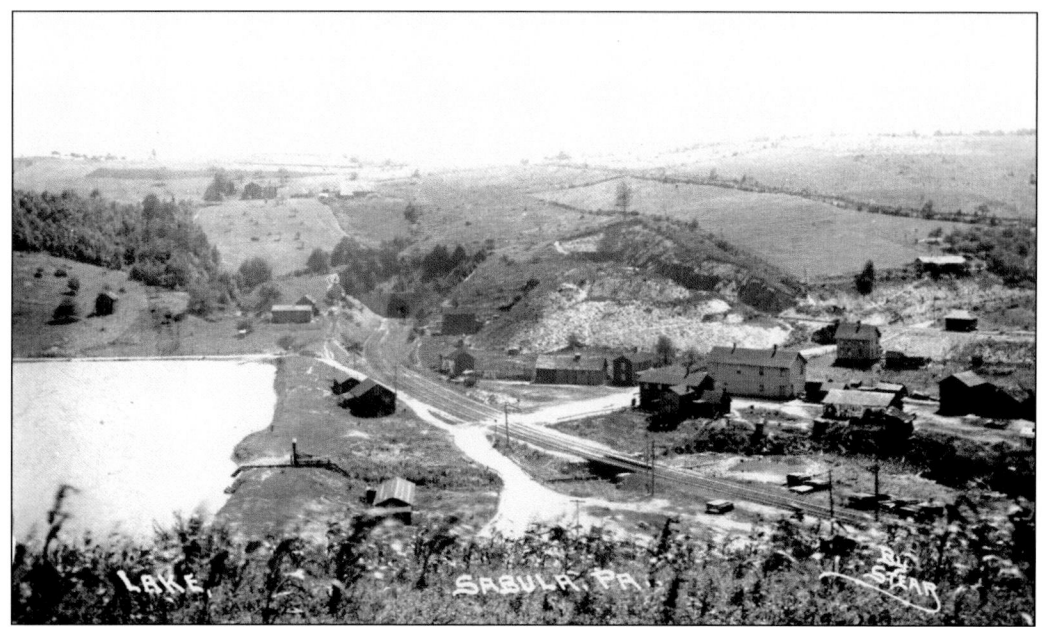

The breast and spillway at the Sabula dam are seen here. The lower railroad is the Pennsylvania Railroad, and the upper one is the Buffalo and Susquehanna Railroad. Each railroad went into one of the two tunnels built in the hillside.

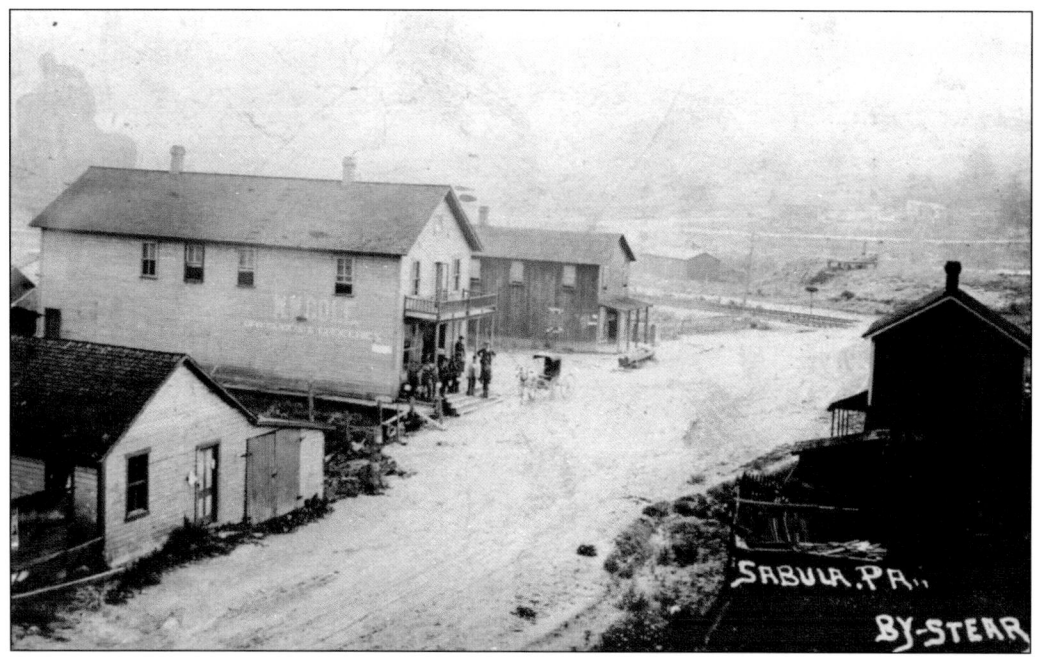

The W. W. Cole store at Sabula served as the post office from 1875 until the store closed in 1925.

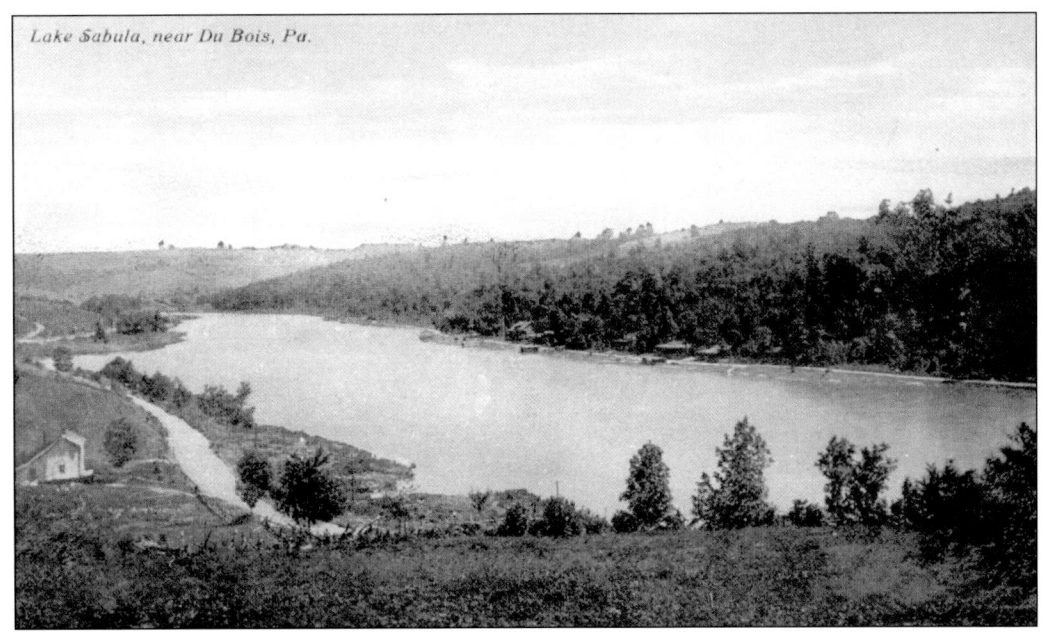
This is a view of Lake Sabula.

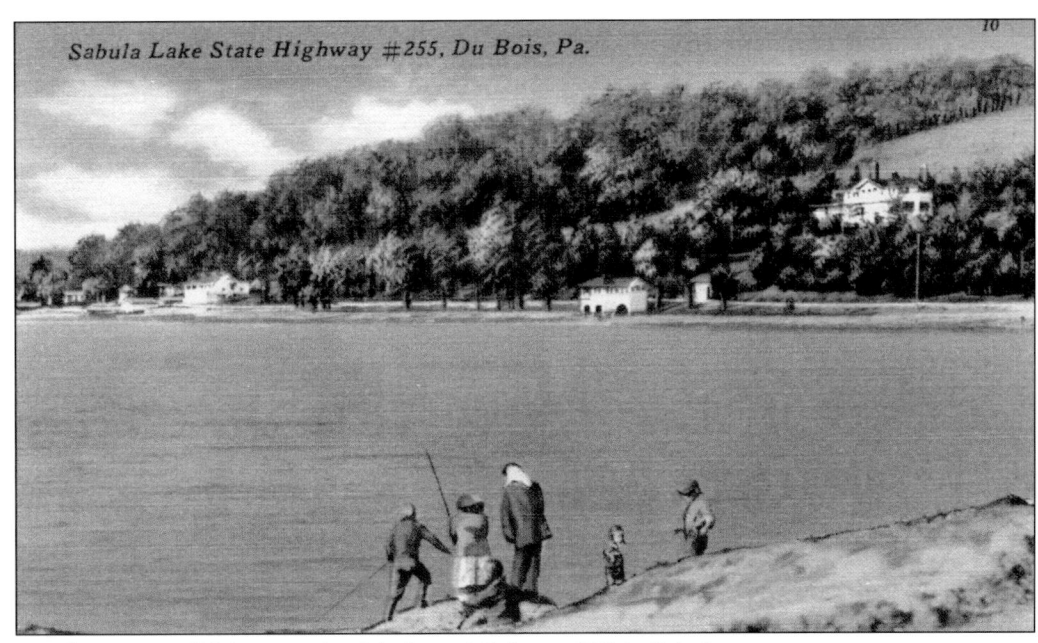
People are seen fishing at Lake Sabula on Highway 255 in Sabula.

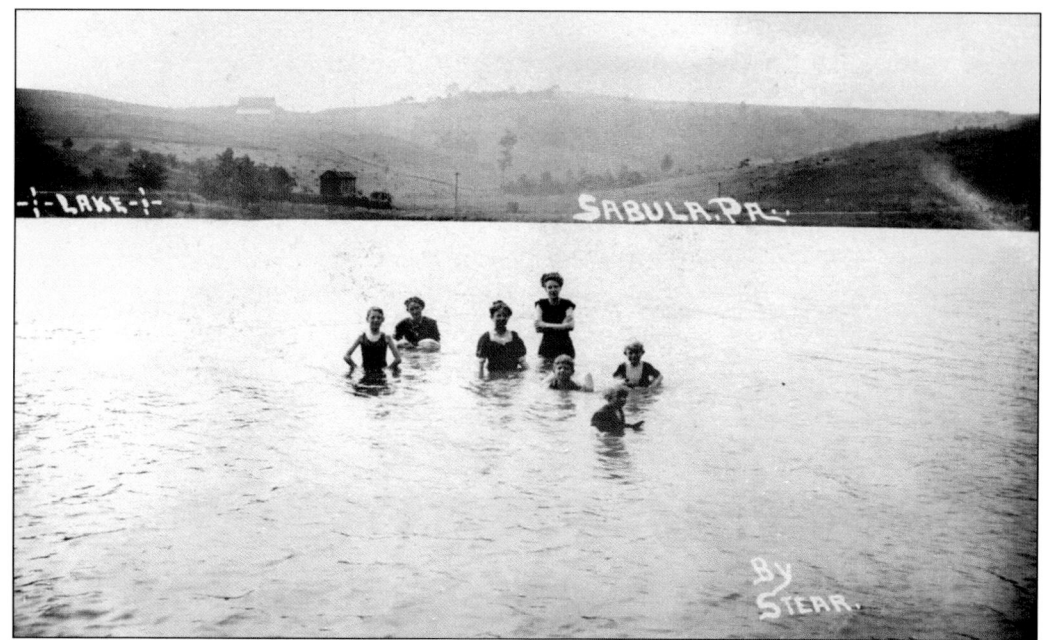
Locals enjoy summer fun at Lake Sabula. The lake was originally a splash dam, or a holding area for logs, used by the DuBois Lumber Company.

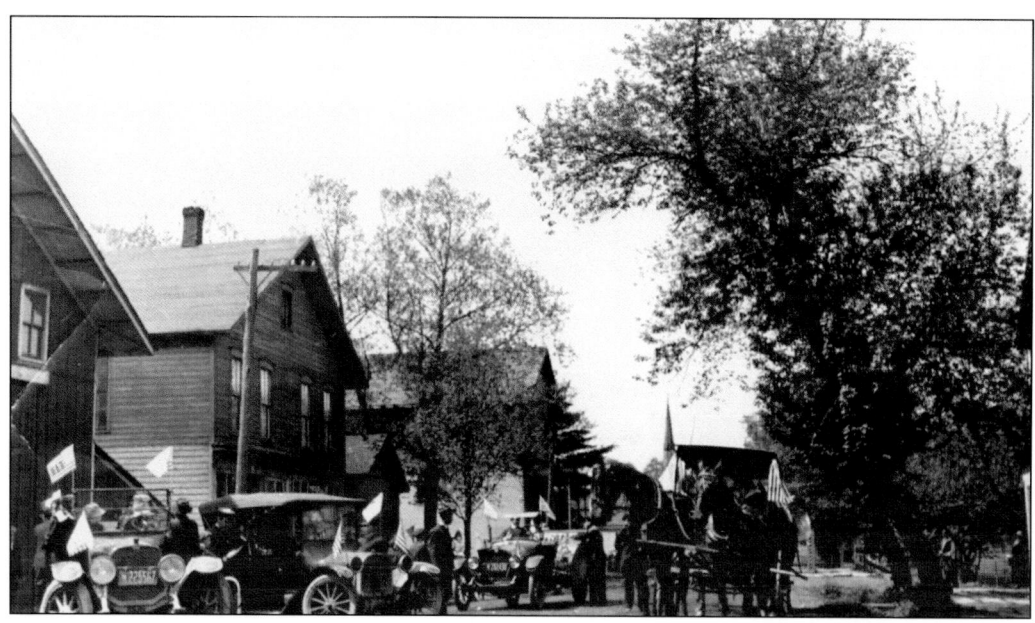
Homes and various forms of transportation are seen along Main Street in Penfield.

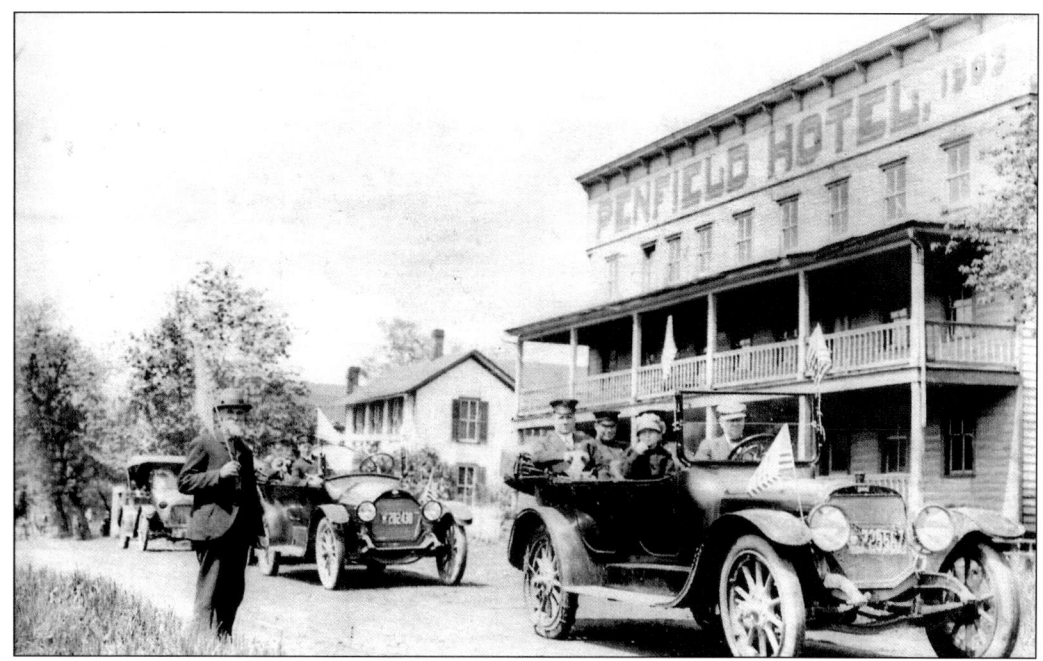

The first Penfield Hotel was built on this spot in 1854 by Jesse Wilson. In 1856, Wilson sold the building to lumber baron Hiram Woodward.

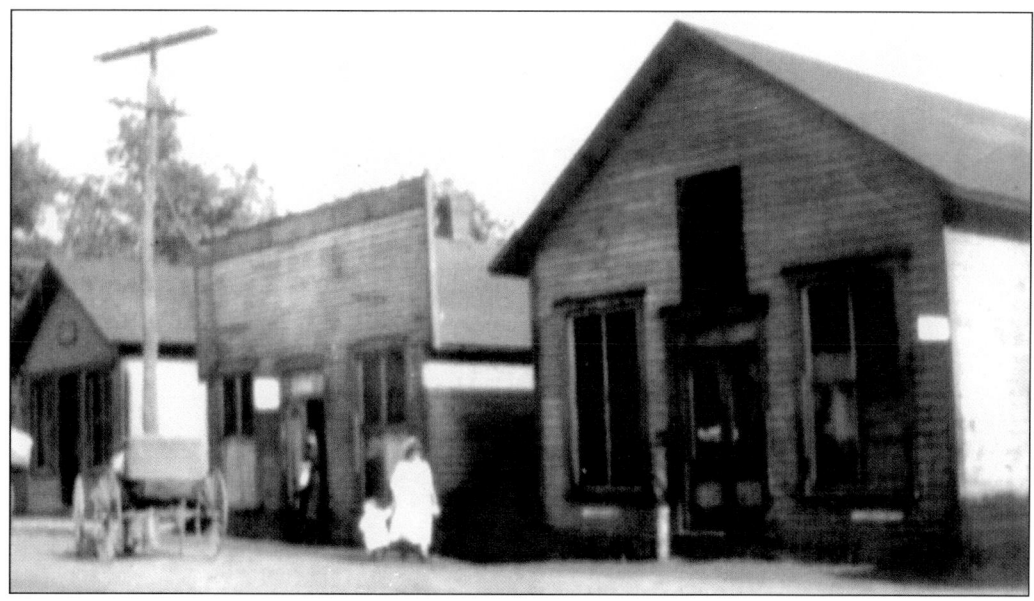

Penfield's first post office opened in 1866 in this building, which was owned for many years by the Riccadonna family. It was razed *c.* 1970.

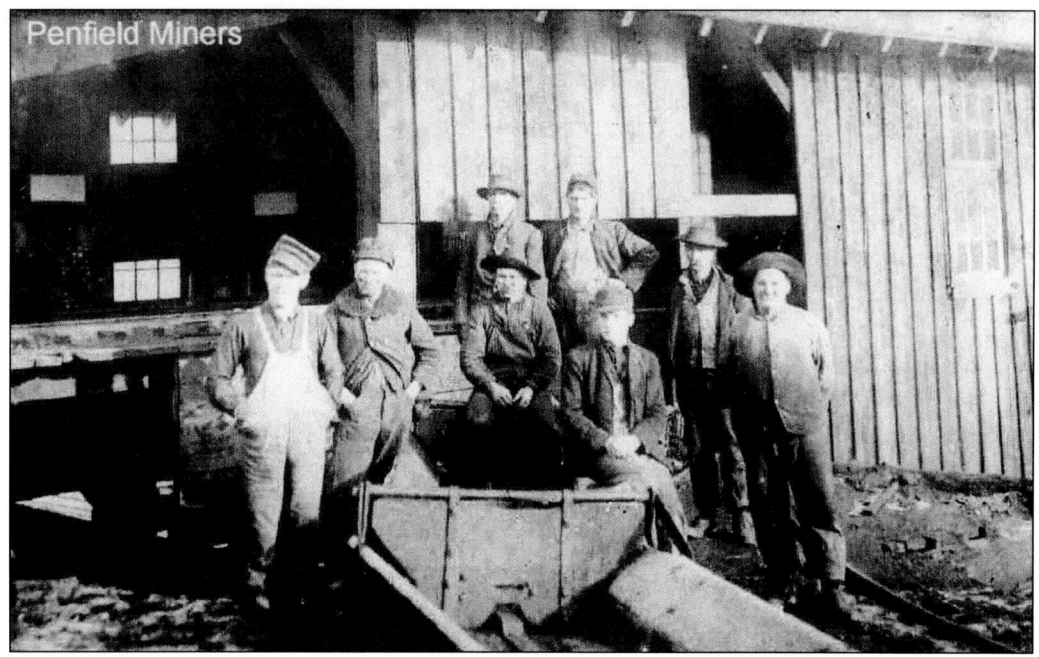
Penfield's coal miners sit in railcars that will take them to work in the mines.

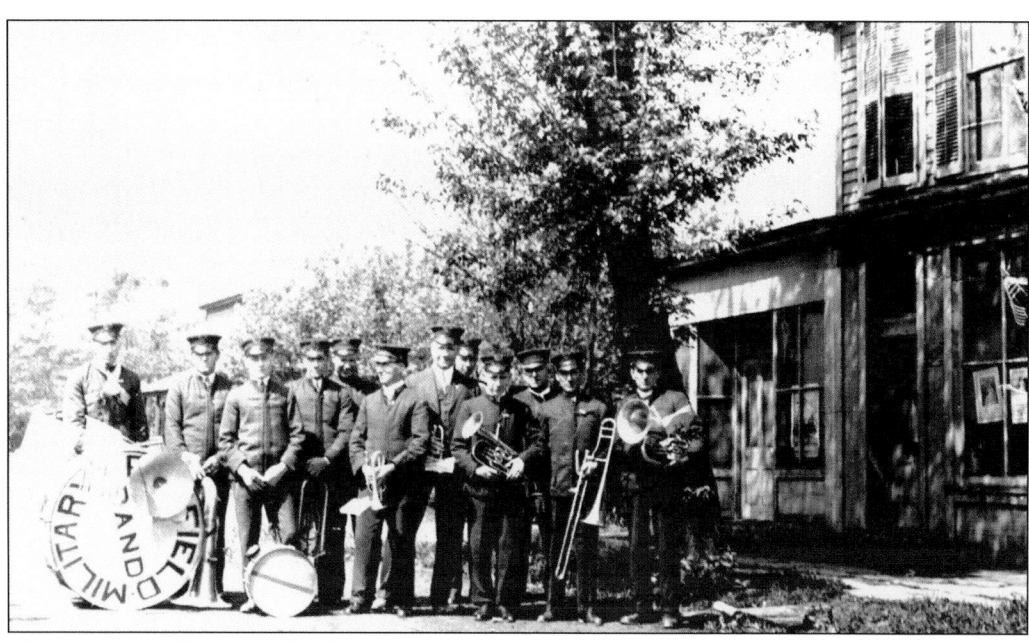
The Penfield Military Band is shown here in 1913. George Rosenkrans is the baritone horn player.

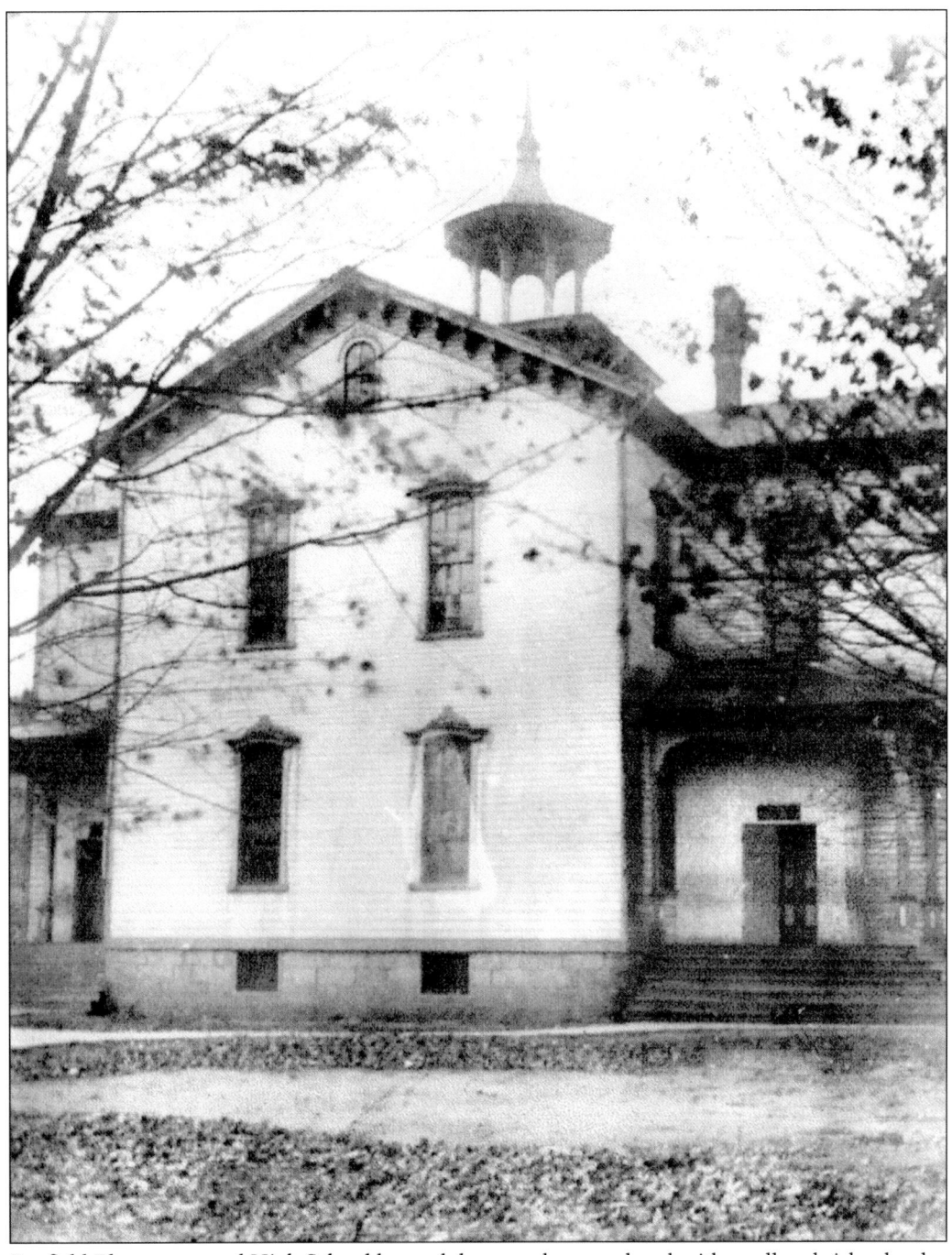
Penfield Elementary and High School burned down and was replaced with a yellow brick school.

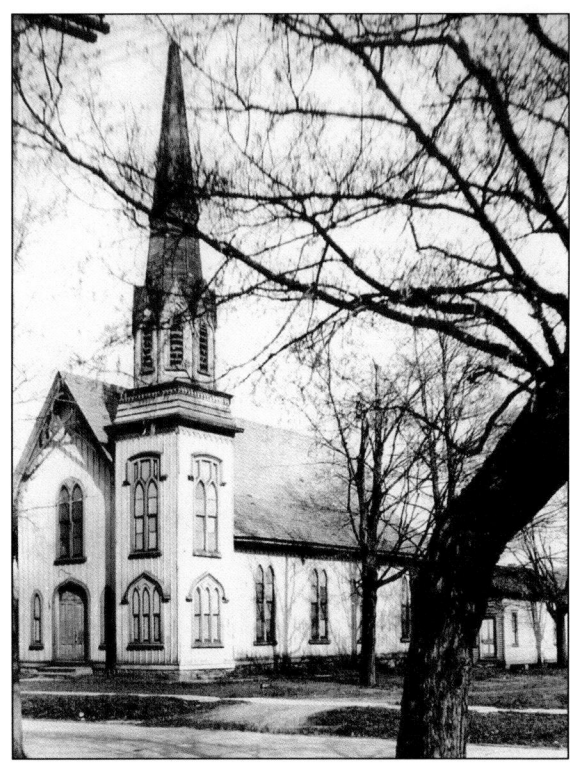

The Presbyterian Church in Penfield was organized in 1872. Hiram Woodward donated a lot, and the church was built in 1873. Rev. Vernon Bell was a pastor from 1881 to 1884. The Presbyterian Sunday School was organized in 1876.

Penfield United Methodist Church dates to the early 1860s. In 1865, the Penfield congregation belonged to the Caladonia Circuit; in 1933, it was part of the Penfield and Benezette Circuit. The congregation joined the Trinity Church in DuBois from 1972 until July 1, 1991. The original church building was about 106 years old. The first baptism and marriage took place in the church in 1878.

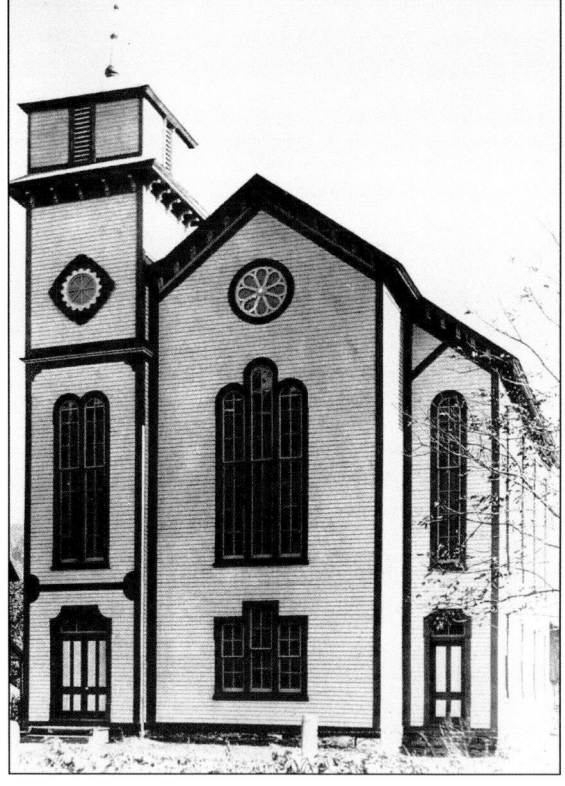

Composer Allen Rosenkrans wrote many hymns. He also delivered mail, using a wheelbarrow to carry the load of mail and packages. Allen Rosenkrans was the father of George Rosenkrans.

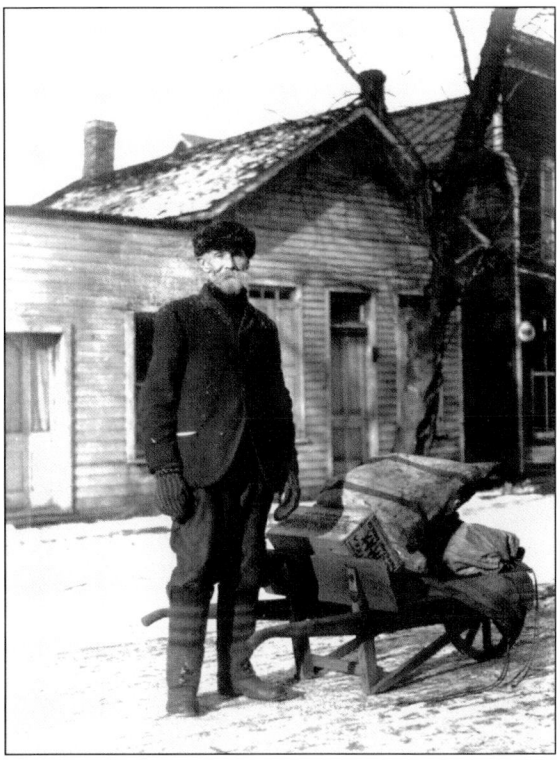

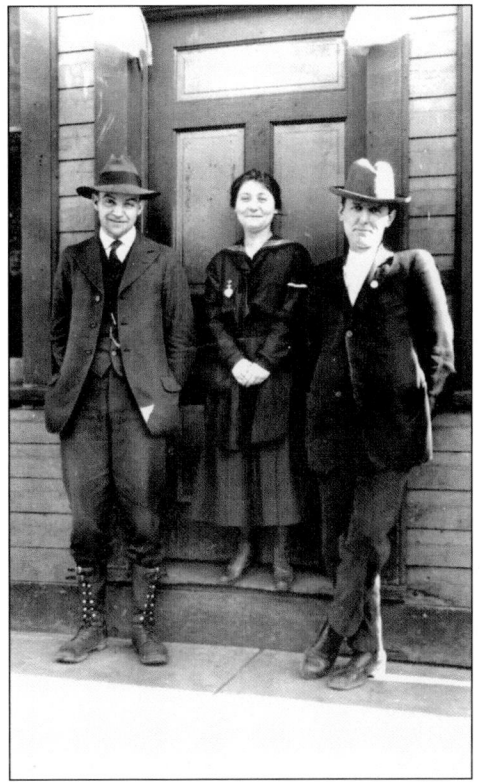

Seen here, from left to right, are Bob Glass, Abbie Robacker, and George Rosenkrans. George Rosenkrans was born in 1881 in Penfield, the son of Allen Rosenkrans, and became a composer of band music. He wrote "All Honor to Glorious Flag," "All Honor to Old Glory," and "Immortal Heroes," which was used at the state funerals for Franklin D. Roosevelt, Dwight D. Eisenhower, Winston Churchill, and John F. Kennedy.

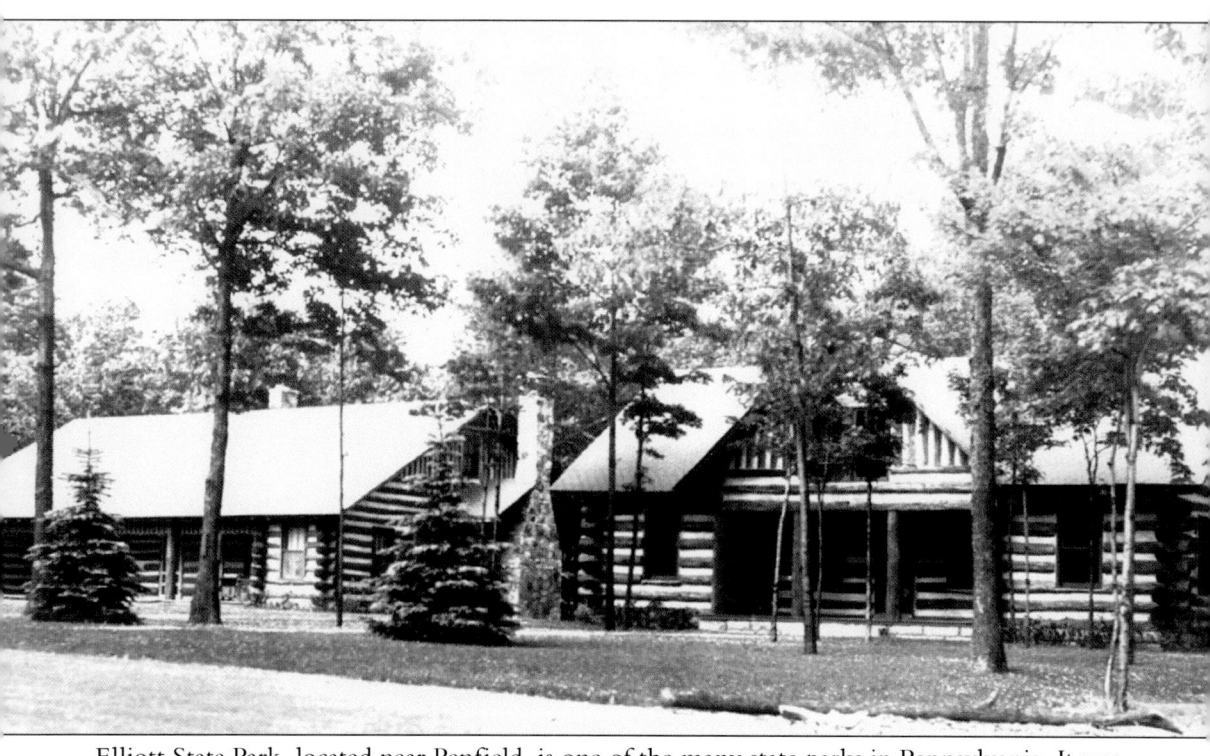
Elliott State Park, located near Penfield, is one of the many state parks in Pennsylvania. It was built during the depression by the Civilian Conservation Corps.

Nine
Reynoldsville and Sykesville

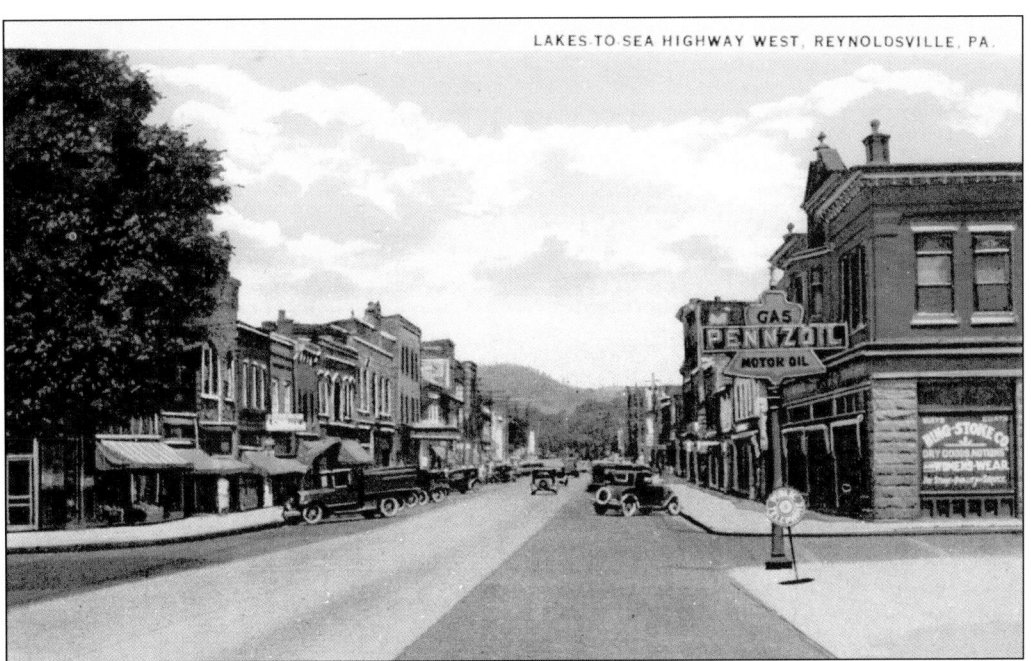

This is the Main Street business district of Reynoldsville. Most of the buildings are still standing and in use today. Main Street was first a plank road in 1893, then a brick road in 1904. It became part of the Lakes to Sea Highway in the early 1920s.

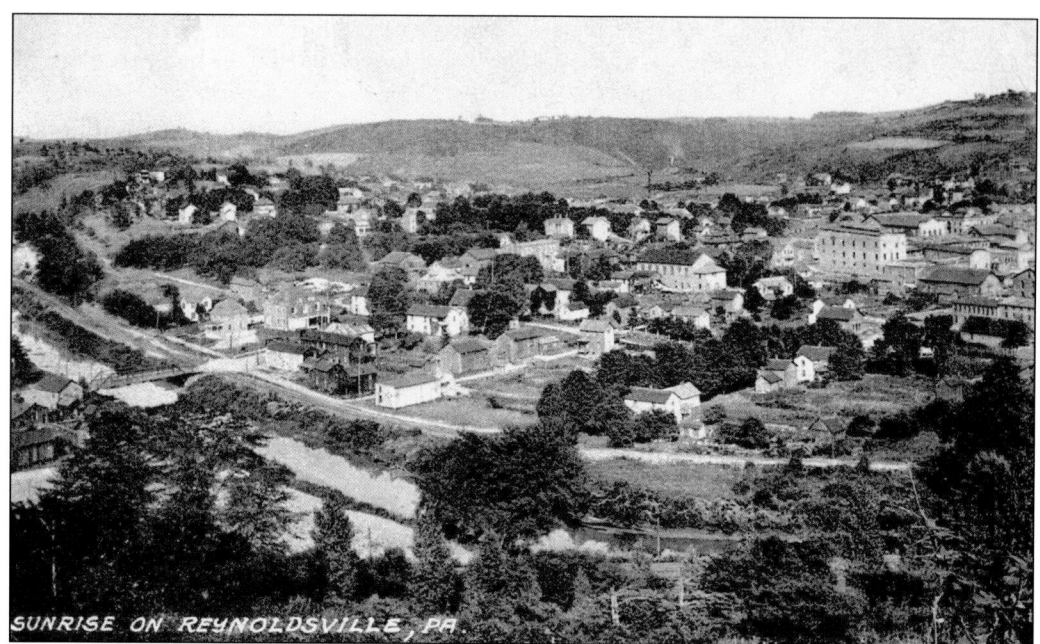
This bird's-eye view shows Reynoldsville.

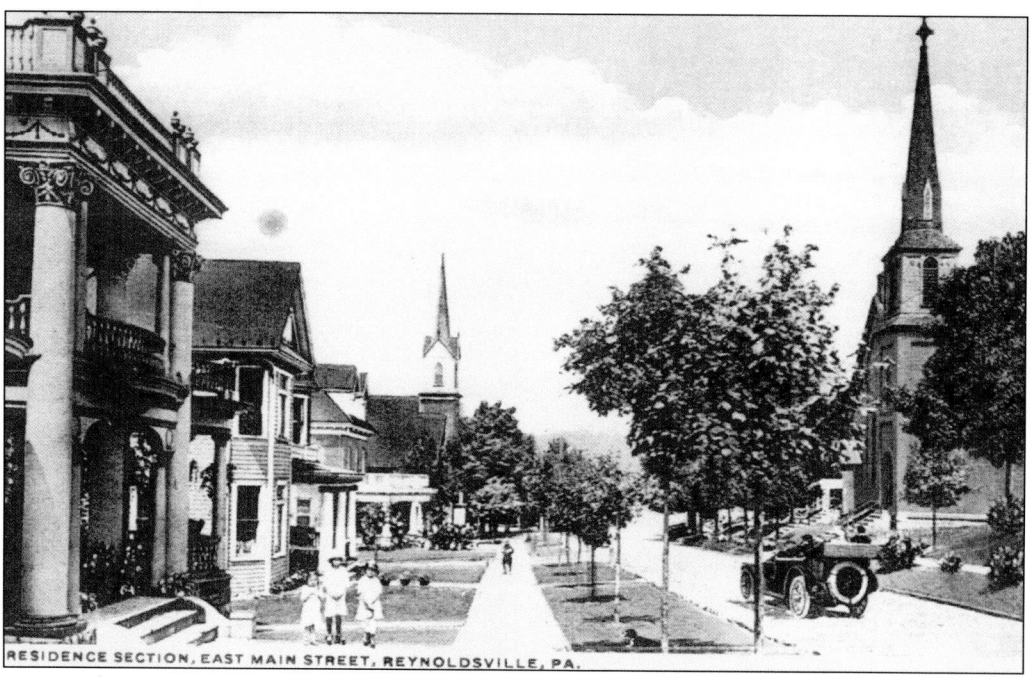
This is a westward view of the residential section of East Main Street. The houses and the Presbyterian church are still there, but a new Catholic church has replaced St. Mary's Catholic Church on the right.

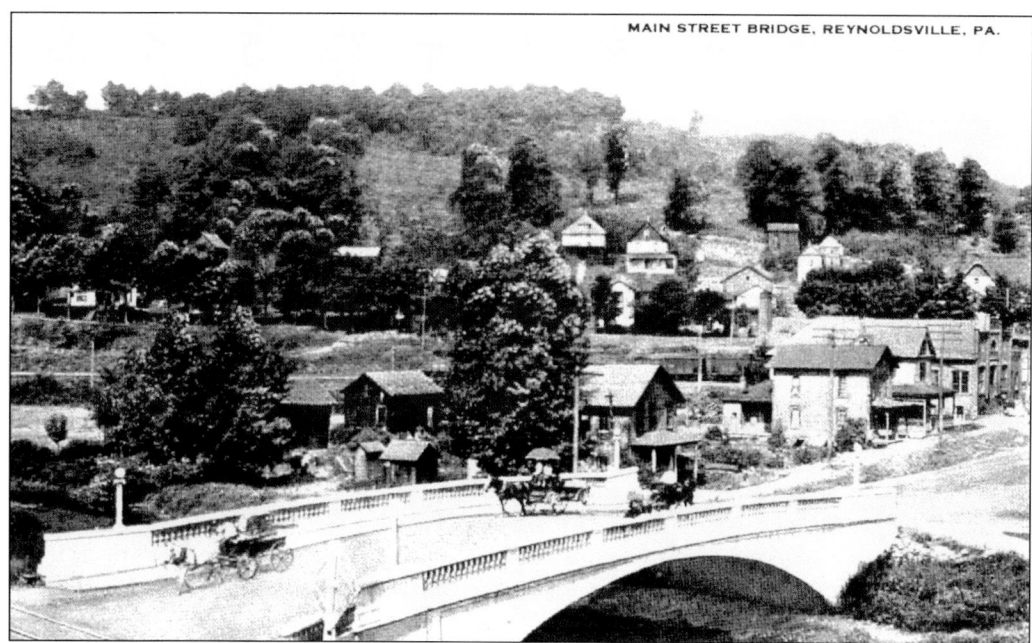

The concrete arch bridge over the Sandy Lick Creek was completed in 1913. There originally were lights at either end, but they no longer exist. Known as the "Tickle Belly Bridge" by many generations, it separated Reynoldsville from Ohiotown and the west side of Reynoldsville. All of these areas were consolidated into one town on April 18, 1914.

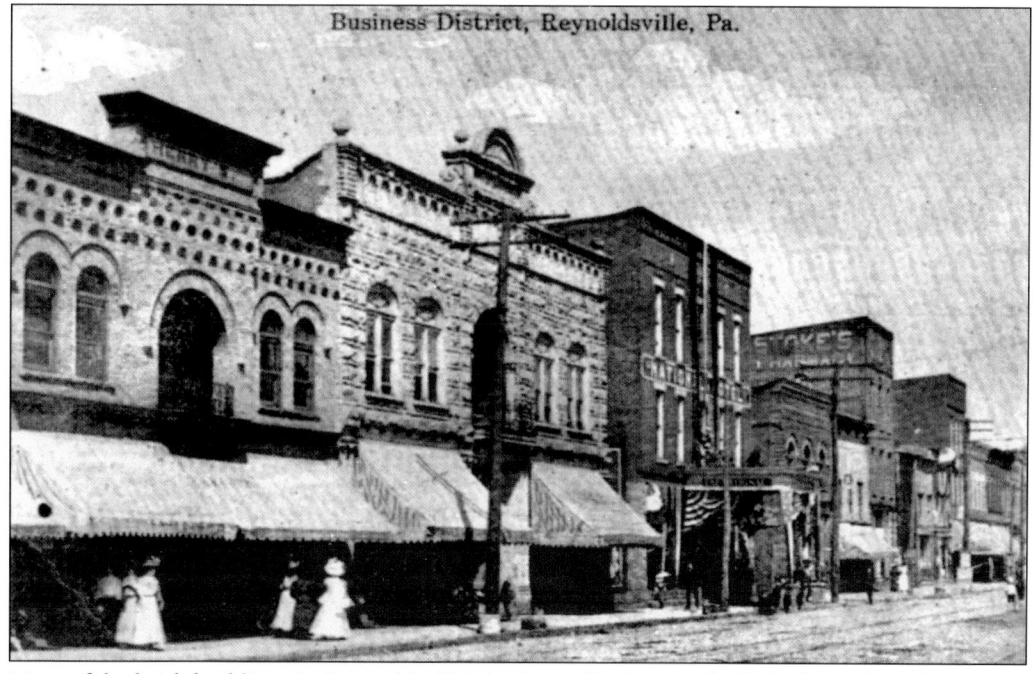

Most of the brick buildings in Reynoldsville's business district were built in the early 20th century.

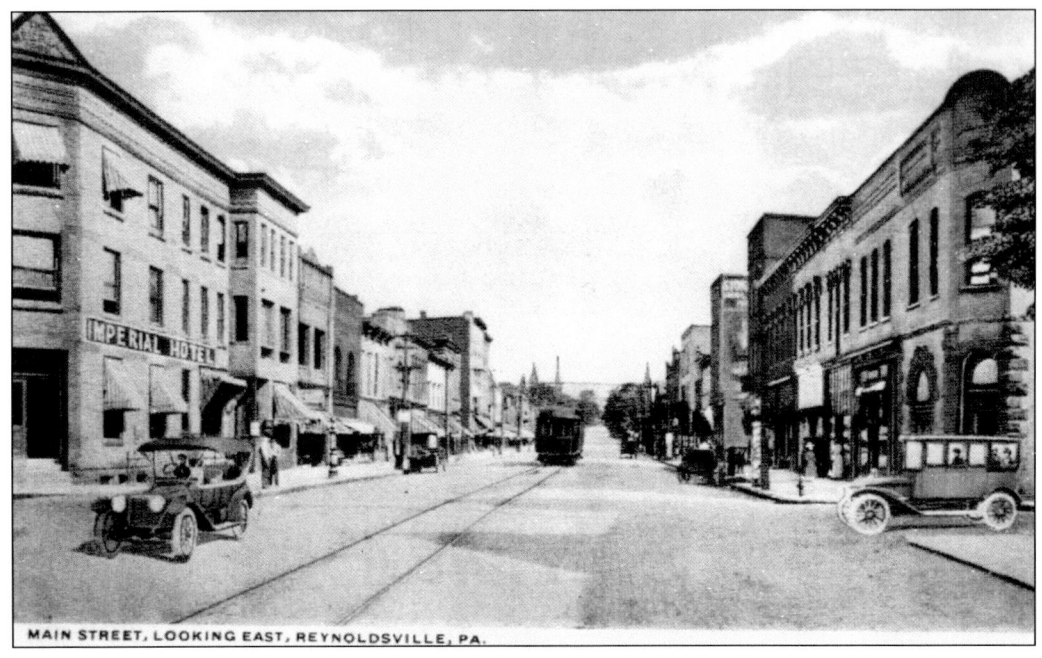

The Imperial Hotel, located on Main Street in Reynoldsville, is shown in this image.

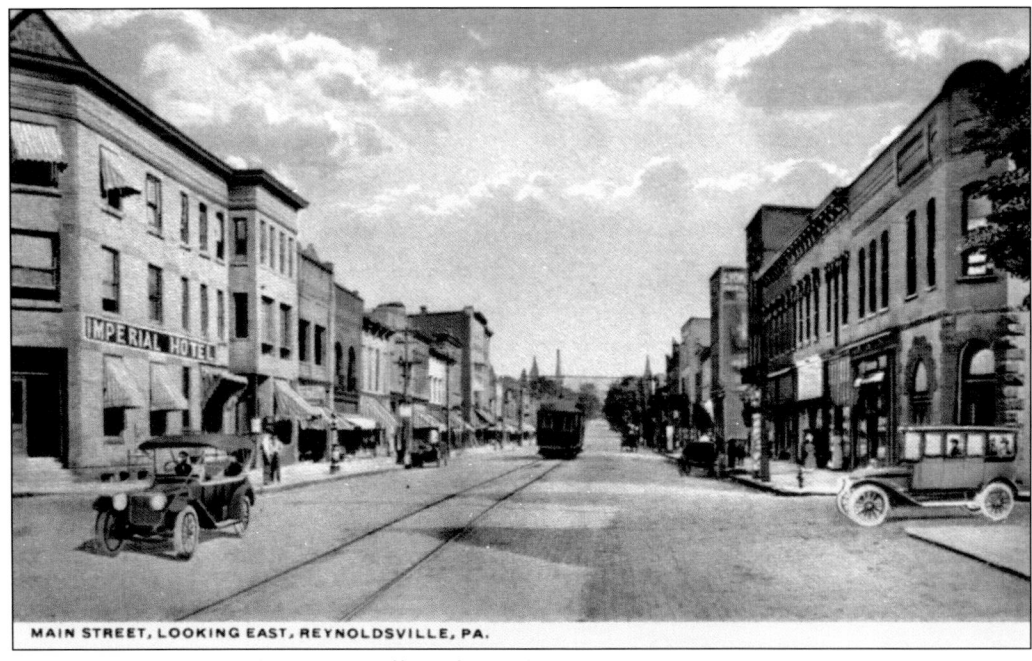

The business district of Reynoldsville is shown here.

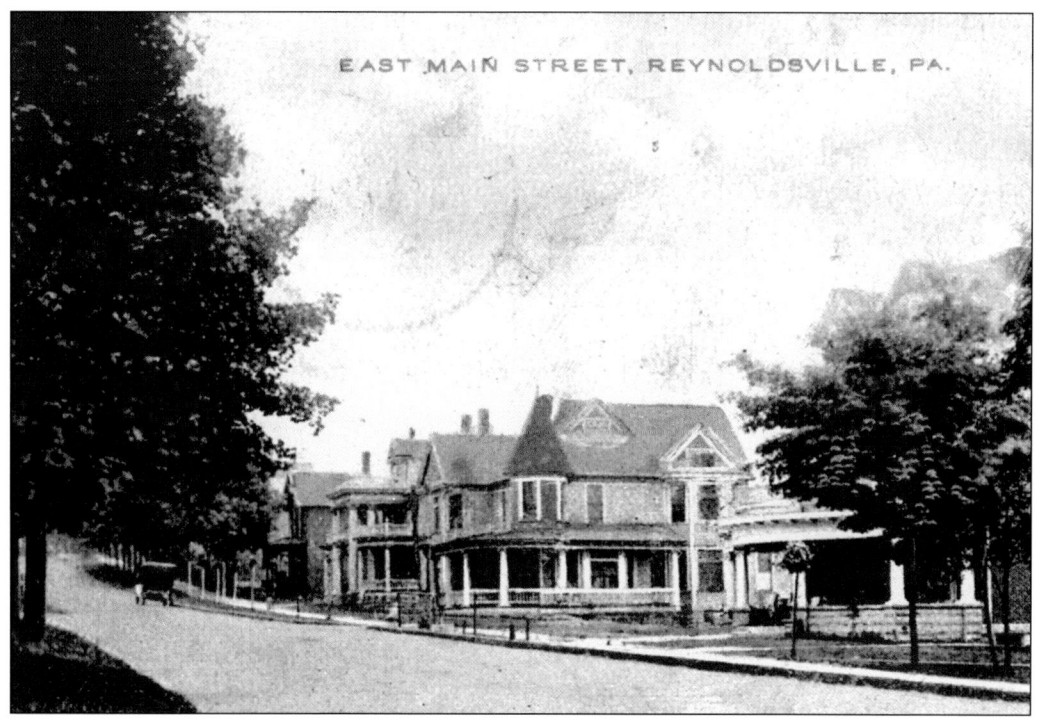
This is the residential area of Main Street in Reynoldsville.

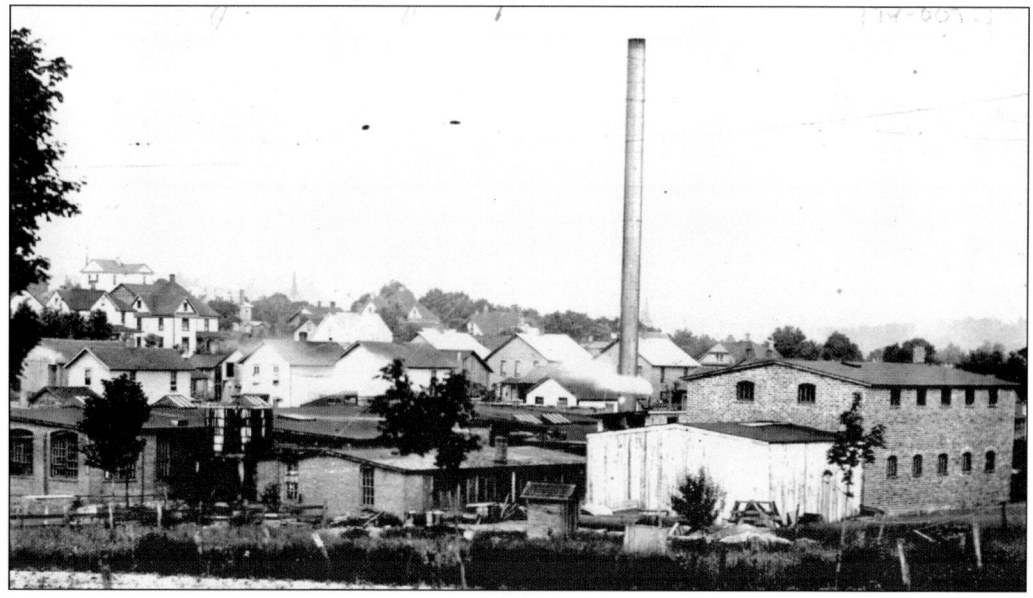
The woolen mill in Reynoldsville is shown here.

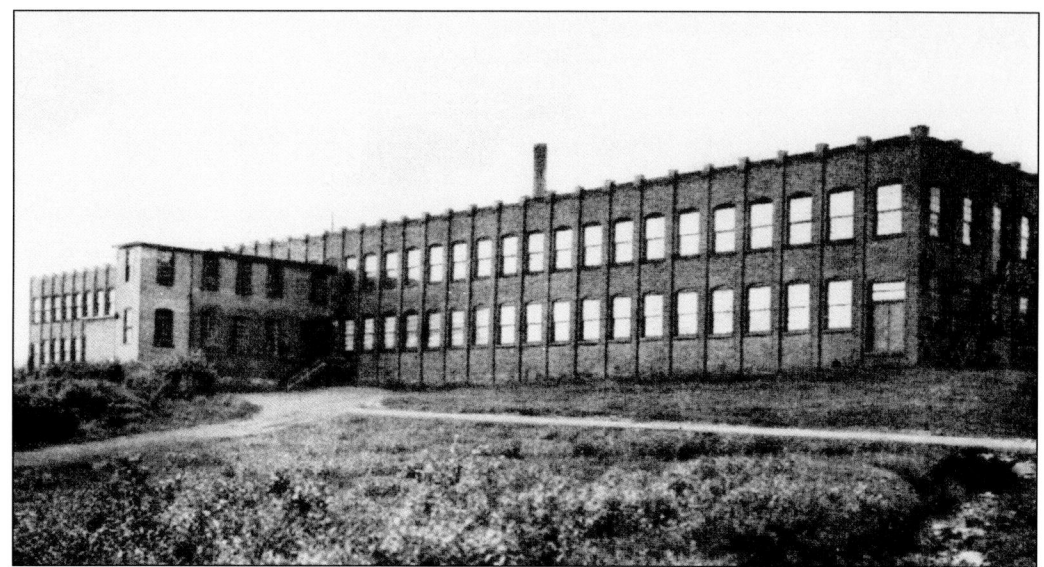
The Reynoldsville Silk Mill, built in 1897, was the first of many companies established in Reynoldsville.

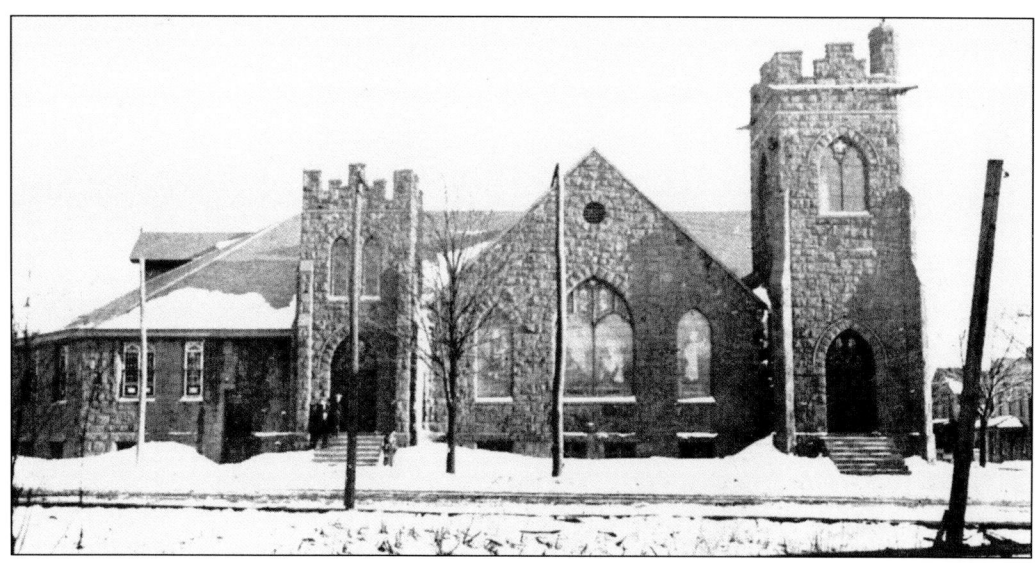
The Methodist Church in Reynoldsville was organized in 1879, and the church building was constructed in 1905. The stained-glass windows are among some of the most beautiful in the area; each window represents a scene from the life of Christ. Andrew Carnegie paid for half of the pipe organ, and the balance was paid by John Reed of Reynoldsville.

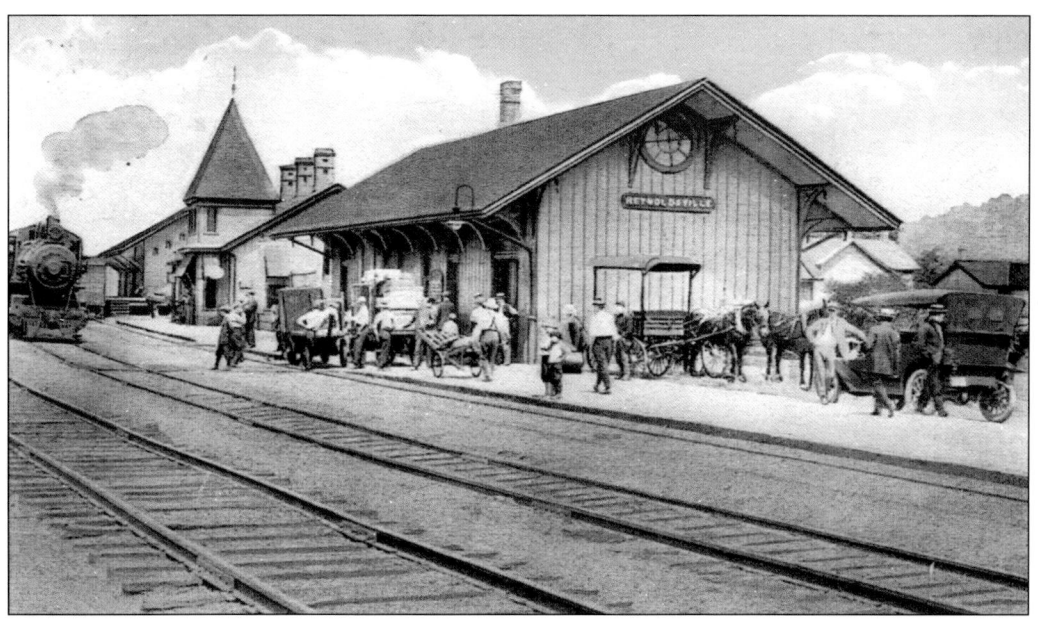
The railroad station in Reynoldsville is shown in the early 1920s.

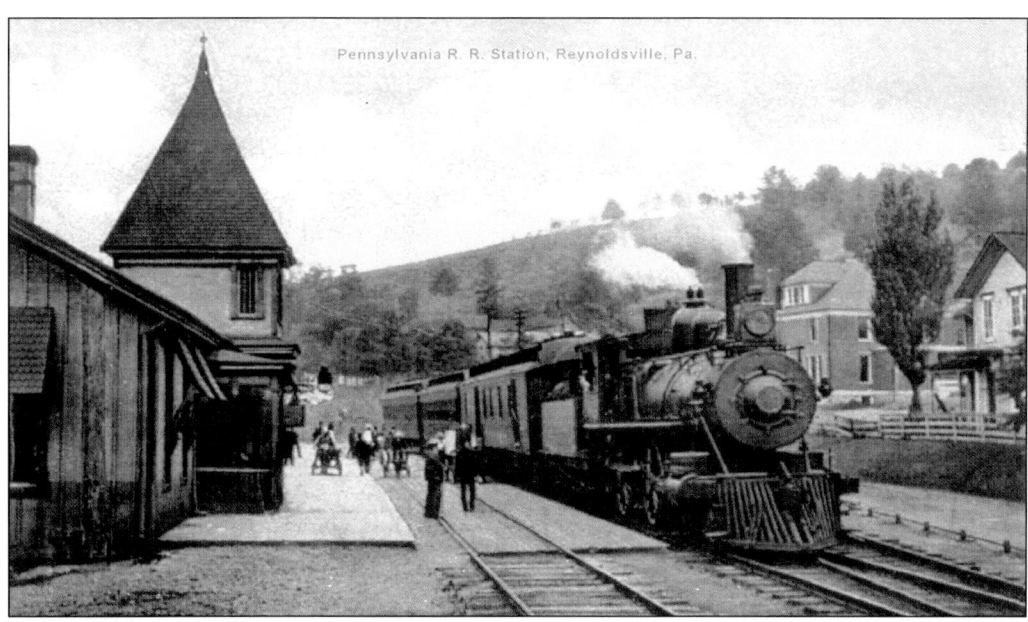
The first locomotive steamed into Reynoldsville on August 5, 1873, via the low-grade division of the Allegheny Valley Railway. The Pennsylvania Railroad Company, offering 10 daily scheduled departures from Reynoldsville, leased this railroad line in 1900. The Reynoldsville Historical Society currently leases the station and plans to use it for a museum in the future.

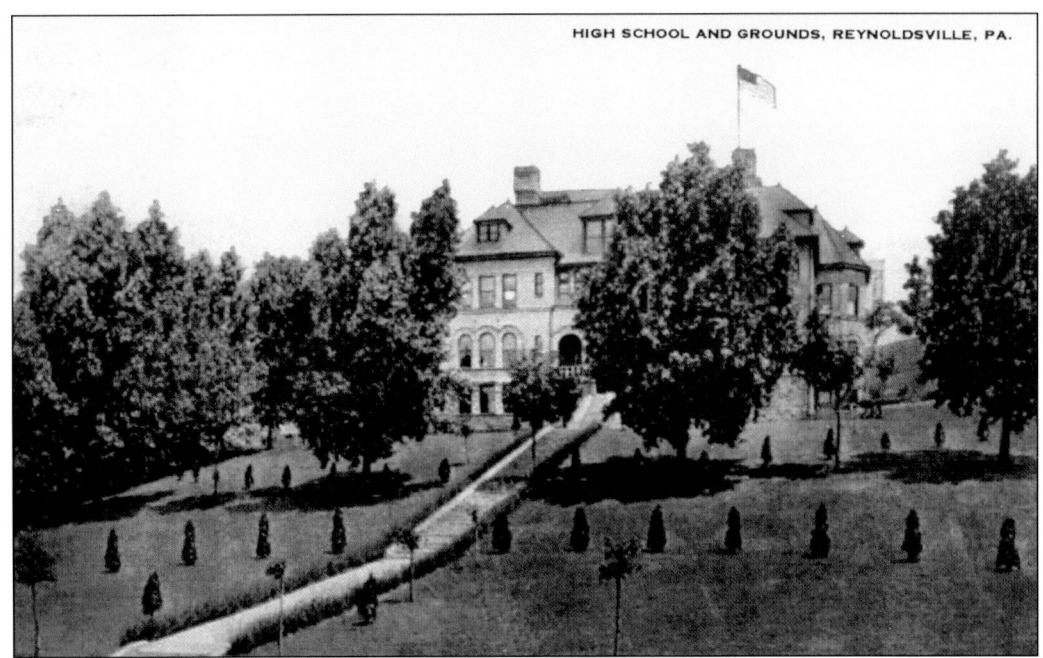

The Reynoldsville High School and grounds were dedicated on September 4, 1896. This yellow brick landmark provided an educational center for Reynoldsville students until 1965. During the flu epidemic of 1917–1918, it served as a temporary hospital. After 1965, it was used as the community center. It was torn down in 1970 to make way for senior citizen apartments.

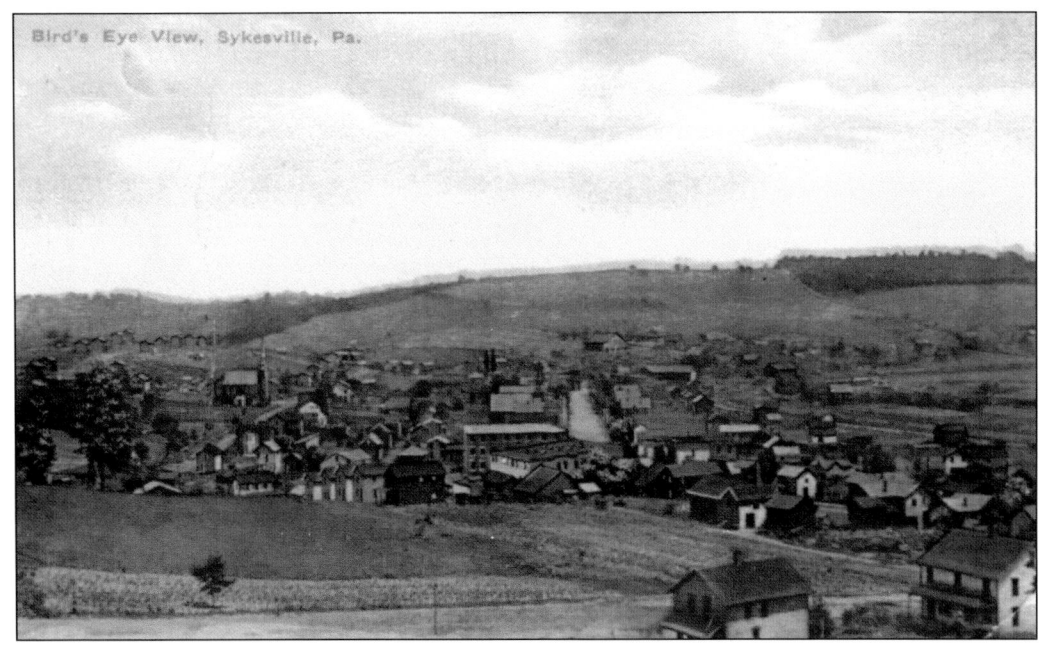

This is a bird's-eye view of Sykesville.

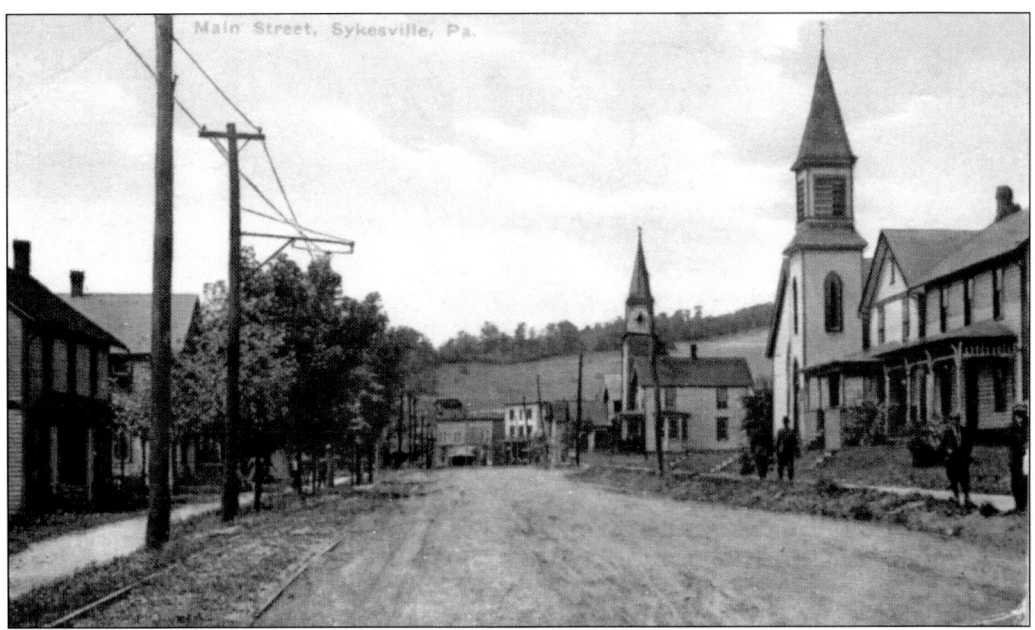

This image of Main Street in Sykesville looks west towards Ideal Products, seen on the left, and Smyer's store, located on the right.

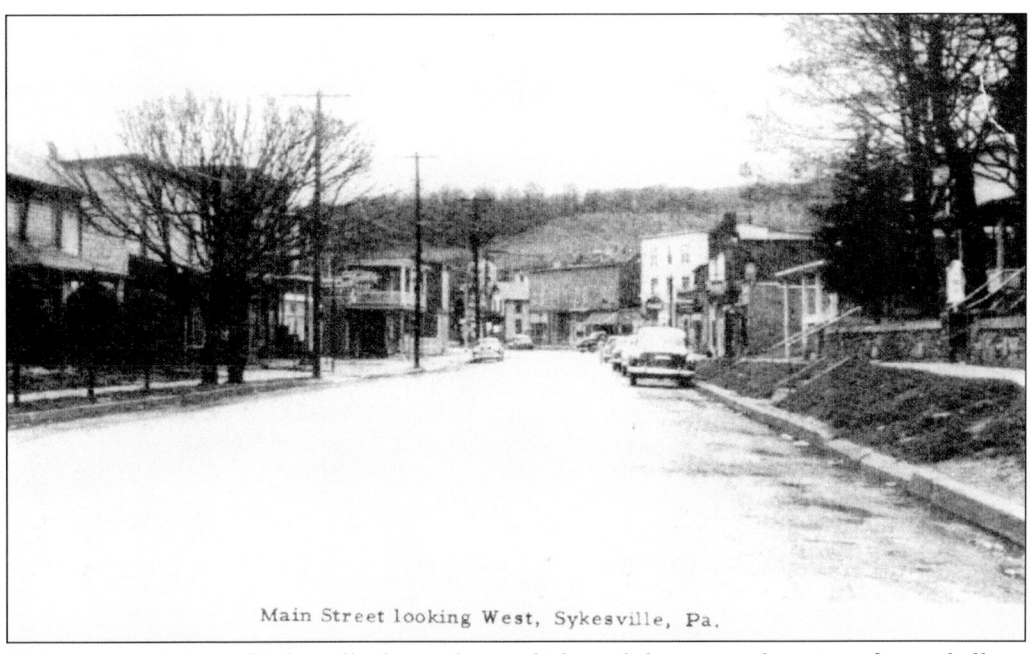

This westward view of Sykesville shows the stoplight and the present location of town hall.

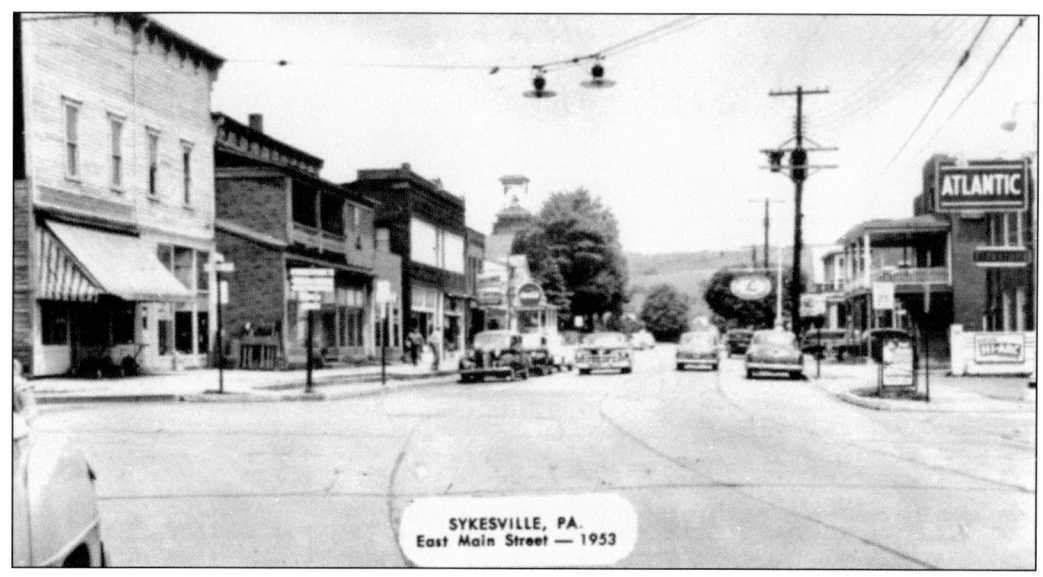

East Main Street in Sykesville is shown here in 1953.

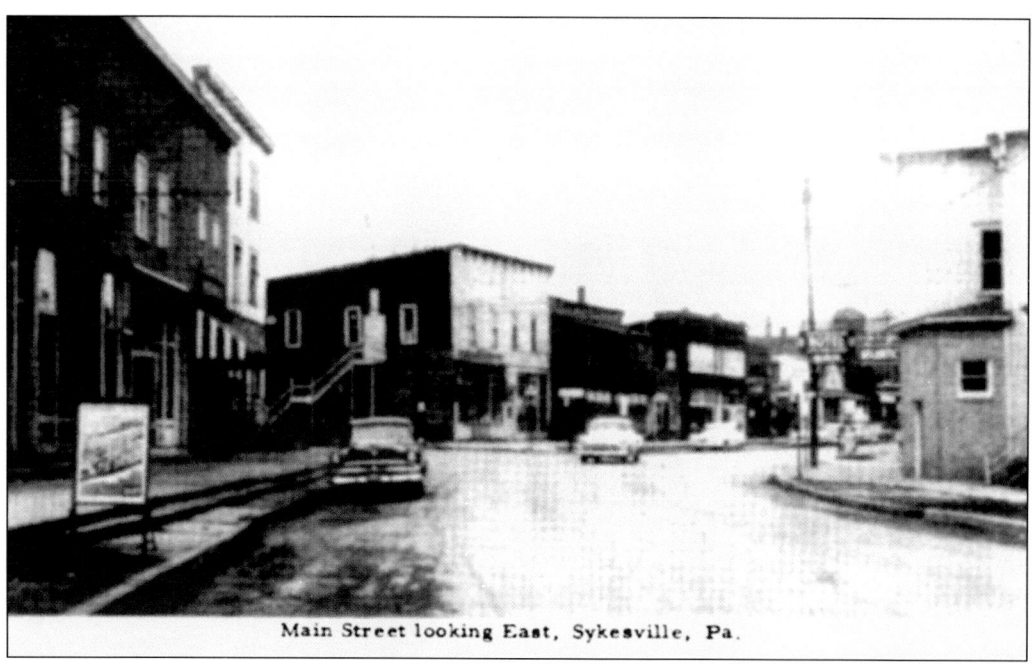

This is Main Street in Sykesville. The Sykesville Hotel, now known as McDermott's, can be seen on the right, and Smyer's store is visible near the center of the image.

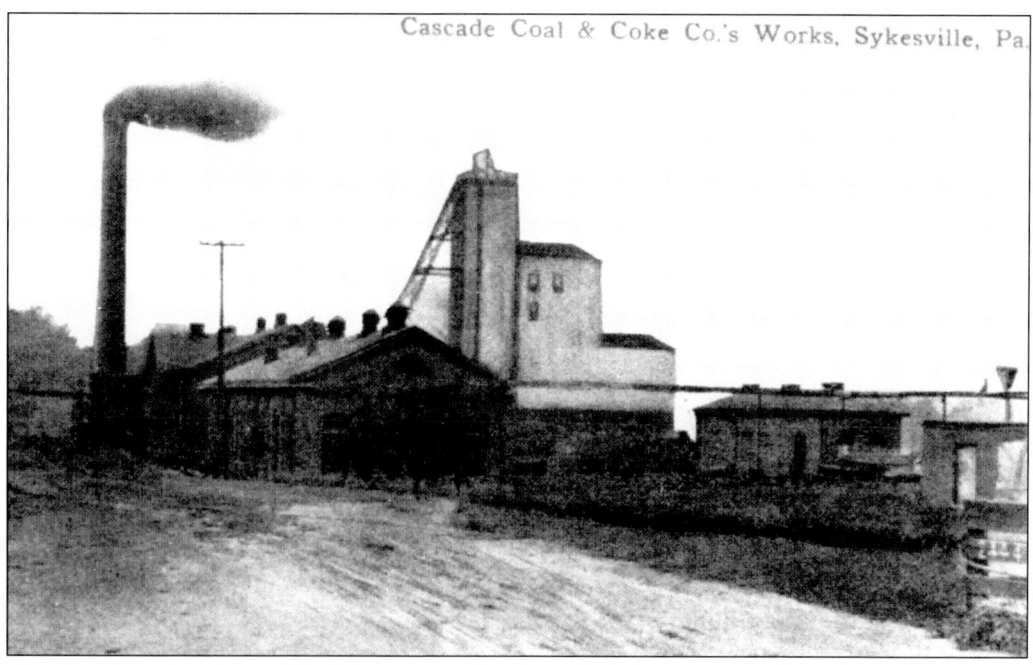

The Goodyear brothers of Buffalo opened the Cascade Mine in Sykesville and another mine in Tyler. The Cascade Mine closed in 1939 after producing 15 billion tons of coal.

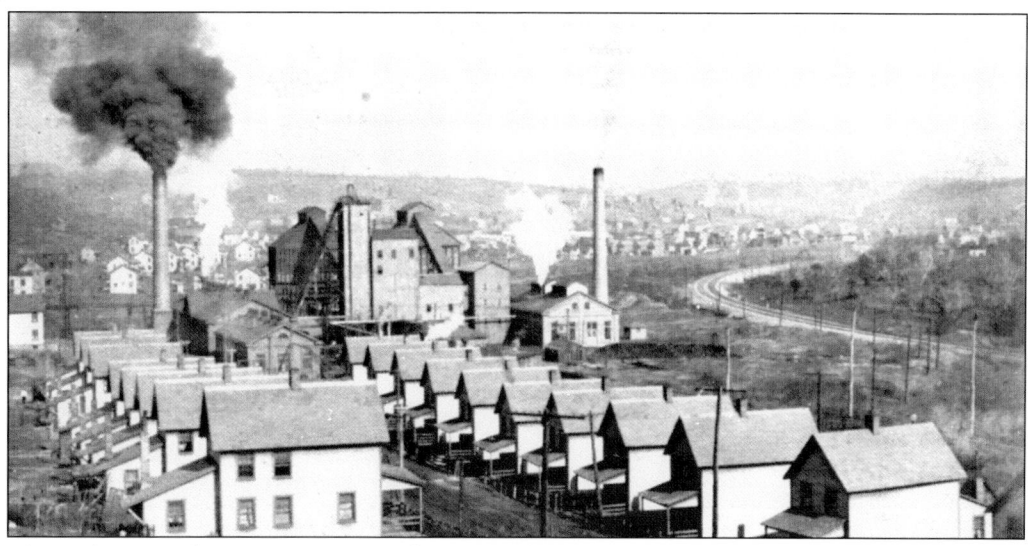

This is the Cascade Mine Company. Shown are the company houses that the miners could rent.

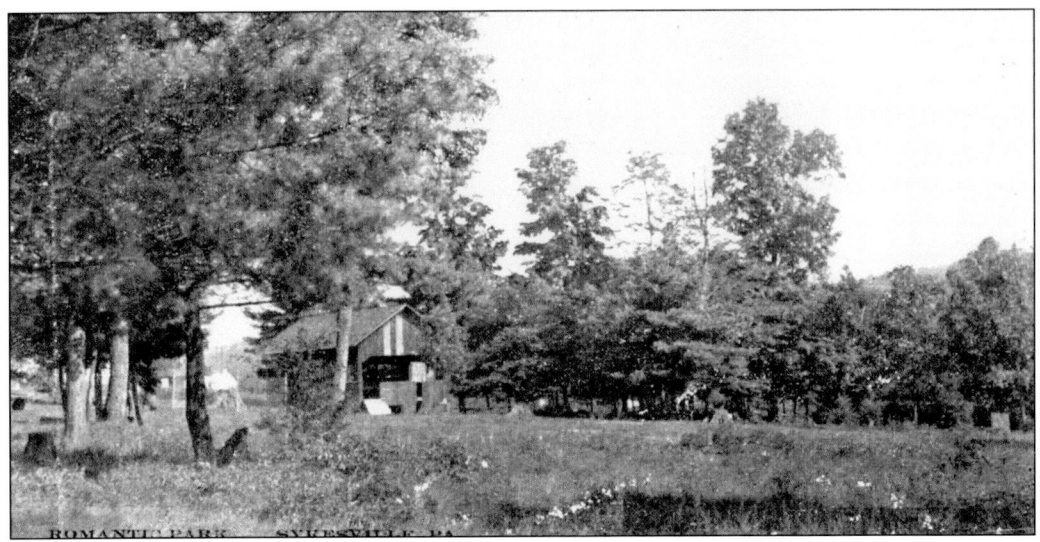
Romantic Park in Sykesville, seen here, is located on the road from Sykesville to Reynoldsville. The park had picnic tables and pavilions for people to enjoy.

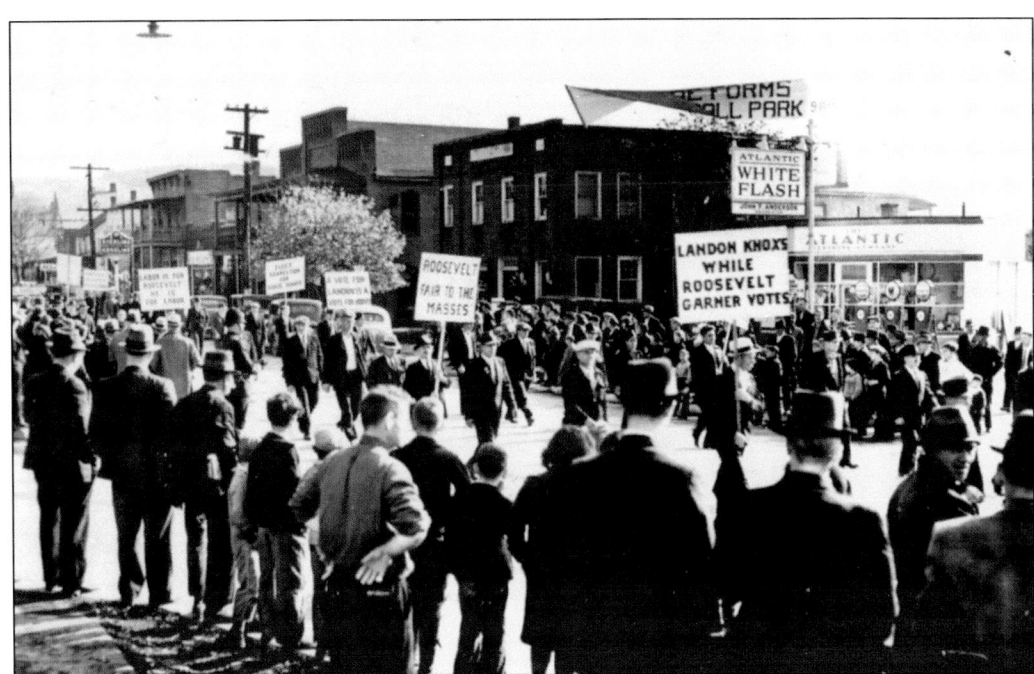
This political parade marched down Main Street in Sykesville during the presidential election of 1936.

Ten

Miscellaneous

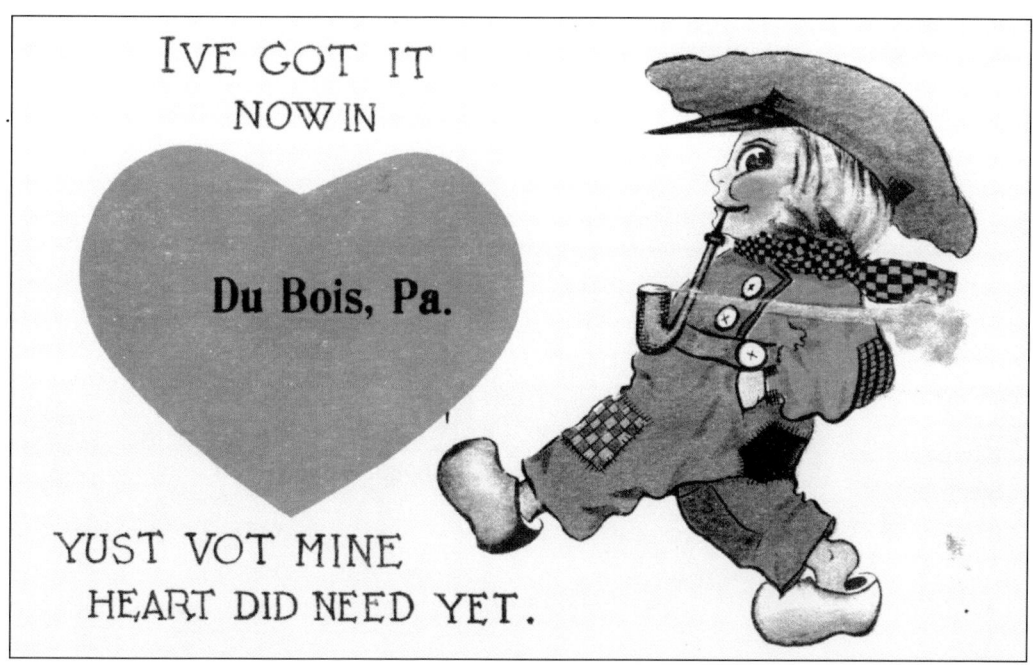

This is a greeting card from DuBois.

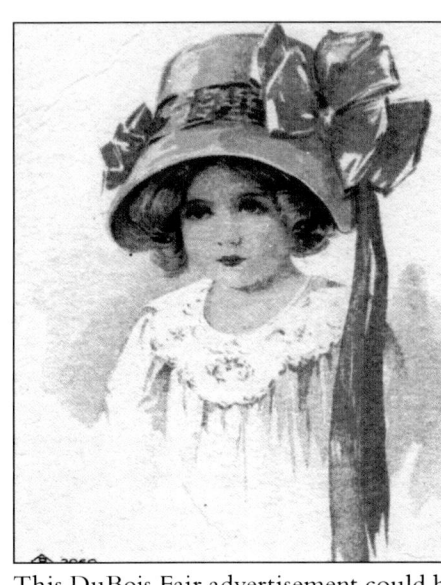

This DuBois Fair advertisement could be used as a free child's admission to the fair.

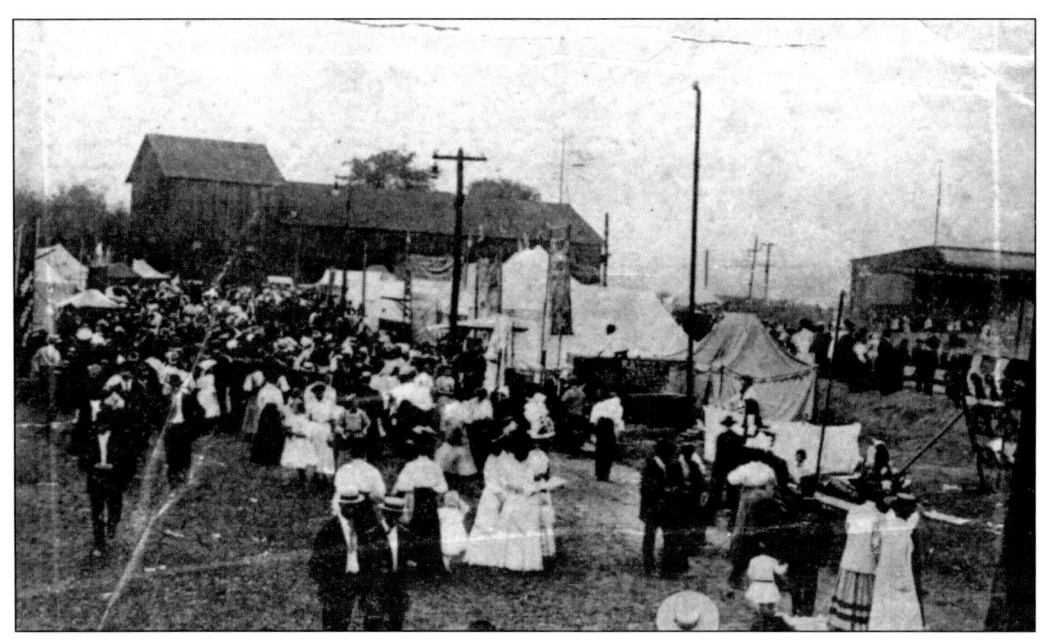

People enjoy the fair in DuBois.

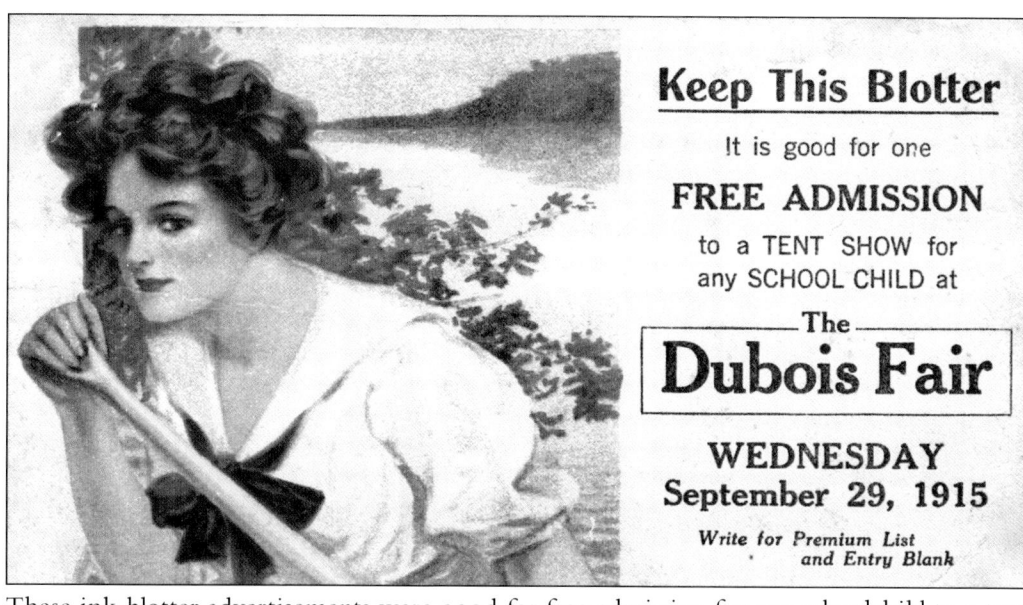

These ink-blotter advertisements were good for free admission for any schoolchild to a tent show at the DuBois Fair.

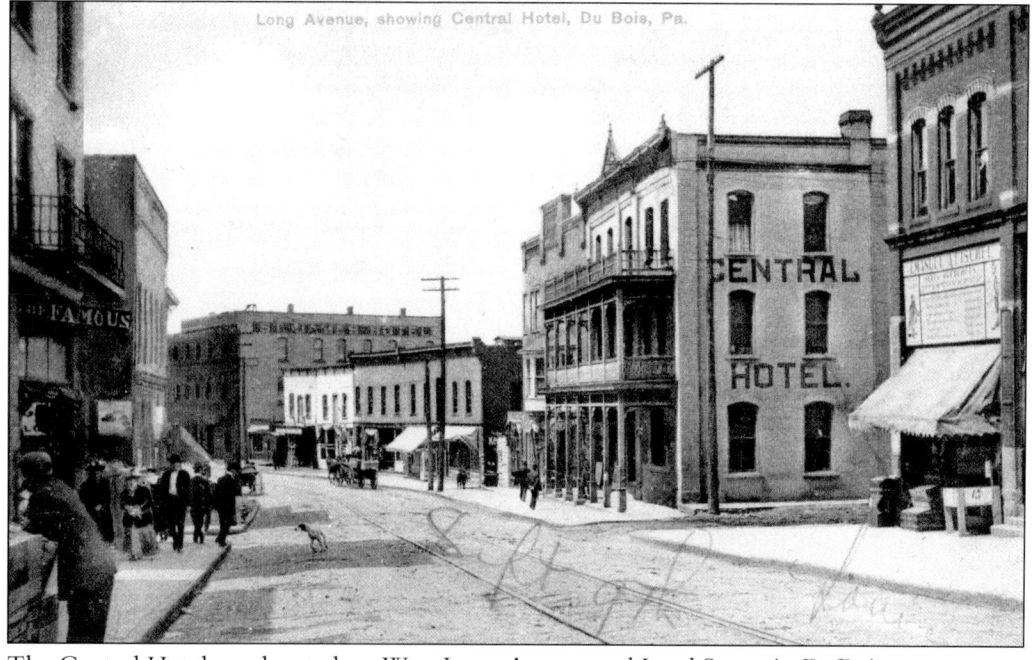

The Central Hotel was located on West Long Avenue and Jared Street in DuBois.

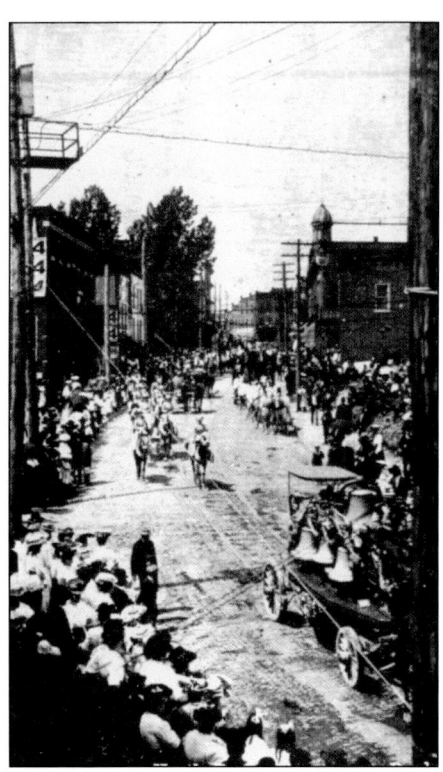

The 1907 firemen's parade marches down Brady Street in DuBois.

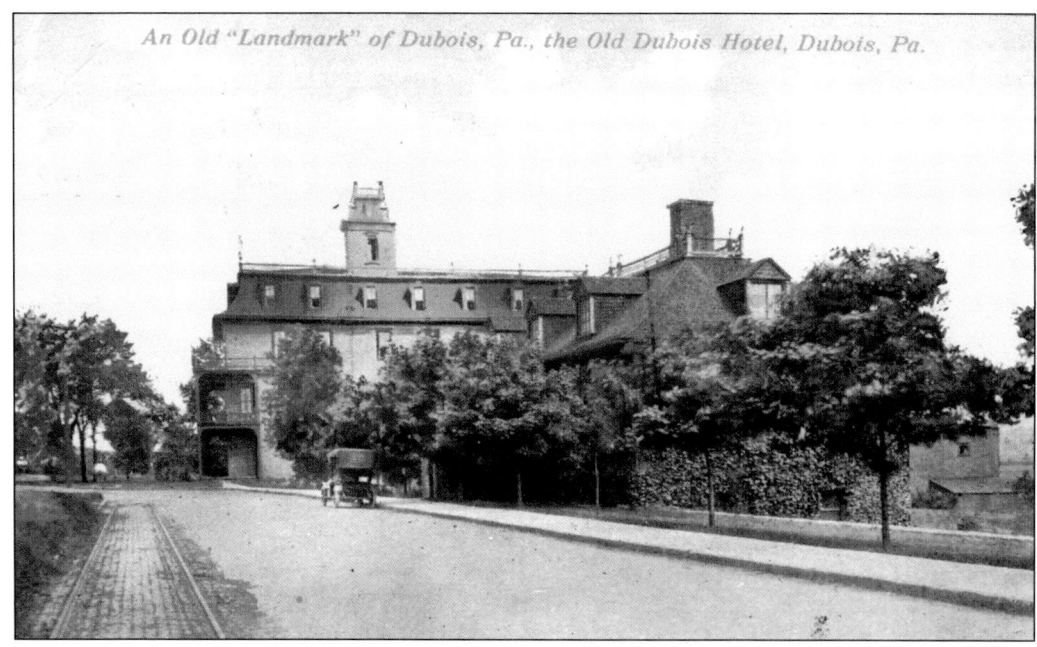

The Old DuBois Hotel is an area landmark.

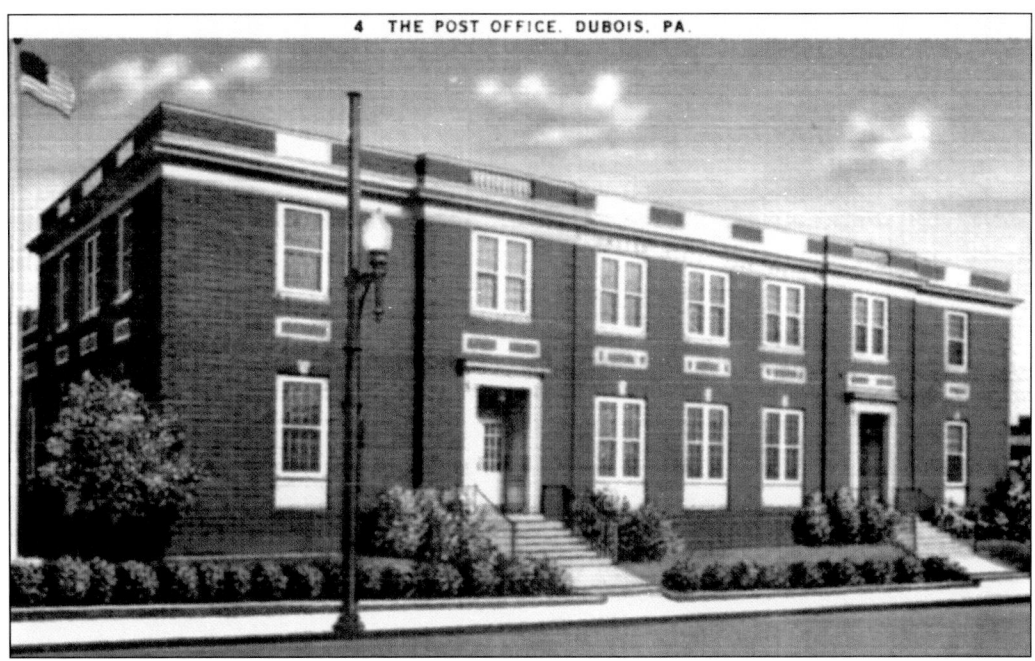
Liberty Boulevard, where the Rockwell plant is located, is shown in the 1950s.

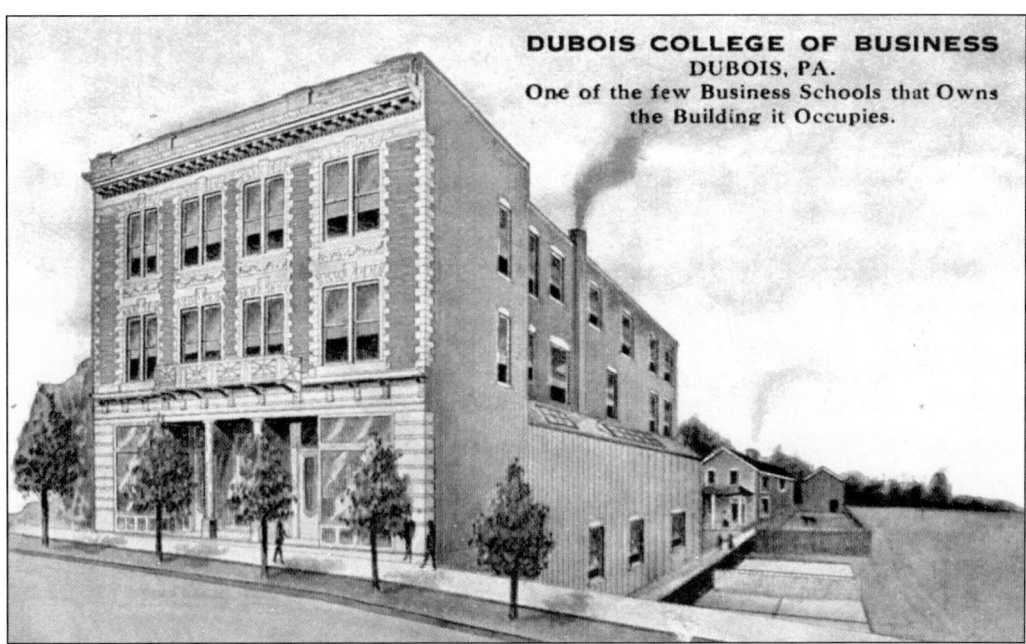
The first building owned by the DuBois Business College was the building now owned by Overdorf Plumbing.

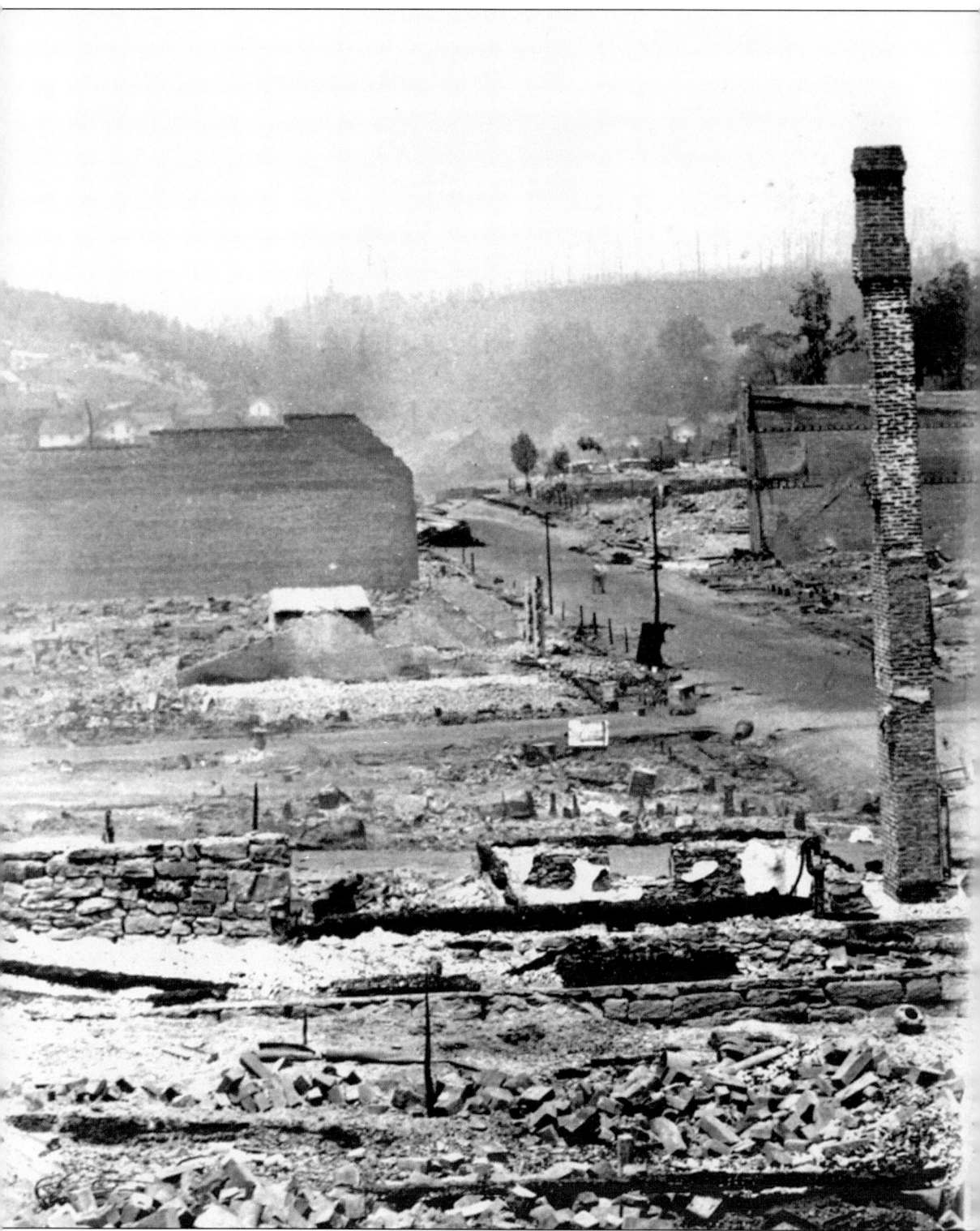
The great fire of 1888 leveled the business district of DuBois.

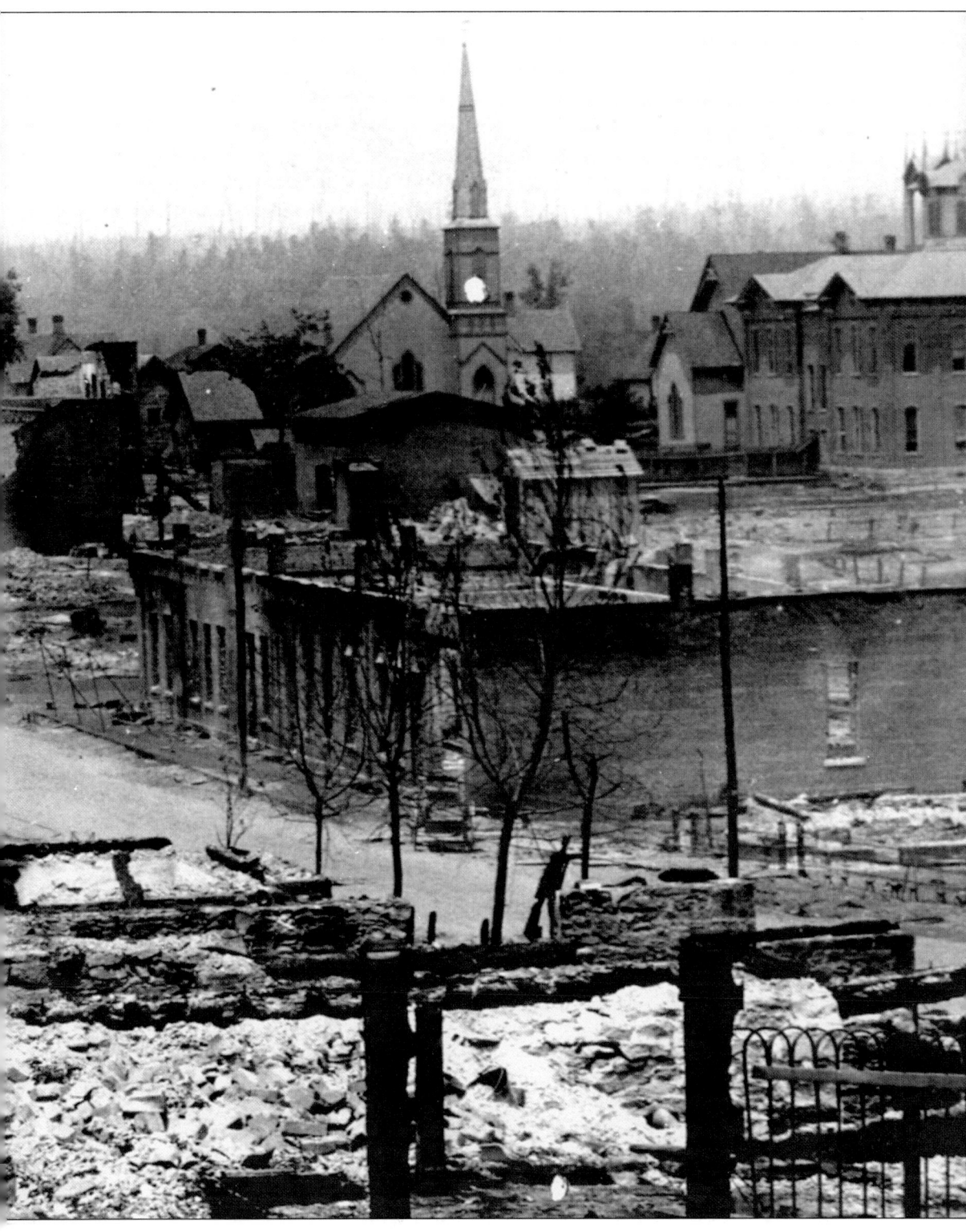

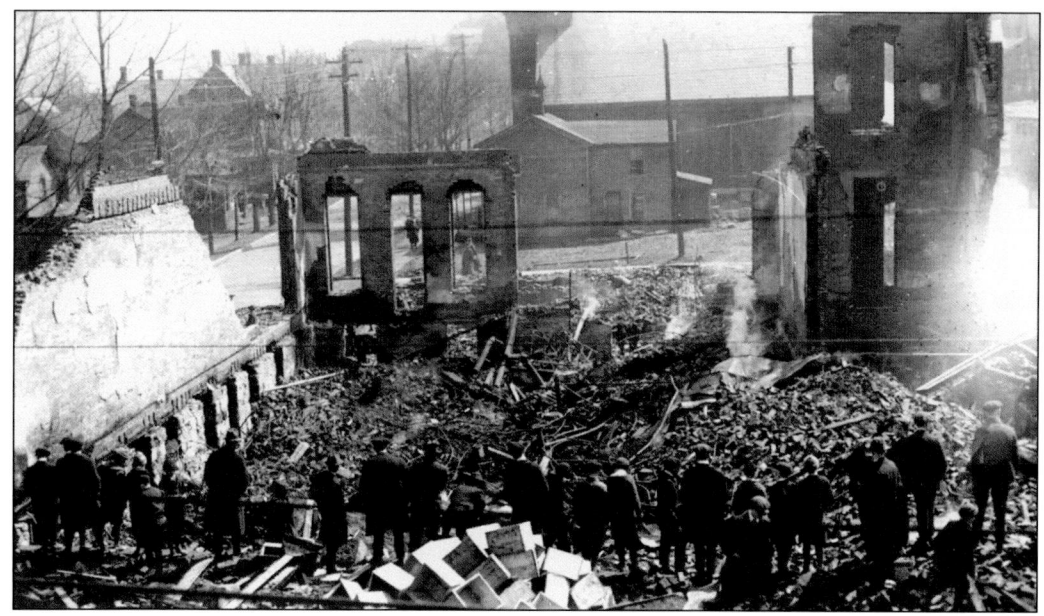
The Broadbent and Martin store was located on the corner of Brady Street and East Scribner Avenue in DuBois. The store burned in 1936.

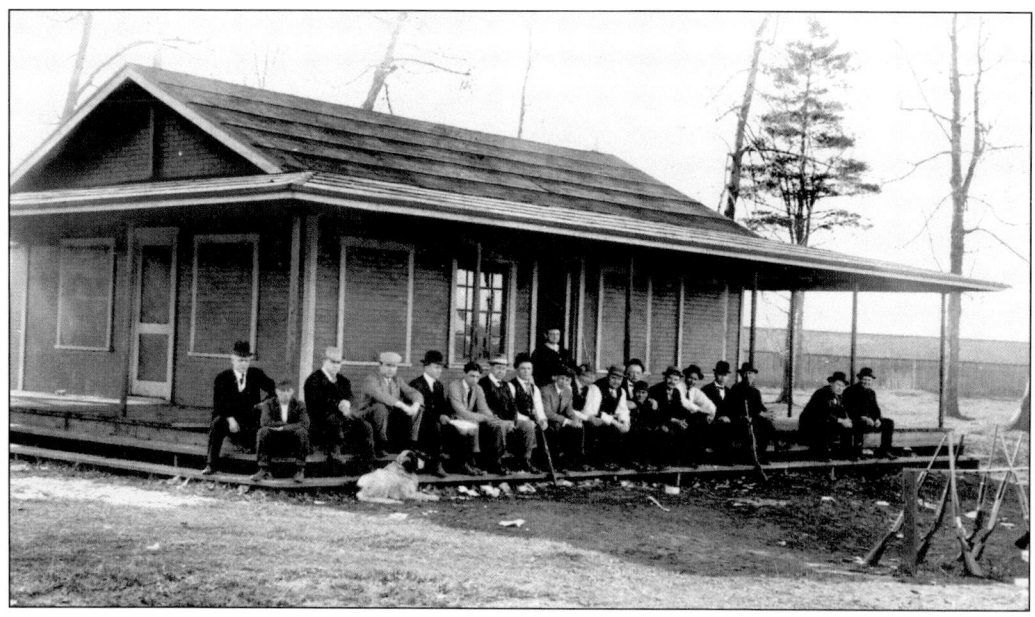
The DuBois Gun Club is pictured here.

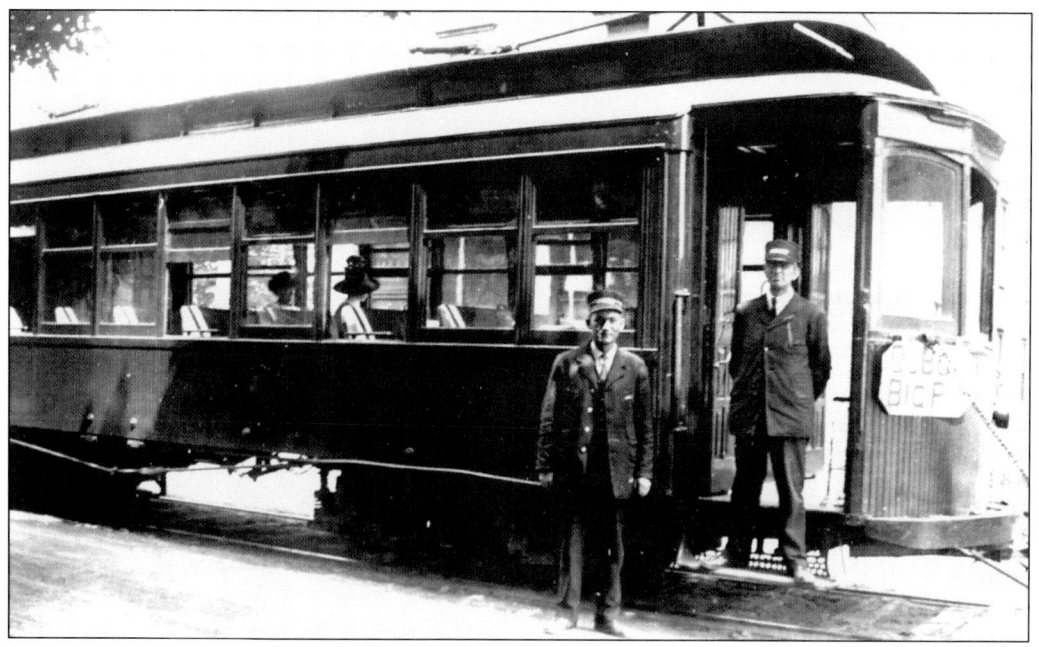
This trolley car ran from DuBois to Big Run.

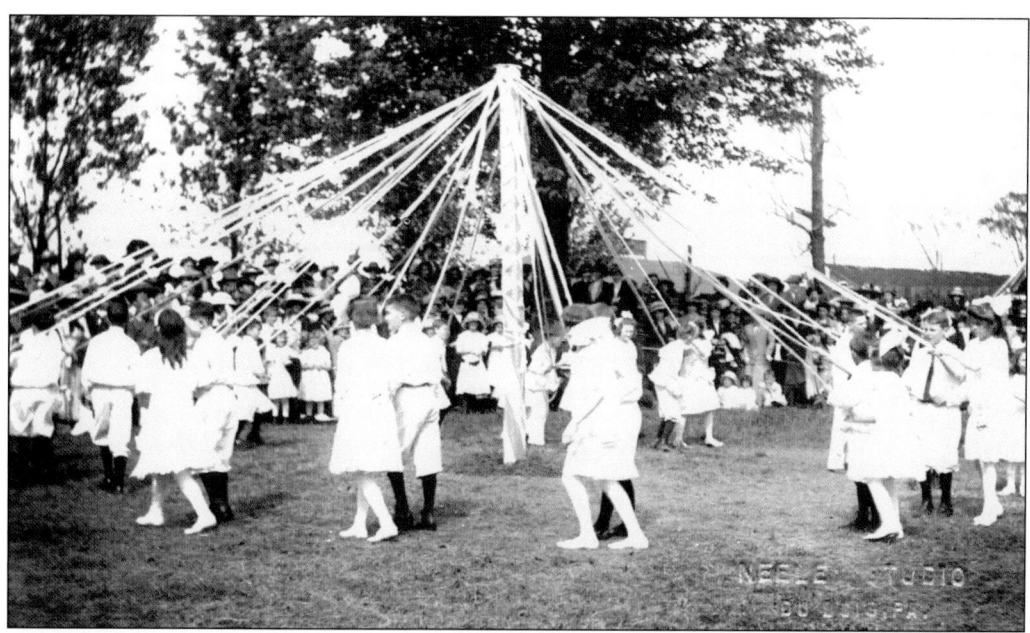
May Day was celebrated on the first of May with a maypole dance performed by local schoolchildren.

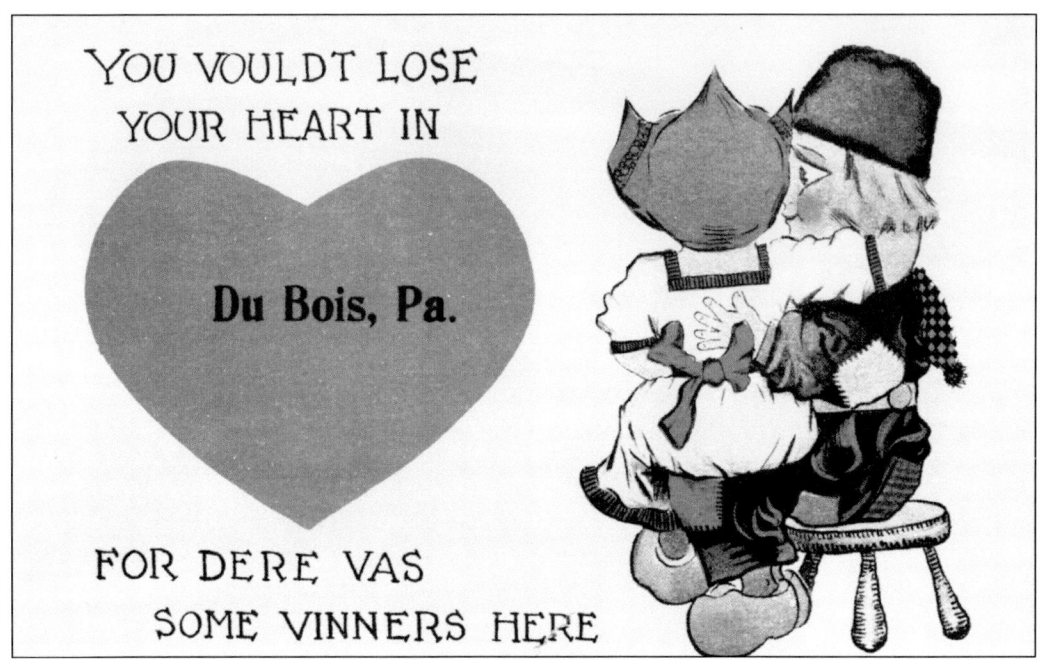

Shown here is a greeting card from DuBois.

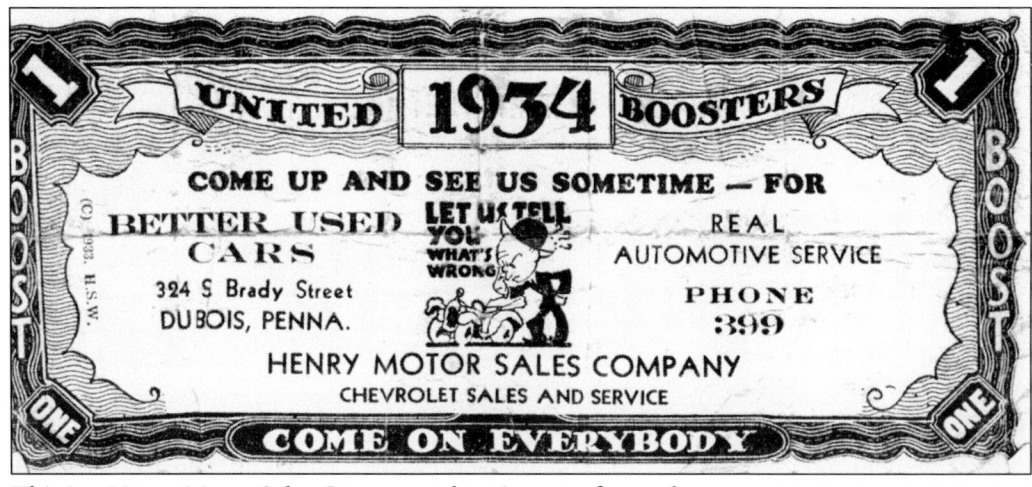

This is a Henry Motor Sales Company advertisement for used cars.

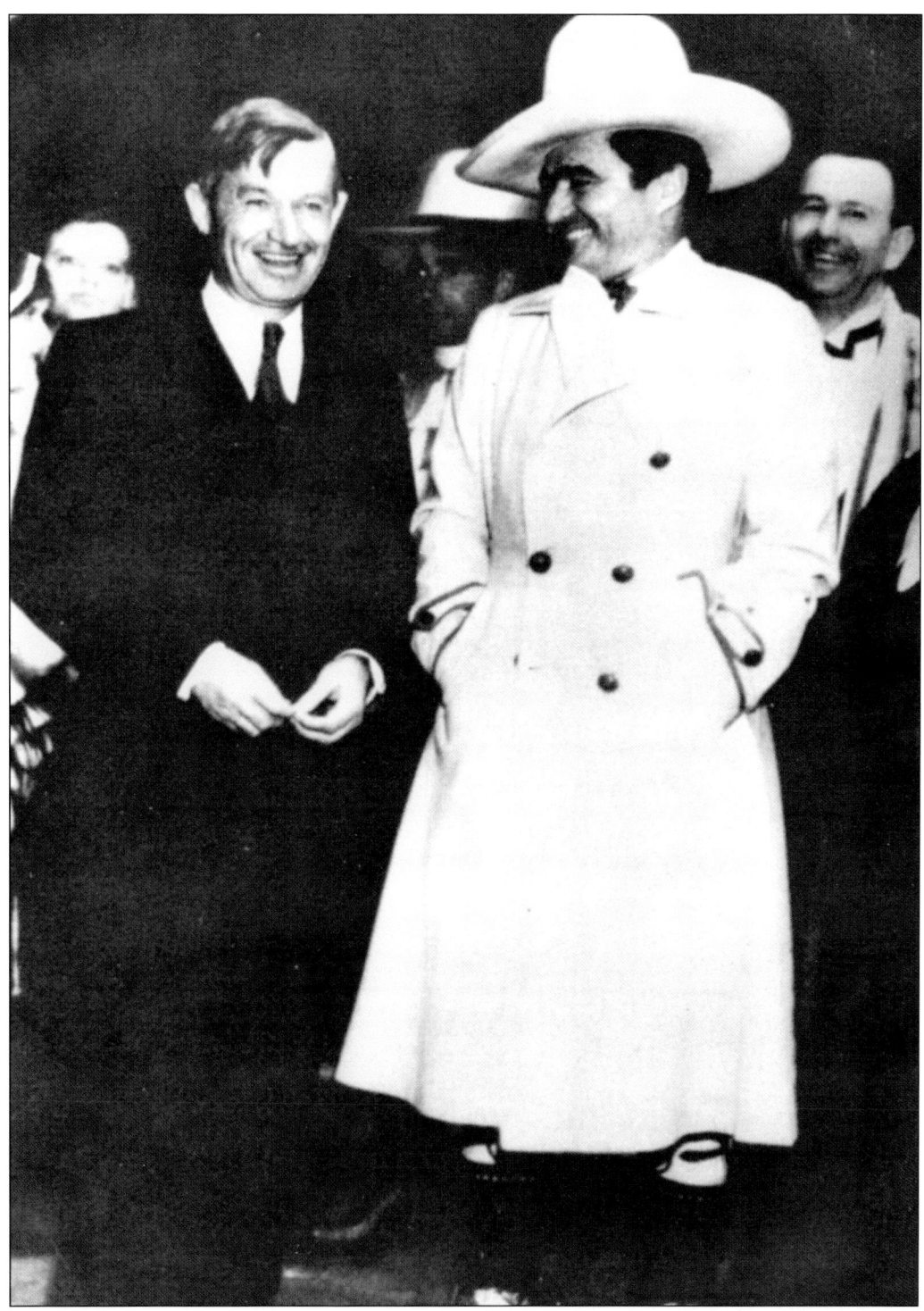
Will Rogers and Tom Mix visited DuBois in the 1930s. Tom Mix was born in Mix Run and came to DuBois with his parents when his father was employed by John DuBois. Tom Mix became a movie star, playing cowboys in Westerns.

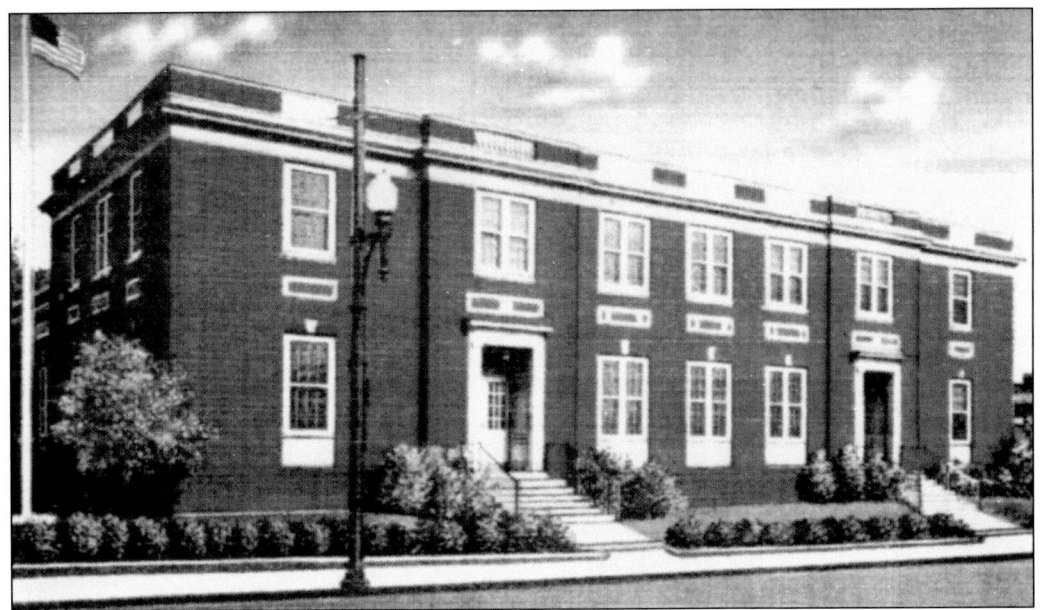
This is the U.S. post office building in DuBois.

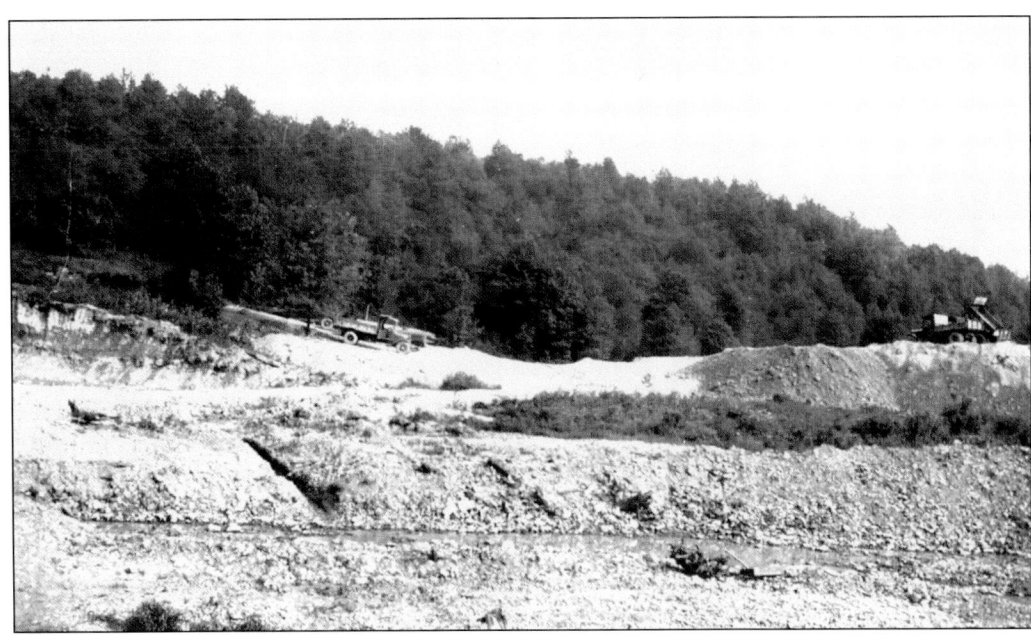
This photograph of the construction of the Anderson Creek Reservoir was taken in 1937, when the height of the spillway was raised three feet.

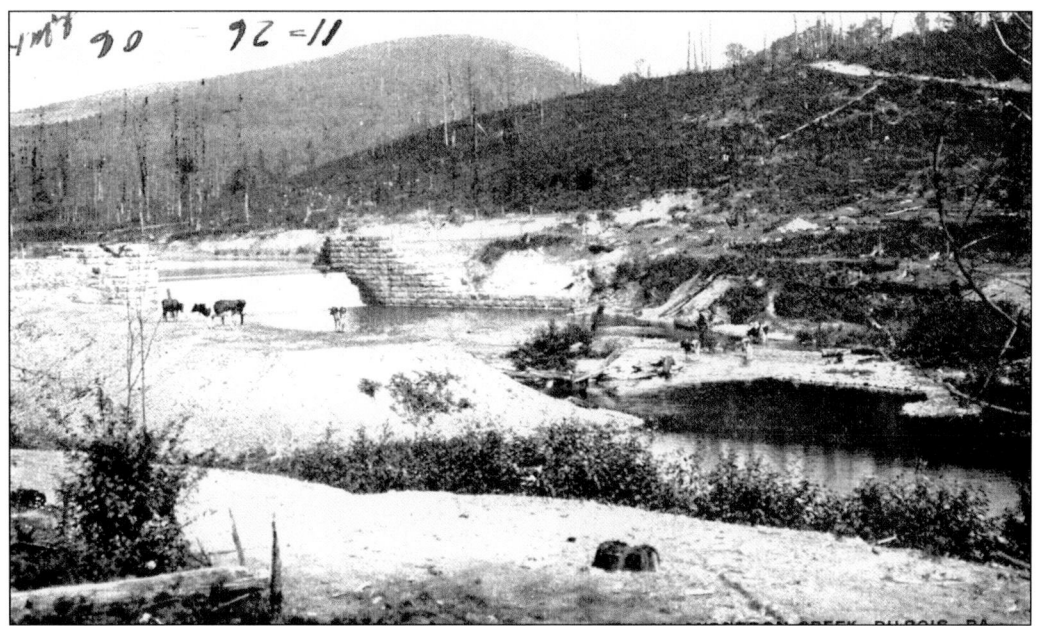
The reservoir is seen here in the early 20th century.

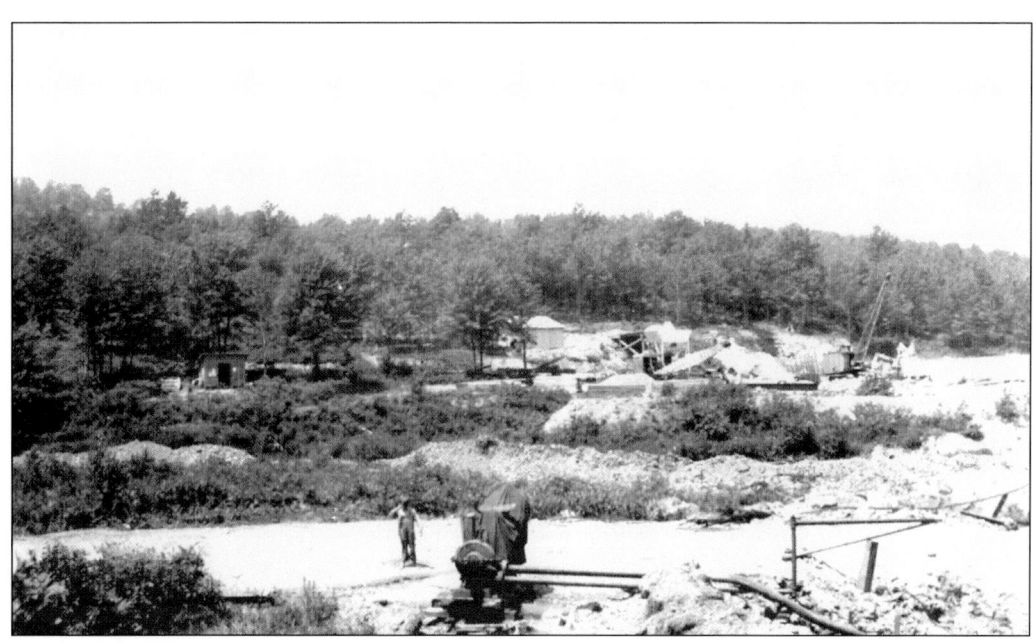
Construction continues on the Anderson Creek Reservoir.

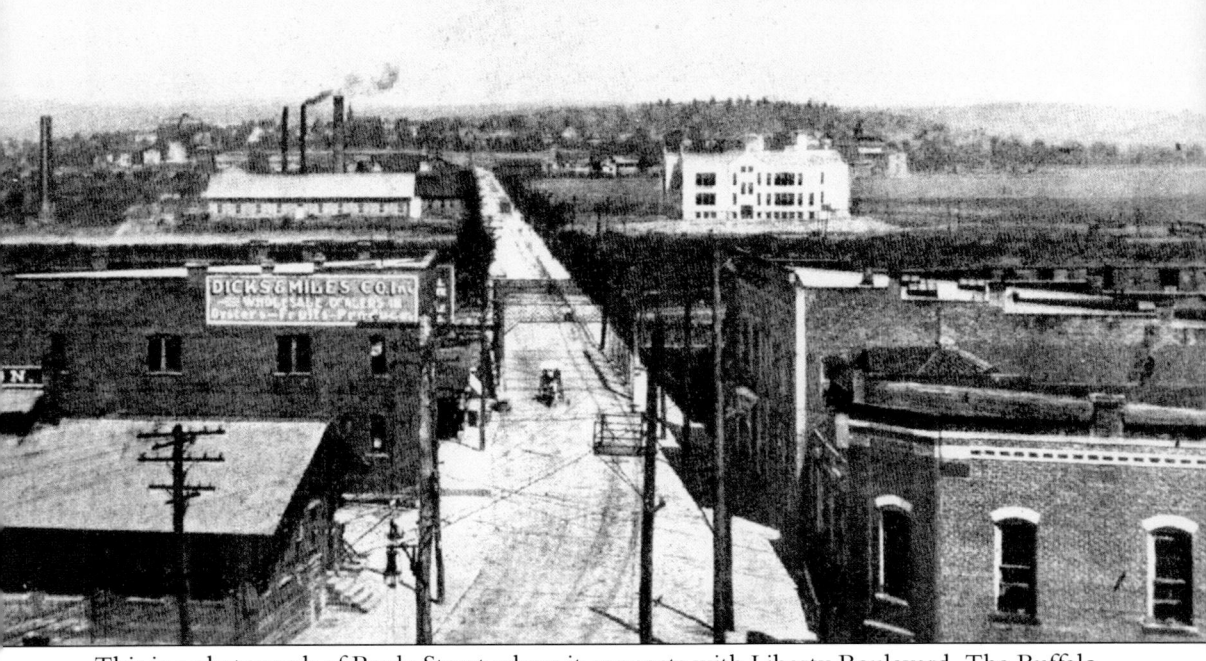

This is a photograph of Brady Street where it connects with Liberty Boulevard. The Buffalo and Susquehanna Railroad station is in the foreground on the left. The high school is located midway along the boulevard on the right. Also visible are the trolley tracks crossing the old iron bridge over Sandy Creek.

Men place forms for the concrete spillway at Anderson Creek Reservoir in 1936.

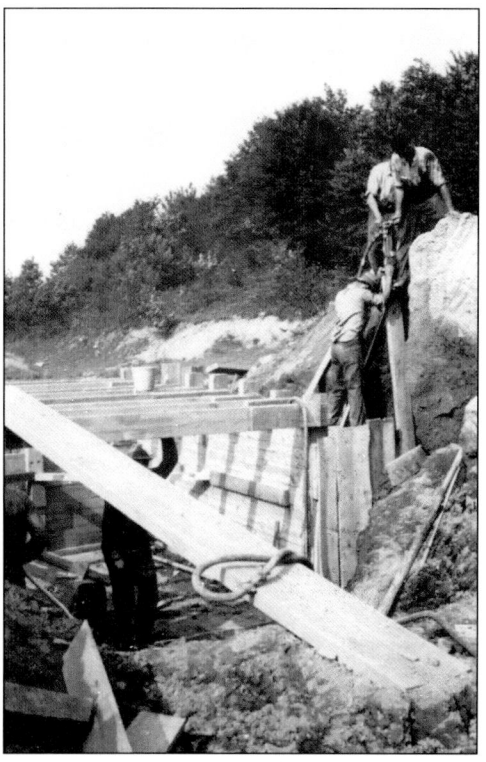

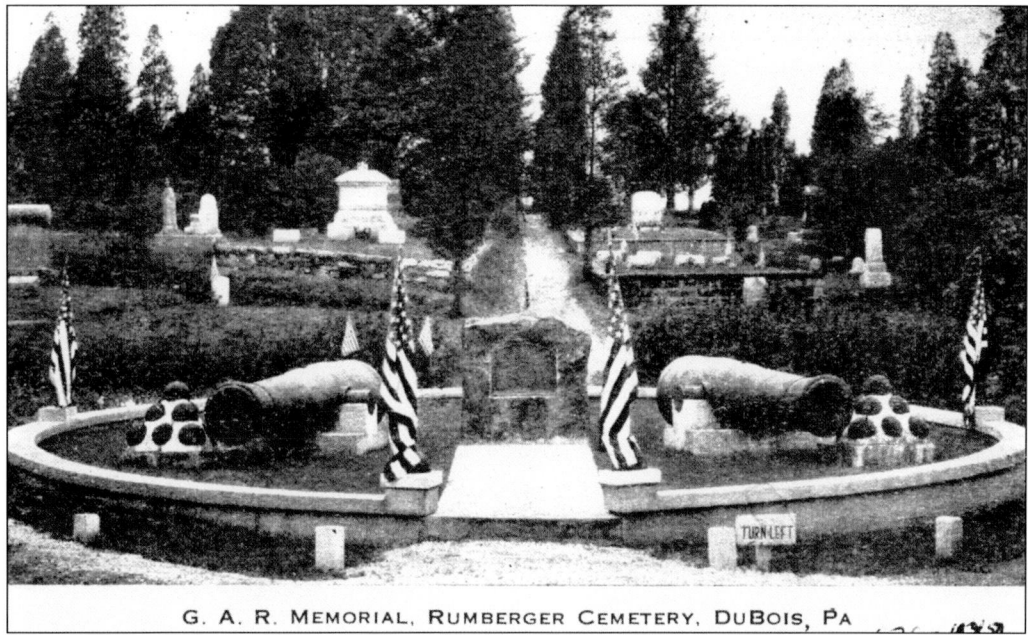

Rumbarger Cemetery, located on South Main Street near DuBois Hospital, dates to 1890. It was originally run by the privately owned DuBois Cemetery Company. In 1898, the cemetery was deeded to Herbert A. Moore and A. L. Cole. It was relinquished to the Rumbarger Cemetery Association in 1977.

The proceeds from this book go to support the DuBois Area Historical Society, located at 30 West Long Avenue, DuBois, Pennsylvania, 15801. The society can be reached by telephone at (814) 371-9006.

The museum and its library are open to the public. Visitors may view the museum from April 1 through December 15 on Tuesdays and Fridays from 2:00 p.m. to 4:00 p.m. and on Wednesdays from 10:00 a.m. to 4:00 p.m. From December 16 to March 31, the museum is open only on Wednesdays from 10:00 a.m. to 4:00 p.m. Special appointments and museum tours may be arranged by calling (814) 371-9006 when the museum is open.

Further information is available by e-mail, history@wrkcs.net, and on the web, http://home.wrkcs.net/history.